MW01000332

The Hemmings Book of

OLDSMOBILES

ISBN 0-917808-77-0
Library of Congress Card Number: 2001092943

One of a series of Hemmings Collector-Car Books. Other books in the series include:
The Hemmings Book of Buicks; The Hemmings Motor News Book of Cadillacs; The Hemmings Motor News Book of Chrysler Performance Cars; The Hemmings Motor News Book of Corvettes; The Hemmings Motor News Book of Hudsons; The Hemmings Motor News Book of Mustangs; The Hemmings Motor News Book of Packards; The Hemmings Motor News Book of Pontiacs; The Hemmings Motor News Book of Postwar Fords; The Hemmings Book of Postwar Chevrolets; The Hemmings Book of Prewar Fords; The Hemmings Motor News Book of Studebakers.

Hemmings Motor News
Collector Car Publications and Marketplaces
1-800-CAR-HERE (227-4373)
www.hemmings.com

The Hemmings Book of
OLDSMOBILES

Editor-In-Chief
Terry Ehrich

Editor
Richard A. Lentinello

Designer
Nancy Bianco

Cover photo by Roy Query: 1956 Super Eighty Eight Convertible

This book compiles driveReports which have appeared in *Hemmings Motor News*'s *Special Interest Autos* magazine (SIA) over the past 30 years. The editors at *Hemmings Motor News* express their gratitude to the following writers, photographers, and artists who made this book possible through their many fine contributions to *Special Interest Autos* magazine:

Terry Boyce	Michael Lamm	Don Spiro
Arch Brown	John Lee	Don Stickles
Ken Gross	Vince Manocchi	Russ von Sauers
M. Park Hunter	Alex Meredith	Josiah Work
Bud Juneau	David Newhardt	Vince Wright
John F. Katz	Roy Query	

We are also grateful to David Brownell, Michael Lamm, and Rich Taylor, the editors under whose guidance these driveReports were written and published. We thank GM Design Staff, GM Engineering Staff, Image International, *Motor Trend* magazine, and the National Automotive History Collection, Detroit Public Library, who have graciously contributed photographs to *Special Interest Autos* magazine and this book.

CONTENTS

Special Interest Autos (SIA) magazine's back issues are referred to in this book by issue number. If in stock, copies may be purchased directly from Hemmings Motor News at 800-227-4373, ext. 550 or at www.hemmings.com/gifts.

1931 OLDSMOBILE

High Value for Hard Times

drive report

by Alex Meredith
photos by Vince Manocchi

B Y RIGHTS, 1931 ought to have been a great year for Oldsmobile. And no doubt it would have been, had it not been for the Depression's ever-tightening grip on the American economy. Bank failures numbered 2,300 that year, wiping out the life savings of hundreds of thousands of depositors, for there was no such thing in those days as a federally insured account. Public confidence sank as unemployment figures rose, and people no longer listened when President Hoover optimistically proclaimed prosperity to be just around the corner.

But in a sense, Olds had a banner year. Production and sales were off only slightly for the car from Lansing, while the industry in general was taking a terrible beating. Oldsmobile's share of the dwindling market increased by a dramatic 39 percent that year, while its sales ranking rose from eleventh to eighth.

No wonder; the 1931 Oldsmobile was an exceptionally attractive automobile.

Big, by the standards of the time, handsome and impressive in appearance, at $845 for the popular two-door sedan it was one of the best bargains the industry had to offer that year. Doubtless it owed a lot of its appeal to the fact that it looked like a much more expensive car than it really was. For a family striving to keep up appearances in the face of hard times, that was an important factor.

And from an engineering standpoint, the Olds was as good as it looked. But we'll come to that, presently.

For years. the Oldsmobile had been General Motors' "hard luck" car. In the very early days, when Ransom Eli Olds was turning out his smart little Curved Dash Runabout, it had been the fastest selling car in the world. But the bloom was already commencing to fade from that particular rose when R.E. Olds departed the company in 1904 and went on to found the REO Motor Car Company. Ransom's erstwhile partners wasted little time in abandoning the

Originally published in Special Interest Autos #82, Jul.-Aug. 1984

1931 Oldsmobile Price and Production Table

	Price	Disc Wh.	Standard (5 wheels) Production Wire Wh.	Wood Wh.	Price	Deluxe (6 wheels) Production Wire Wh.	Wood Wh.	Total*
Coupe (2-passenger)	$845		1,364	1,059	$ 910	802	475	3,700
Sport coupe	$895		858	687	$ 960	2,067	1,288	4,900
Sedan, 2-door	$845	1	2,803	2,519	$ 910	2,077	1,756	9,156
Sedan, 4-door	$925	26	3,090	3,620	$ 990	5,177	5,309	17,222
Patrician sedan	$960	5	443	510	$1,025	3,457	4,383	8,798
Convertible roadster	$935		233	124	$1,000	1,965	1,179	3,501

Grand total, 1931 model year production   42,277

*Totals include both Standard and Deluxe models.

(The reader will note that despite the severely depressed state of the economy in 1931, the Deluxe models, overall, outsold the Standard cars by 29,935 to 17,342 — a margin of 72.6%.)

Sources: *Automobile Trade Journal*, April 1931; Jerry Heasley, *The Production Figure Book for U.S. Cars*

low-priced field; they took aim, instead, at the luxury market.

The results were catastrophic. Oldsmobile's market share, which had amounted to 35.3 percent in 1903, plunged to 1.7 percent five years later, and the company's ledgers were awash in red ink.

It was at that point — 1908 — that William Crapo "Billy" Durant took over Oldsmobile, absorbing it into the new organization that he had dubbed General Motors. Doubtless to his dismay, Durant found that the debilitated Olds organization hadn't developed a new model for the 1909 season. Quickly, then, the resourceful Billy cobbled together the Model 20, which was really nothing more nor less than a stretched Buick. It sold for less than half the price of the cheapest 1908 Oldsmobile, and it paced the division to a sixfold sales increase.

One might expect that Durant would elect to stay with this winning formula. But in 1910 he positioned Olds once again in the luxury market with one of the most spectacular — not to say outrageous — automobiles ever produced: the Oldsmobile Limited.

Constructed on a wheelbase of 130 inches, later stretched to 138, the Limited stood so tall on its 42-inch wheels that two steps were required to board the monster, Power came from a 707-cubic-inch F-head engine, doubtless endowing the Limited with an almost unlimited thirst! One is left to imagine what a chore it must have been to crank this behemoth to life, for the electric self-starter was still a couple of years down the road.

It was the Limited, incidentally, that inspired William Harnden Foster's famous painting, "Setting the Pace," which depicts one of these great machines in a headlong race with the New York Central's crack 20th Century Limited passenger train. Whether such a contest ever took place is debatable, but no matter; the painting is one of the masterpieces of automotive art!

No doubt the big car enhanced Olds-

Comparative Specifications
1931 General Motors Lower-Medium-Priced Convertibles

	Oldsmobile	Buick 50	Oakland	Pontiac
Price	$935	$1,095	$995	$745
Net weight (pounds)	2,800	3,095	3,105	2,710
Engine	L-head 6	ohv str. 8	L-head V-8	L-head 6
Bore and stroke	33/16 X 41/8	2⅞ x 4¼	3 ⁷⁄₁₆ x 3 ⅜	3 ⁵⁄₁₆ x 3 ⅞
Displacement (cubic inches)	197.5	220.7	251.0	200.0
Compression ratio	5.06:1	4.75:1	5.0:1	4.9:1
Hp @ rpm	65 @ 3,350	77 @ 3,200	85 @ 3,400	60 @ 3,000
Hp per c.i.d.	.329	.349	.339	.300
Main bearings	4	5	3	3
Axle ratio	4.56:1	4.54:1	4.55:1	4.55:1
Brake lining area (square inches)	160.5	182.0	232.0	214.0
Lbs per square inch lining area	17.4	17.0	13.4	12.7
Tire size	5.25/18	5.25/18	5.50/18	5.00/19
Wheelbase (inches)	113.5	114	117	112
Lbs./hp	43.1	40.2	36.5	45.2
Lbs./c.i.d.	14.2	14.0	12.4	13.6

Primary source: *Automobile Trade Journal*, April 1931.

1931 OLDSMOBILE

Right: Headlamp design is Oldsmobile's own, but, **below and below right**, body is shared with '31 Chevrolet cabriolet, and such items as the graceful landau bars and folding windshield interchange between the two makes.

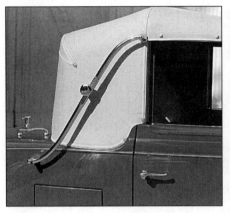

tag was nearly three times that of the contemporary Cadillac. By 1912, Oldsmobile's market share was down to three-tenths of one percent.

What followed was a decade of confusion at Olds. Seemingly uncertain as to its place in the automotive world, or even in the General Motors structure, Oldsmobile offered a proliferation of four-, six- and eight-cylinder models — and even, from 1919 to 1923, a line of light trucks. Nothing seemed to work, at least not for very long. Oldsmobile's share of the market rose to 2.4 percent in 1919 — not much, compared to what it once had been, but the best the division had seen since the days of the pseudo-Buick a decade earlier. But then the bottom fell out again, and by 1922 that elusive market penetration had shrunk once more, to less than one percent.

By this time, however, Alfred Sloan had come to power at General Motors, and Sloan had plans for Olds. Installing A.B.C. Hardy, formerly of Chevrolet, as Oldsmobile Division's president, Sloan prepared to position the Olds just above Chevrolet on the price ladder he was

1931 Oldsmobile Color Schemes

Color Spec.	Model	Body Reveals	Window	Moulding	Stripe	Fenders	Wood Wheels Wheels	Wire Wheels
400	Standard Coupe	Black		Black	Tokio Ivory	Black Enamel	Black Enamel	Cream
401	Sport Coupe	Upper-246-30116 Pottery Brown; Lower-246-30111 Crockett Brown		246-30116 Pottery Brown	Cream Medium	246-30116 Pottery Brown	Spokes-Crockett Brown Enamel; Hub-Pottery Brown Enamel	Cream
402	Two-dr Sedan	Upper-Black; Lower-246-30114 Fenway Gray	246-30112 Dunsmuir Gray	Black	Aurora Red	Black Enamel	Spokes-Dunsmuir Gray Enamel; Hub-Fenway Gray Enamel	Black
403	4-dr sdn	246-30107 Bennington Blue	246-30115 Martini Brown	246-30107 Bennington Blue	Cream Med.	Black Enamel	Spokes-Martini Brown Enamel; Hub-Black Enamel	Cream
404	Patrician Sedan	Upper-246-30105 Argonne Green Lower-246-30108 Bingham Green		246-30105 Argonne Green	Tokio Ivory	246-30105 Argonne	Spokes-Bingham Green Enamel; Hub-Black Enamel	Cream
405	Optional on all closed cars	*Viceroy Maroon	246-30117 Royden Red	*Viceroy Maroon	Gold Bronz	Black Enamel	Spokes-viceroy Maroon Enamel; Hub-Black Enamel	Black
406	Conv. Roadster	246-30121 Venetian Blue	Saddle Panel-Argent	246-30121 Venetian Blue	Silver Blue	246-30121 Venetian	Spokes-Venetian Blue Enamel; Hub-Argent	Cream
407	Conv. Roadster	246-30118 Tokio Ivory		Black	Tokio Ivory	Black Enamel	Spokes-Tokio Ivory Enamel Hub-Black Enamel	Black
408	Conv. Roadster	246-30106 Beau Brummel Brown	Saddle Panel-246-301188Tokio Ivory	246-30109 Caromel Brown	Tokio Ivory	246-30109 Caromel Brown	Spokes-Beau Brummel Enamel; Hub-Caromel Brown Enamel	Cream
409	2-dr sdn	Upper-246-30113 Faunce Green Lower-246-30119 Valdez Gray		246-30113 Faunce Green	Gold Bronze	Black Enamel	Spokes-Valdez Gray Enamel; Hub-Faunce Green Enamel	Black

(Color numbers and names are duPont Duco)

Above: *Flying bird mascot was factory accessory.* **Left:** *Single stop/taillamp illuminates the rear.* **Below:** *Natural wood wheels with painted accent are especially successful on this car.* **Bottom:** *Overall appearance is graceful and pleasing.*

developing for the corporation.

By late in 1923 a new Oldsmobile appeared. This was the Model 30, a six-cylinder car bearing more than a passing resemblance to the Chevrolet. With its advent, all other Olds models, including the truck, were dropped. And so was the price: At $850, the new six sold for $245 less than the four-banger whose place it took!

The publicity people pulled out all the stops. "Cannonball" Baker, a prominent race driver of the day, was hired to drive a Model 30 coast-to-coast *with the transmission locked in high gear!* Baker's car was equipped with oversized gas tanks, and refueling was accomplished by raising the rear wheels off the ground in order to keep the engine running. The trip, an advertising tour de force, took 12½ days to complete. That it could be accomplished at all was no mean feat, in 1923.

Sales began to climb. By 1924 Oldsmobile production had more than doubled from the figure of two years earlier.

Late in 1925, in a trend-setting move that helped to establish Olds as GM's avant-garde division, radiator shells began to appear in chrome, rather than nickel plate. For 1927 the engine was bored to 185 cubic inches, up from 169.3, and four-wheel brakes were fitted for the first time. Styling had been updated in 1925, though the resemblance to the Chevrolet was stronger than ever, and that year the practice commenced of finishing the cars in

Duco. In certain body styles Fisher coachwork had been featured since 1923, and by 1925 nearly all Oldsmobiles came with bodies from the new Fisher plant, located in a nearby factory that had once belonged to General Motors' founder Billy Durant.

But the real breakthrough for Olds

Driving Impressions

Joe Ferreira, a Chino, California, dairy rancher, first saw his 1931 Oldsmobile convertible roadster at a swap meet, back in 1975. The "For Sale" sign posted in its windshield caused Joe to quickly huddle with his wife Tina, for both of them are long-time Oldsmobile drivers as well as vintage-car enthusiasts. It wasn't long before they hauled the ragtop home, to take its place beside the '31 Ford DeLuxe phaeton whose restoration was just then nearing completion.

Ferreira disassembled the Olds and commenced the long and arduous job of restoration. But several hundred head of dairy cattle can place heavy demands on a man's time, and eventually Joe concluded that the job was simply more than he could handle. By that time he had already farmed out some of the work to Paul Batista's excellent restoration shop, Batista Automotive, in nearby Montclair. Finally, in 1978 the Oldsmobile was transported — in pieces. of course — to Batista's facility.

Someone in the convertible's mysterious past had attempted to restore it. A wretched paint job had been applied, the wrong bumpers had been fitted, and the fenders had been subjected to some severe, ham-fisted clouting. The hardwood framing of the Fisher body was largely rotted away, but fortunately the sheet metal was straight and free from rust And the wooden artillery wheels, happily, were in excellent condition, needing only to be cleaned up and refinished.

The Oldsmobile was very nearly complete, just as Joe Ferreira had purchased it. But the few missing parts proved to be critical, and eventually a parts car — a '31 Olds sedan — was purchased in order to complete the job. In addition to furnishing the radiator shell, some of the dashboard instruments, the differential, brake hardware, and assorted nuts and bolts, the sedan served as a model for the reassembly of the convertible; since Batista and his staff hadn't disassembled the car, putting it back together promised to be a challenging task!

A full, body-off restoration was undertaken, a project which eventually consumed 3,500 man hours at Batista Automotive. But the result is a car that must literally be better than new. The finish is flawless; the body is so carefully rebuilt that the doors close at the touch of a finger, and the mechanical components have been restored to equally high standards. There's even a rare radiator cap ornament, located by good fortune at the Hershey swap meet.

Not surprisingly, then, the Oldsmobile was named First Junior Winner, Class 20A, at Hershey in 1982. This was followed by a Senior Award at the 1983 AACA National Spring Meet, and a Presentation Award at the AACA Palm Springs event in October 1983.

It was *SIA*'s privilege to drive Joe Ferreira's Oldsmobile on what might be termed its "maiden voyage." Everywhere it had gone since the restoration, it had traveled by trailer; its total mileage when we slipped behind the wheel was less than ten! Joe Ferreira was kind enough. however, to permit us to drive the convertible several miles to Vince Manocchi's photo location, forming impressions and recording notes along the way.

The '31 Olds has a novel arrangement in which the throttle, starter, and choke are all inter-connected. Thus, when the starter pedal (located on the floor to the right of the accelerator) is depressed, the throttle is slightly open and the choke is closed. We can see the potential for all kinds of grief with such an arrangement; it's not, in our view, the most impressive feature of the car.

The driver sits comfortably in a fairly erect position on the adjustable seat. Leg room is adequate, even for the tall driver. Visibility to the side is impaired by the absence of a quarter-window, but of course that's to be expected in a convertible of this vintage.

There's a full panel of instruments, at the top of which is a knob that at first we were unable to identify. Upon experimentation, we learned that it controls the radiator shutters. In its normal position it is pushed all the way in, and the shutters are open.

But to increase engine heat — there being no thermostat — the knob is pulled out. Just the thing for a cold January morning — say, in Bennington, Vermont!

The newly rebuilt engine is, of course, very stiff. The clutch operates smoothly, and acceleration is more rapid than we expected, particularly in view of the fact that we were just commencing the breaking-in process. Engine noise is not obtrusive, and the second gear is just as quiet as Oldsmobile's advertisements claimed it to be. Shifts are easy. with fairly long throws to second and third gears. But the synchronizers — though they were replaced when the gear-box was overhauled — aren't as effective as they might be. The downshift from high to second is clash-free, even if the lever is moved rapidly. We found, however, that it is advisable to double-clutch the upshifts.

There's a distinct vibration, very noticeable but not terribly bothersome, when the Olds is accelerating hard. Paul Batista tells us that this is characteristic of the F-31 Oldsmobile, resulting from a leather couplet that is used in lieu of a universal joint at the forward end of the driveshaft; an economy move, no doubt, and not a particularly felicitous one.

At speed, however, the Olds is smooth and quiet. The body of the 1931 model was lighter than had been the case in previous years, yet it is better insulated, and the result is very satisfactory. The ride, for a car of this age and class, is good. The single-acting shock absorbers permit a certain amount of choppiness; still, with Paul at the wheel we were able to take legible notes, writing on a clipboard held in our lap.

It was interesting, as we drove, to feel the engine gradually "freeing up." After a few miles, the difference was readily noticeable. We'd like to have an opportunity to drive the Olds again after it has a few hundred miles on it, just for the sake of comparison.

The Oldsmobile corners with relatively little roll. Steering is heavy. It's acceptable enough under ordinary driving conditions, but parking the car requires lots of muscle.

If the Olds can be seriously faulted in any area, it seems to us it must be with respect to its brakes. Not that they're really *bad*. The action is peculiar. Heavy pedal pressure is required, then there is a slight pause as the brakes seemingly energize themselves. And then they take hold, bringing the car to a halt in reasonably competent fashion. We have a suspicion, however, that the binders might be susceptible to fading under hard use; for the Oldsmobile carries 40 percent more weight per square inch of lining than, for example, either the '31 Pontiac or the comparably priced Nash 660.

In General Motors' price structure — "Alfred Sloan's ladder," as *Fortune* magazine once put it — Oldsmobile, in 1931, was positioned squarely between the Pontiac and the Series 50 Buick: $190 higher than the former, in convertible form; $160 lower than the latter. It may have been a better value than either of them; certainly no more serviceable or attractive automobile could be had at the Oldsmobile's comparatively modest price.

came in 1928, with the introduction of the vastly improved L series. Gone were the boxy lines, the Chevrolet-inspired appearance. The new L-28 Oldsmobile was bigger, heavier (by about ten percent), sleeker and far more handsome than the previous model. Its power came from a completely redesigned engine. Still a side-valve six, it was both stouter and smoother than its predecessor. Its bore was greater and its stroke shorter, increasing the displacement to 197.5 cubic inches. Horsepower was increased to 55, up from 40 in the 1927 model. The compression ratio was also increased; the crankshaft was cradled in four main bearings instead of three, and fuel was fed by a camshaft-driven fuel pump instead of the vacuum tank that was still the norm for most of the industry.

Predictably, sales took another spurt. Olds was still outproduced by sister division Buick by a ratio of something like two-and-a-half to one, despite the Oldsmobile's $270 price advantage and its more advanced styling. But the division's share of the market was the best it had been in a decade. Olds had at last found its place in the scheme of things at General Motors!

The smart styling of the F-28 Oldsmobile created, in its price class, a sensation not unlike that which greeted the LaSalle, a year earlier. Longer and lower, with its wheelbase extended by three-and-a-half inches, its lines were smooth and sweeping. The cowl was high and long, a trend-setting design feature, and the windows were long and low. Compared to most of its competitors, the design of the new Oldsmobile was at least a year ahead of its time.

The F-28 Olds was, in fact, a totally new car, not merely a modification of the Model 30. A million road miles had been racked up by a fleet of 14 experimental cars, each of which differed from the others in certain important respects. Test driving during the developmental process was done by amateurs — not professionals — on the theory that an expert driver might instinctively com-

pensate for any flaws in the cars' performance, while in the hands of this army of klutzes any possible short-comings would be instantly revealed!

The final version borrowed the best features of each of the 14 test cars, the declared objective being to produce an automobile that would deliver 50,000 miles of service without major mechanical attention. By the standards of 1928 that was an ambitious goal, but evidently it was fully achieved.

The remarkable F series engine, in fact, remained in production, with periodic modifications, for more than two decades. For 1929 horsepower was increased to 62, chiefly by means of

another boost in the compression ratio.

Two years later a new downdraft carburetor raised it to 65, and eventually — bored to 238.1 cubic inches and given a 6.5:1 compression ratio — it reached 100 horsepower. But in 1931, when our driveReport car was built, that day was still a decade In the future.

Improvements were substantial in 1931's F-31 series. The frame was strengthened by means of deeper side rails and beefed-up crossmembers. A new transmission from the Muncie Products Division of General Motors featured quiet, helical gears and synchronized second and third speeds. In addition to the new Stromberg downdraft

illustrations by Russell von Sauers, The Graphic Automobile Studio

© copyright 1984, Special Interest Autos

specifications

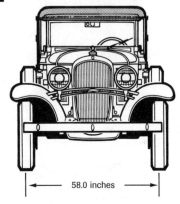

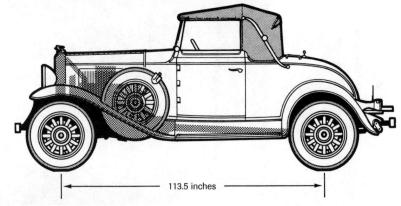

58.0 inches

113.5 inches

1931 Oldsmobile F-31

Price	$1,000
Standard equipment	6 wood-spoke artillery wheels with sidemounts; trunk rack; front and rear bumpers; Lovejoy hydraulic shock absorbers; rear view mirror; automatic windshield wiper; fold-down windshield; two spare tires and tubes; spare wheel locks
Options on dR car	White sidewall tires; clock mirror; shatterproof glass; natural finish wood spoke wheels; radiator ornament

ENGINE

Type	L-head 6-cylinder, cast en bloc
Bore x stroke	3.1875 inches x 4.125 inches
Displacement	197.5 cubic inches
Max. bhp @ rpm	65 @ 3,350
Taxable horsepower	24.4
Max. torque @ rpm	95 @ 1,000
Compression ratio	5.06:1
Induction system	1.25-inch Stromberg DRX-2 downdraft carburetor with an automatic heat control; mechanical fuel pump
Lubrication system	Full pressure
Main bearings	4
Electrical system	Delco-Remy 6-volt

CLUTCH

Type	Single dry plate
Diameter	8.875 inches
Actuation	Mechanical, foot pedal

TRANSMISSION

Type	Muncie 3-speed selective, sliding gear. Synchronized second and third gears; quiet second gear
Ratios: 1st	3.06:1
2nd	1.63:1
3rd	1.00:1
Reverse	3.44:1

DIFFERENTIAL

Type	Spiral bevel
Ratio	4.56:1
Drive axles	Semi-floating

STEERING

Type	Worm and three-tooth sector
Turns lock-to-lock	4
Ratio	16:1
Turn circle	38 feet

BRAKES

Type	4-wheel duo-servo mechanical
Drum diameter	12 inches
Total swept area	160.5 square inches

CHASSIS & BODY

Frame	6-inch channel iron, 5 cross-members
Body construction	Steel over hardwood framing
Body style	Deluxe convertible roadster

SUSPENSION

Front	35.5-inch x 2-inch semi-elliptical leaf springs; solid axle
Rear	54.5-inch x 2-inch semi-elliptical leaf springs
Tires	5.25 x 18
Wheels	Wood artillery, natural finish

WEIGHTS AND MEASURES

Wheelbase	113.5 inches
Overall length	173 inches (inc. bumpers)
Overall height	69.25 inches
Overall width	68.5 inches
Front track	58 inches
Rear track	58 inches
Ground clearance	8 inches
Shipping weight	2,875 pounds
Height	13.4 inches

CAPACITIES

Crankcase	6 quarts
Cooling system	13 quarts
Fuel tank	16 gallons

PERFORMANCE FACTORS

Weight per c.i.d.	14.6 pounds
Weight per bhp	44.2 pounds
Hp per c.i.d.	.329
Top speed	75+ mph (factory figure)
Acceleration 0-60	18.0 seconds*
Standing ¼ mile	21.9 seconds

* Theoretical acceleration figures (computed according to formulae supplied to *SIA* by Alex Tremulis)

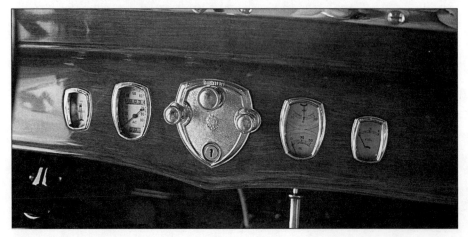

1931 OLDSMOBILE

was improved, contributing to better performance, but oddly enough, the compression ratio was reduced from 5.2:1 to 5.06:1.

Six body styles were offered, each available in either standard or deluxe trim. The former was "stripped" to the extent that bumpers and even the spare tire cost extra. But the latter, in addition to bumpers front and rear and a pair of sidemounted spares as standard equipment, even supplied a folding trunk rack and locks for the spare tires. At $65 the deluxe package was a bar-

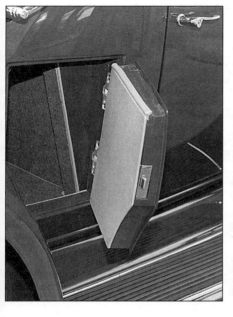

Facing page: Woodgrained dash carries symmetrical instrument layout. **This page, far left:** A further touch of class, golf bag door was standard. **Left:** Generous entry and exit room for driver or passenger. **Below left:** Flathead six was thoroughly up to date with mechanical fuel pump and downdraft carburetor. **Below:** Seats and door panels are very plain in design. **Bottom left:** Rumble seat offers cushy perch, good leg room. **Bottom:** driveReport car has been restored with authentic, old-style grease fittings.

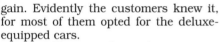

gain. Evidently the customers knew it, for most of them opted for the deluxe-equipped cars.

Ten different color schemes were offered, but options were limited to no more than three for any given body style. The convertible roadster, for instance, was available in Tokio Ivory with black fenders, Beau Brummel Brown with Caromel Brown fenders, or solid Venetian Blue. Our driveReport car left the factory finished in the latter hue, and although it suffered a nondescript beige paint job at some point in its career, it has been restored to the splendor of its original color.

An unusual Oldsmobile feature for 1931 was the buyer's option, in either the standard or deluxe cars, of wood spoke, or wire wheels. Sedans could even be had with disc wheels, but few cars were so equipped. The price was the same in any case, though natural spoke (rather than painted) wooden wheels fetched a premium of ten dollars the set. Mohair or whipcord, at the buyer's option, was used for the interior of the closed models, while the convertible roadster offered a choice of whipcord or genuine leather upholstery. ෙ

Acknowledgements and Bibliography
Automobile Trade Journal, *various issues;* Automotive Industries, *various issues;* Dennis Casteele, The Cars of Oldsmobile; *Beverly Rae Kimes,* Oldsmobile, the First Seventy-Five Years; Oldsmobile factory literature.

Our thanks to Paul and Frank Batista, Montclair, California; Ray Borges and Linda Huntsman, Harrah Foundation Library, Reno, Nevada; Dave Brown, Durham, California; Jim Edwards, Operations Manager, Harrah's Automobile Collection, Reno, Nevada; Vince Manocchi, Azusa, California; Rick Sullivan, Montclair, California. Special thanks to Mr. and Mrs. Joseph C. Ferreira, Jr.,

That's How It Was, in 1931

The Depression was playing hob with the economy in 1931. Unemployment was up; the gross national product was down; new car registrations were off 52 percent compared with 1929's record total, and an atmosphere of gloom pervaded the nation.

And yet, in some respects it was business as usual!

• Gangster Jack "Legs" Diamond, who had just been acquitted on a kidnapping rap, was shot to death in an Albany, New York, boarding house.

• The waters of Niagara Falls tore away about a million cubic feet of rock on the American side.

• Pope Pius XI, on the occasion of the ninth anniversary of his coronation, de-livered a radio address which was carried by stations all across the United States. In some parts of the world, however, the broadcast was "jammed" by the Soviets.

• The Reverend Doctor Harry Emerson Fosdick dedicated the $4 million Riverside Church in New York City.

• The United States purchased from Denmark, for $25 million, the Danish West Indies. We know them now as the Virgin Islands.

• An act of Congress declared "The Star Spangled Banner" to be the national anthem.

• A group of Massachusetts congressmen presented a resolution calling for the repeal of prohibition. Within two years, the "long drought" would end.

• The Empire State Building, at 102 floors, 1,449 feet, the tallest in the world at that time, was opened. For a dollar, the sightseer could catch the high-speed elevator and take in the spectacular view from the observation platform near the top.

• Radio telephone service was established between the Pacific Coast and the Far East.

• Notre Dame football coach Knute Rockne was killed in an airplane crash. (The following year the Studebaker Corporation, with which Rockne had long been associated, would name its new, low-priced car in his honor.)

• And the 20 millionth Ford car, a Model A DeLuxe fordor, came off the assembly line at Dearborn.

1935 Oldsmobile 6 vs. 8

by Arch Brown
photos by Bud Juneau

FOR as long as most Americans can remember, Oldsmobile has been riding high on the sales charts. But it wasn't always so. Consider this: It took 37 years from the founding of the company until that day in 1934 when the millionth Oldsmobile was built. By way of contrast, Nash — never a hot seller — also passed the million mark during 1934, less than 17 years after the marque's debut.

As recounted in *SIA* #82, there had been a time, back in the early years of the century, when Olds was literally the world's best-selling automobile. But then Sam Smith, who with his two sons owned a controlling interest in the company, forced Ransom Olds out, and Oldsmobile abruptly changed direction. Instead of concentrating on the popular $650 Curved Dash Runabout, the firm went upscale, with 1906 prices ranging as high as $2,250. The Smiths promoted this top-of-the-line model as "the best thing on wheels." Possibly it was, but sales fell precipitously.

Billy Durant acquired the troubled firm in 1908, as part of his newly organized General Motors Corporation. He quickly cobbled together a Buick-based Olds for the 1909 season. Selling for less than half the price of the cheapest 1908 model, it paced the division to a sixfold sales increase. But then, in a move that defies explanation, Oldsmobile abruptly dropped the smaller car and returned to the luxury market. Once again, sales plummeted.

But if its volume was down, at least Olds was building some of the most spectacular automobiles ever conceived. By 1911 the big Limited series rested on a wheelbase of 138 inches and was powered by a huge T-head six of 707 cubic inches' displacement. This gargantuan

stood so high, on its 42-inch wheels, that two steps were required in order for passengers to climb aboard. Prices ranged as high as $7,000 for the limousine. (To put these figures in perspective, the Cadillac limo sold, in those days, for $3,000, while Packard's version was priced at $4,400.)

Over the succeeding years a variety of four- and six-cylinder models were offered, and between 1916 and 1923 there was even an Olds V-8. Prices bobbed up and down in a manner that seemed to suggest some corporate confusion with respect to Oldsmobile's intended market target. And sales went no place. Production reached the 10,000 level for the first time in 1916, but that year Olds was outsold ten-to-one by corporate rival Buick.

It wasn't until Alfred P. Sloan, Jr., took command at General Motors that order was restored. During 1923 the existing four- and eight-cylinder series were dropped in favor of a new six, the Model 30. Undercutting by $245 the price of

Originally published in Special Interest Autos #111, May-June 1989

the earlier four, it became GM's second-lowest-priced car. By 1924 Olds sales were more than double the 1922 figure — though the numbers were still modest enough.

Duco finish and chrome-plated trim were among the features pioneered by Oldsmobile during 1925. Then for 1927 the engine was bored an eighth of an inch, raising the horsepower from 41 to 47. Four-wheel brakes were adopted that same year. But it wasn't until 1928 that the Model 30 was replaced by the first in a long line of "F" Series cars. Heavier by 270 pounds than its predecessor, and 17 percent more powerful, the F-28 featured an advanced new engine. The stroke/bore ratio was substantially reduced, four main bearings replaced the previous three, the compression ratio was raised from 4.7:1 to 5.0:1, and the troublesome vacuum tank gave way to a modern, camshaft-driven fuel pump.

Equally important from a sales standpoint, the F-28 was a beauty. Longer, lower and smoother of line than the Model 30, it was one of the most stylish automobiles in its class. Certainly it was handsomer and more modern in appearance than the contemporary Buick, and it undercut the price of Buick's Standard Six by $270. Model year production reached 84,635, a new record for Olds, but still Buick outsold it by two-and-a-half to one.

Horsepower was increased to 61 in 1929's F-29 series, and production topped the 100,000 mark for the first time, narrowing somewhat the sales gap between Olds and Buick. A "companion" car, the Viking V-8 (see SIA #10), made its appearance in Oldsmobile showrooms that March. Priced at $1,595 — $620 higher than the Olds — it was intended to broaden the division's market coverage. A big, impressive car, 700 pounds heavier than the Oldsmobile, the Viking bore a striking resemblance to the LaSalle. It even shared the LaSalle's 125-inch wheelbase.

But the Viking was no LaSalle, and it was no sales sensation, either. No doubt the Depression, coming along so soon after the new car's introduction, contributed to its early demise, and it is doubtful that the market really needed another upper-medium-priced car, in any case. At least equally important, however, was the matter of the Viking's engine, which had two peculiarities. The first of these was its use of horizontal valves, resulting in an odd configuration for the cylinder heads and a sharp bend in the head gaskets. But the critical factor was the Viking's adoption of a single-plane crankshaft, a practice abandoned several years earlier by Cadillac and other builders of V-8 engines.

In any event, the Viking lasted only through the 1930 season.

For 1931, the six-cylinder F-31 was Oldsmobile's sole offering. Production came to 47,316 for the model year — barely more than a third of Buick's output for the same period, but not too bad by Depression standards. The bottom dropped out in 1932, however, despite the introduction of a new straight-eight, the L-32, to supplement the six-cylinder F-32 series. Sales were at the lowest point since 1921, another Depression year, and for a time Oldsmobile's future seemed in doubt.

Fortunately, there was a dramatically restyled Olds for 1933. From the sloping, V-shaped grille to the "beavertail" rear, this one was as modern as it was handsome. Fenders were deeply skirted, wheels were of the new steel artillery type, and — best of all — prices were sharply cut. Sales increased significantly as Olds moved from twelfth place to ninth — still behind Buick, but gaining fast. (It's a reasonable assumption, in fact, that Oldsmobile would probably have edged past Buick during 1933, had it not lost sales to Pontiac's smart new bargain-priced straight-eight.)

The big moment came in 1934, when for the first time ever, Oldsmobile sold more cars than Buick. Sales, in fact, were more than double the 1933 figure as Olds built its millionth car and leap-frogged over Studebaker and Pontiac, as well as Buick, to capture sixth place in the production race.

It was a well-deserved success. Consider now what Oldsmobile had to offer for 1934:

• Prices of the six-cylinder F-34 were lowered once again, ranging now from $650 for the business coupe to $785 for the touring sedan. (Perhaps we should explain here that the term "touring," in mid-thirties parlance, indicated a built-in trunk, a comparatively recent innovation at that time.)

• Horsepower, in the case of the best-selling F-34, was increased from 80 to 84, though the bore was smaller by a sixteenth of an inch, leading to a reduction in displacement from 221 to 213 cubic inches. (Evidently the critical factor here was an increase in the com-

pression ratio from 5.3:1 to 5.7:1.) The L-34's output remained at 90 horsepower, a very competitive figure for a car that sold for less than a thousand dollars.

• Ride and handling were substantially improved through the use of independent front suspension. Unlike Pontiac, which shared with Chevrolet the somewhat fragile Dubonnet system, Oldsmobile's "knee action" was of the "wishbone" variety, a sturdy and serviceable arrangement.

• Hydraulic brakes were employed. Apart from the new LaSalle, which was in many respects an Olds derivative, the 1934 Oldsmobiles were the first General Motors cars to be fitted with this critically important feature. Not for another two years would either Buick or Cadillac follow suit.

• Styling, which featured this time a sharply sloping, gently vee'd grille, was even more modern looking than before — and more massive appearing as well, especially in the case of the L-34.

In short, Oldsmobile had come up with an attractively styled and technically advanced automobile, offering outstanding comfort and more than adequate performance at very reasonable prices. No wonder it was a good year. Second only, in fact, to Olds's all-time peak of 1929.

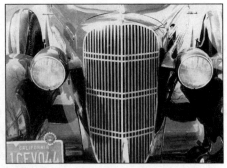

Above left and right: Differences between six and eight cylinders extend right through to the grille design with eight carrying three more horizontal bars. **Below:** *In Olds's model jargon both cars were catalogued as coupes, but the eight is the more familiar coupe.*

warned that the steel top would be noisy. It would be hot. It would kill the effectiveness of the popular roof antenna, a wire screen hidden under the customary fabric insert.

That last point was valid, of course, though other types of antennae were at least equally effective. The first two objections, however, were nonsense, as the public was quick to perceive, and as rapidly as GM's competitors could tool up for it, nearly all of them adopted the seamless steel roof.

Wheelbases were longer, by one inch in the case of the six, two inches on the eight, bringing those measurements to 115 and 121 inches, respectively. Smaller wheels and fatter tires (6.25/16 vs. 5.50/17) were adopted for the F-35, partly for styling considerations and partly in order to cope with a 150-pound weight increase. Frames were strengthened at the rear by boxing in the side rails, and an additional cross-member was fitted. It was claimed that torsional frame stiffness was increased by one-third. New, three-point engine mountings, in combination with additional crankshaft counterweights, provided smoother engine operation.

Brakes, too, were improved. Double-piston wheel cylinders replaced the previous single-piston type; brake shoes were wider and drum size was increased. Even the front suspension was refined and strengthened. And the six was returned to its previous cylinder dimensions, raising the horsepower from 84 to 90. Oil pump capacity of this engine was increased, the crankshaft was redesigned, and connecting rods were strengthened. A redesigned cylinder head, meanwhile, helped to raise the eight-cylinder engine from 90 horsepower to 100.

Eight body styles were offered on both the F-35 and the L-35 chassis, with the price differential between the two series averaging about $150. There were three coupes: "business," "club," and "sport." The first of these was a two-passenger job, while the others accommodated auxiliary riders — on "jump" seats in the case of the limited-production club coupe, or out in the sport coupe's rumble seat. The two-door sedan was called a "five-passenger coupe," which must have caused some degree of confusion. Or, equipped with a built-in trunk, the same car became the "touring coupe." There were two four-door types, the trunk-back "touring sedan" being by far the more popular of the pair.

Some items of equipment that would today be taken for granted were still classed as options in 1935. Oldsmobile's "Group A," for instance, included bumpers, bumper guards, rear spring covers, and a spare tire. This group, factory-installed, was virtually a mandatory option," the idea being to keep

Model year production came to 126,768 cars in 1935 — 25 percent higher than the division's previous all-time record. Calendar-year production looked even better at 183,152 units, thanks to the early introduction of the 1936 models.

Styling was completely revised for 1935. Lines were more softly rounded. An impressive die-cast grille was used (or rather, a pair of them, for the bridgework of the L-35 was readily distinguishable from that of the smaller F-35). Some people irreverently suggested that either style might well have served as a shield for one of King Arthur's knights, but for

the most part both versions were well received. Both the F-35 and the L-35 used two-piece "Vee'd" windshields in lieu of the previous single flat pane, and in both instances chromed, cigar-shaped (or was it dirigible-shaped?) vents decorated the hood side panels. Front-opening "suicide" doors were adopted throughout the line, a practice that would be abandoned the following year.

By far the most significant styling innovation for 1935 was the one-piece steel "Turret Top." Touted as an important safety feature, it appears to have thrown the competition into a state of near-panic. Prospective buyers were

And you thought the '63 Sting Ray was the first split-window from GM!

Side vent design in hoods is identical, as are hood latches.

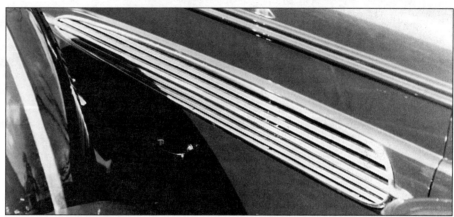

the advertised price as low as possible. The price was $37.50 on the F-35, $45.00 on the L-35. "Group B," another factory installation, consisting in this instance of dual trumpet horns, twin windshield wipers with booster pump, and a right-hand sun visor, was priced at a reasonable $12.50. Twin, side-mounted spares cost $47.50 on the six-cylinder cars, $50.00 on the eights.

Other extras included a choice of two radios ($57.50 and $66.25) and two heaters ($13.90 and $18.65). Fender skirts, lacquered to match the body color, were remarkably inexpensive at $11.50. Safety glass windshields and vent wings were supplied as standard issue, but probably most buyers paid the extra ten bucks to have the laminated glass installed in all windows. Oversize tires came to $30.00, and a luggage compartment light cost two whole dollars, while a starboard tail-lamp — standard on the L-35 — could be supplied for an extra $5.50 on the six-cylinder cars.

The best was yet to come, but for 1935, a time when most automakers — including all the other GM divisions —

were still struggling to shake off the lingering effects of the Depression. Olds sold more cars than ever before. Seventy percent more, in fact, than its intracorporate rival, Buick. At long last, Oldsmobile had emerged from comparative obscurity to become a potent force in the automobile market.

Driving Impressions

I recall the time when Dad's friend Alfred turned up at our place, driving a brand new Oldsmobile straight-eight. An L-35 touring sedan it was, though I couldn't have identified it that precisely at the time.

Dad, a Scotsman to the core, about dropped his teeth, Alfred had been driving a four-cylinder Plymouth, which made a lot of sense — though initially

there had been just an edge of suspicion about the hydraulic brakes. But this big thing? An Olds six would have been easy enough for Dad to rationalize, but for Alfred to have popped the extra $150 for the eight seemed somewhat out of character. Not just on account of the initial outlay, either. Two more cylinders to feed; that was — presumably, at least — the worst of it.

So I've been looking for a chance to compare the six-and eight-cylinder versions of Oldsmobile's highly successful 1935 model. The opportunity came when, at Sacramento's Capitol Concours, I met the family that seemingly must own half the 1935 Oldsmobiles in California: the brothers Benjamin, Marco, and Victor Gonzalez and their brother-in-law, Bob Wise. Among them, these four guys own 17 of these cars.

1935 Oldsmobile: Table of Prices, Weights and Production

Body Style	Prices		Weights		Production	
	F-35	L-35	F-35	L-35	F-35	L-35
Business Coupe	$675	$660	3,110	3,335	6,468	1,226
Sport Coupe	$725	$895	3,150	3,380	2,865	959
Club Coupe	$725	$670	3,115	3,340	200	74
Coupe, five-passenger	$755	$695	3,225	3,460	14,765	670
Touring Coupe	$765	$900	3,235	3,465	19,821	4,662
Sedan, 4-door	$790	$940	3,265	3,530	13,009	2,976
Touring Sedan	$620	$970	3,295	3,545	34,647	18,056
Convertible Coupe	$800	$950	3,155	3,390	1,596	910
Production Totals:					95,413	29,035

As might be expected, eight-cylinder car offers more acceleration. Both cars sacrifice flat cornering for smooth riding qualities.

Both hood ornaments are pure thirties in their design, though the six-cylinder car has the more stylish one.

Some are restored units, some are decent originals, some are in progress, and some are awaiting their turn. A few will end up as parts cars.

For *SIA*'s purposes, it was an ideal situation. We selected as our photo subjects two of the nicest cars, a restored L-35 business coupe and a largely original F-35 five-passenger coupe. (The latter body style, as we've noted above, is really a flat-back, two-door sedan. Somebody in the advertising department evidently favored fancy titles, however confusing they may have been.)

Perhaps we should explain that technically our comparisonReport L-35 belongs jointly to Victor and Bob, while the F-35 is Marco's. But the entire enterprise is so completely a cooperative

undertaking that distinctions of ownership tend to become blurred.

It was Bob Wise who was responsible for getting this unusual family hobby under way. Back in 1972 Bob had collected an alarming number of speeding tickets, and he purchased an F-35 sedan (for $700) on the assumption that it would tend to temper his driving habits. Which, of course, it did; a 1935 Olds is no hot rod.

As time went along, Wise joined the Oldsmobile Club of America, and at a Fresno wrecking yard he found the L-35 business coupe. Shortly afterward he talked Marco into buying the F-35 five-passenger coupe, and it wasn't long before Benjamin caught the fever and acquired an F-35 touring sedan. Then

came the joint purchase, from a southern California collector, of ten passenger cars and an L-35 Henney ambulance. Included in this group was a rare L-35 convertible, now awaiting restoration.

Marco's car was purchased in Redlands, California, from its second owner. At that time the odometer read 54,000 miles, evidently the actual figure. Marco and his wife Becky drove the Olds home to Sacramento — a trip of more than 400 miles — without incident. Apart from a new paint job in the original Buckingham Gray color, little has been done to the car to bring it to the condition in which it is shown here.

The L-35 coupe was another matter, however. The frame had been cut by a hot-rodder and had to be replaced by a unit robbed from a parts car, but the body was straight and solid. The engine, which — at 52,000 miles — had never been rebored, was reasonably sound apart from three broken valve springs.

Specifications: 1935 Oldsmobiles, Series L-35 and F-35

	L-35 (8-Cylinder)	F-35 (6-Cylinder)
Price, model tested (f.o.b. factory)*	$860	$725
Options on feature cars	Dual sidemounts, wsw tires, beauty rings, bumper guards, radio, heater, leather interior, clock	White sidewall tires, beauty rings, bumper guards, radio, heater
Engine	8-cylinder, in-line	6-cylinder, in-line
Bore x stroke	3″ x 4¼″	3 5/16″ x 4⅛″
Displacement (cu. in.)	240.3	213.3
Compression ratio	6.20:1	6.00:1
Maximum bhp @ rpm	100 @ 3,400	90 @ 3,400
Maximum torque @ rpm	182 @ 1,800	165 @ 2,000
Taxable horsepower	28.8	26.3
Valve configuration	L-head	Same
Valve lifters	Mechanical	Same
Crankshaft	Fully counterweighted, fitted with vibration damper	Same
Main bearings	Thin wall, replaceable steel-	Same
Number main bearings	5	4
Induction system	Duplex downdraft carburetor, automatic choke, mechanical fuel pump	Single downdraft carburetor, manual choke, mechanical fuel pump
Lubrication system	Pressure to main, con rod, camshaft brgs and piston pins; spray to other parts	Same
Exhaust system	Single	Same
Electrical system	6-volt	Same
Clutch	Single dry plate	Same
Diameter	9⅞″	9″
Actuation	Mechanical, foot pedal	Same
Transmission	3-speed selective, floor lever, synchronized 2nd and 3rd gears	Same
Ratios	2.94/1.66/1.00 (3.78 reverse)	Same
Differential	Spiral bevel	Same
Ratio	4.44:1	Same
Drive axles	Semi-floating	Same
Torque medium	A)S rings	Same
Steering	Jacox worm-and-roller	Same
Ratio	20.4:1	19.0:1
Turns, lock-to-lock	3.90	3.75
Turn circle	38 feet	37 feet
Brakes	4-wheel internal hydraulic	Same
Drum diameter	12″	11 1/16″
Effective area (sq. in.)	207	190
Construction	Body-on-frame	Same
Frame	Rigid X-girder type	Same
Body construction	Composite steel and wood	Same
Body style, test car	Business coupe	Five-passenger coupe
Front suspension	Independent, coil springs	Same
Rear suspension	Conventional, semi-elliptic longitudinal springs, ride stabilizer	Same
Shock absorbers	Double-acting hydraulic	Same
Wheels	Steel artillery	Same
Tires	7.00/16	6.25/16
Wheelbase	121″	115″
Overall length	193 23/32″	188 11/32″
Overall width	72″	Same
Overall height	67 7/16″	67″
Front track	58″	Same
Rear track	59″	Same
Minimum ground clearance	8″	7¾″
Shipping weight, model tested	3,335 pounds	3,225 pounds
Crankcase capacity	7 quarts	6 quarts
Cooling system capacity	15 quarts	12¾ quarts
Fuel tank capacity	18 gallons	Same
Horsepower per cubic inch	.416	A22
Weight per horsepower	33.4 pounds	35.8 pounds
Weight per cubic inch	13.9 pounds	15.1 pounds
Weight per sq. in., brakes	16.1 pounds	17.0 pounds
Estimated top speed (factory figures)	85-90	80-85

* With standard equipment

The optional leather interior, however, was a mess. It has been replaced by high-quality vinyl, using the old upholstery as a pattern. The restoration of this car, completed in 1986, required an enormous investment of time, Victor reports. Time well spent, for it is one of only 43 L-35 business coupes to have been fitted with factory sidemounts.

Both of these automobiles are used regularly as tour cars. They're displayed occasionally at club meets and other events, but no one pretends that either machine is in concours condition. Victor, the family's ace mechanic, tells us that the 1935-36 Oldsmobiles were prone to snapping axles, but to date, fortunately, none of the Wise/Gonzalez cars has experienced that problem.

We drove the F-35 first. The front leg room, while hardly generous, was fully adequate, and the front bucket seats offer a measure of lateral support. Doors are wide, providing easy access to the rear compartment, and back seat passengers can stretch their legs to full length.

Same stamping, different treatment. Six has plain taillamp lens and simple trim ring, while eight gets fancier lens and fully plated housing.

Above: *Handsome, fully enclosed sidemount cover hides artillery-style steel wheels. Both cars use this anachronistic wheel design.* ***Below:*** *Leather interior on eight is most inviting; both cars use this "deco" design on scuff plates.*

The clutch is smooth and light, but gearshift action is sloppy — more so on this car than on the L-35, though the latter is no model of precision, either. Acceleration couldn't be called brisk, but keeping up with the flow of traffic is no problem. Steering, we found, is reasonably quick, and easier than one might expect. Suspension is soft, providing a smooth ride. But at a price, for

the car leans heavily in hard cornering. Brakes, for a mid-thirties automobile, are excellent.

Acceleration is noticeably faster in the eight-cylinder car. We're sure the difference would be even more apparent in hilly terrain, but unfortunately for our purposes, Sacramento is as flat as a table top. Steering is a trifle slower in the L-35, and noticeably heavier. No

problem here, however, it's just that the F-35 steers exceptionally easily. Braking action is not quite as effective on this car as on the six, possibly because identical binders are used to stop a somewhat heavier car. Suspension, again, is soft, but the L-35 leaned a bit less in the turns and was somewhat easier to control. The shocks, which are in better shape on this car than on the six, doubtless have something to do with the difference.

We dislike "suicide" doors for more reasons than one, a view that must have been widely held, since Olds used them for only one season. But our major gripe about the business coupe has to do with its restricted visibility to the rear. The back window is small, and there are no quarter-panes; so backing up is a hazardous undertaking.

Taken all-in-all, we like the 1935 Oldsmobiles. Both of them. They are not exciting automobiles, to be sure. But they are handsome, comfortable, easy to drive, and certainly a solid value for the money — as motorists were quick to recognize, back in 1935.

Which brings us back to Dad's friend, Alfred. Did he make the right choice in selecting the eight-cylinder Oldsmobile, rather than the less expensive six?

In balance, we'd have to say, yes, Alfred chose well. Had the Olds been intended primarily for his wife's around-

Coupe certainly wins the space race in the back.

town use, the lighter steering and shorter overall length of the F-35 would have made it the car of choice. But Alfred made frequent trips from his home in Berkeley to his family's ranch in the Sacramento Valley, covering well over 250 miles on each occasion. The L-35's greater weight and longer wheelbase combined to give it a distinct edge in riding comfort. And the big straight-eight rendered Alfred's car capable of sustaining higher cruising speeds than the six could have done.

And as to Dad's objection about fuel consumption: Not to worry. Assuming an overall city/highway average of 14 miles to the gallon for the L-35, 15.5 for the F-35 (and these figures come pretty close to the truth); and estimating Alfred's annual mileage at 10,000, that's 69 additional gallons consumed each year by the eight-cylinder car. At sixteen cents a gallon, the going rate for "regular" in those days, the extra outlay comes to just $11.04 per annum.

Alfred would consider that money well spent. ☙

Acknowledgements and Bibliography
Automobile Trade Journal, *January 1935 and March 1935;* Automotive Industries, *February 23, 1935; Dennis Casteele,* The Cars of Oldsmobile; *Beverly Rae Kimes (ed.),* Oldsmobile, the First Seventy-Five Years; *Beverly Rae Kimes and Henry Austin Clark Jr. (eds.),* Standard Catalog of American Cars, 1805-1942; *Richard M. Langworth and Jan P. Norbye,* Complete History of General Motors; Motor, *January 1935;* Oldsmobile factory literature.

Our thanks to Ray Borges, William F. Harrah Automobile Foundation, Reno, Nevada; Dave Brown, Durham, California. Special thanks to our comparisonReport car owners.

Above and below: Family resemblance between six- and eight-cylinder engines is readily apparent.

Both cars boast uncluttered, attractive rear styling.

PHOTOS BY DON STICKLES

by Ken Gross,
Feature Editor

drive report

Because of the numerous steps to conserve scarce metals, many buyers felt then and enthusiasts still feel now that the '42s were inferior cars. Let's test that theory with this original and very representative...

1942 OLDSMOBILE B-44

THE YEAR 1942 has always had a peculiar fascination for me—as I suspect it has for a lot of other car enthusiasts. The fact that all U.S. auto production actually stopped for three years makes for an incredibly rare run of special-interest cars; also the stoppage created that unprecedented later demand for postwar cars.

Michael W.R. Davis wrote about "The Year That Wasn't" in *SIA* #6, and our 1942 Ford driveReport (*SIA* #29) also elaborated on this unusual period. To recap briefly, though:

The year the cars stopped came as no sudden surprise to Detroit. Automakers began getting heavily into defense armaments in 1939-40, when most 1942 cars were on the drawingboards. In February 1941, the WPB (War Production Board) said "no more non-defense heavy tooling," and the government imposed quotas and production cutbacks. The WPB, in fact, said that automakers could build only half the cars for 1942 that they'd sold in 1941. As it turned out, no company made even that many.

There were limitations, too, on scarce metals like zinc, aluminum, nickel, and chromium. These restrictions forced great engineering and styling compromises and caused the widespread substitution of plastic, stampings, and paint. The greatest problem that faced Detroit at that time was to keep up with the flurry of new Washington orders; also to make their 1942 cars halfway appealing in the process.

The axe fell in February 1942. By February 10, when the last Fords and Mercurys rolled off the line, only 1,175,484 cars had been built—the lowest model run since 1932. Toward the end, many '42s had their chrome plating painted over in response to WPB regulations. Whitewalls were almost non-existent that year to save zinc oxide, and diecastings were sometimes replaced with steel stampings or molded plastic.

Because of the numerous steps to conserve scarce metals, many buyers felt then and enthusiasts still feel the '42s were inferior cars. They were planned before the war and were built to last for the duration. Although the industry saved many pounds of critical ingredients through careful planning and new production techniques, every make's advertising naturally emphasized that the '42s were quality built. Frequently, manufacturing costs were increased due to the necessity of using substitute materials. Quality did suffer.

Oldsmobile's promotional approach to 1942 was a very patriotic one. The 1942 Olds catalogue is liberally sprinkled with military scenes. The first page doesn't even show the new B-44 (not a new medium bomber, but Oldsmobile's 1942 model designation). Instead, amid an industrial panorama showing oil wells, factories, a P-38 twin-engine Lightning fighter, and an Army gun crew firing a 155mm howitzer, was the announcement, "Defense comes first with Oldsmobile!"

Oldsmobile Division began producing howitzer shells in April 1941. Automatic cannons for fighter planes went into production in Lansing a few months later. Olds, like so many car manufacturers, told buyers that, in cooperation with the defense program, specifications might have to change, and they reserved the right to discontinue models.

Olds ad copywriters had a military wordfest with the B-44s. Double-duty bumpers, dreadnaught frames, and turret tops were just a few of the warlike descriptions. The catalogue showed as many soldiers and sailors admiring the new models as civilians.

"You can always count on Olds," the copy read, "...it's quality built to last." In truth, the new B-44 was described a bit like a medium tank, and the factory claimed its new car "...was better built than any Olds in 44 years." There was a bit of license taken here as Ransom E. Olds had built his first car in 1896.

Despite the defense cutbacks, Oldsmobile started 1942 with a full deck: three wheelbases, five series, two 6s, and three 8s. The 60 and 70 series (see chart) had a choice of engines, while the 90 series dropped its 6 in '42 and offered the 257-cid 8 as standard equipment. Hydra-Matic, pioneered by the division for 1940, was a $100 option on all models.

Olds claimed its 4-speed Hydra-Matic gave 10%-15% more gas mileage than its standard transmission. This was justified by the Hydra-Matic's 3.63 axle vs. 4.30 with standard transmissions. GM tests in 36 cities using a device called the "Effort-meter," which counted clutch pushing and gearshift motions, also showed H-M saved an average of 419 operating motions per hour of city driving.

GM actively promoted its new automatic transmission. Olds dealers offered a booklet which gave "...complete, confidential information" about Hydra-Matic's advantages. Over 130,000 H-M's had been sold by the start of the 1942 model year; 45% of all Oldsmobile buyers opted for the Hydro. Still a novelty, the '42 Olds proudly displayed Hydra-Matic script on the hood sides and trunks of models so equipped.

Oldsmobile offered a fastback 2-door club sedan in its Special series for 1942 for the first time. The fastback style had appeared in the Dynamic Cruiser range previously. Oldsmo-

The 98 series' hood extended right to the windshield, eliminating the conventional cowl ventilator. To replace it, Custom Cruisers had ducts which opened under the front fenders and ventilator doors inside the car to control the flow of air.

Under the hood, the in-line Econo-Master 8 (and its little brother, the 238-cid 6) remained largely unchanged from 1941. Along with many makes, Olds was forced to replace aluminum pistons with cast-iron ones. Oldsmobile used an alloy called Armasteel—a pearlite malleable iron developed by GM's Saginaw Malleable Iron Division.

Although the new 4-ring pistons were heavier than the aluminum ones they replaced (24 vs. 16 ounces), they didn't affect engine smoothness. Olds engineers redesigned the combustion chambers and raised the 8's compression from 6.3:1 to 6.5:1. Connecting rods were made heavier to support the beefier pistons, and the crankshaft was stiffened by increasing the thickness of the throws. By the time they were through with lower-end refinements, Olds engineers felt the reversion from aluminum to cast-iron pistons would go unnoticed.

Die castings were virtually eliminated at Oldsmobile to conserve valuable zinc. The total weight of die castings in the 1942 vs. the '41 dropped from 40 to 6.5 pounds—chiefly through the use of chrome-plated steel stampings. When the engineers and metalurgists finished their zinc reduction program, the only zinc components outside the Olds were the door handles. On the 6s, a cast-iron carburetor bowl and lower body saved nearly two pounds of zinc on each car.

The '42's self-energizing brakes were ¼-inch wider in front than the '41's—the Dynamic and Custom Cruiser 8s had larger brakes than the Special and Dynamic 6s.

The 98 Custom 8 Cruiser was heralded as a "...massive, long-wheelbase 8 of custom quality in the field of medium price." Much was made of the elimination of runningboards from the 98's new bodies and the addition of rear fender skirts—Olds called them fender panels. As befitted the "...largest, most luxurious car in the entire Oldsmobile line," the interiors had broadcloth seats, velvety carpets, and nearly every Olds accessory for the Special and Dynamic series was standard. The 98s had a push-button starter, but other Oldses kept the floor-mounted variety.

Although the 98 had most of the Olds add-ons, you could still plump for a few extras. Accessory lovers could choose from the Condition-aire heater and defroster at $39.95; the deluxe Master radio, $68.50; a unique In-a-car fold-down bed for $19.50, and directional signals for only $11.40. Convenience and dress-up items included a $4.50 backup light, a pair of $11.50 fog lights; trunk and hood lights for $1.25 each, and even a visor vanity mirror equipped with a thermometer-for just $1.35.

You could accessorize your 98 right into the middle of the Buick price range.

Our driveReport B-44 Custom 8 Cruiser belongs to R.G. (Bob) Hellstrom of East Hampton, Connecticut. Bob owns a number of immaculate special-interest Oldsmobiles, in-

bile, like all its GM brethren in '42, had fenders that swept back across the front doors. Rear fenders on all three new Custom Cruiser bodies reached forward to a point midway in the rear door panels. The 98s had a 24-inch-lower roofline and a 24-inch-longer wheelbase than their '41 predecessors. The biggest Oldsmobile's lower, wider body styles included a convertible, 4-door sedan and 2-door club sedan.

Olds's styling innovation for 1942 was its massive dual front bumper/grille combination. Called the double-duty bumper, the Olds frontal treatment consisted of two horizontal grille bars connected by vertical bumper guards. Rugged channel steel braces top and bottom reinforced the grille and joined it to an additional crossmember at the front of the car's frame. The frame siderails had been extended six inches forward to provide extra firm bumper support and—although they didn't publicize it then—an extra measure of crush area.

Oldsmobiles were unmistakable from the front, with their big chromey grilles. It would be 1958 before the division's offerings again carried so much brightwork.

On the fadeaway fenders, a ribbed, broad-band belt molding provided an art deco styling touch. Strother MacMinn's new instrument panel clusters set off the dashboard.

cluding a 1941 4-door convertible and a '48 station wagon. The '42 is one of his favorites.

He located the car in Virginia in 1969 from an ad in *Hemmings*. Incredibly original, the car still has its "C" gas rationing sticker on the rear window. Up front, the car's 1945 Pennsylvania inspection decal is still visible on the windshield. A faded '42 Hydra-Matic instruction sheet is still in its original place on the driver's sun-visor.

Although buyers could choose a number of attractive bright colors in '42—with names like Warwick tan, New ivory, and Condor blue—and 2-tone paint combinations were only $10 extra, Bob's 98 was finished in a deep, lustrous black that was one of the most popular colors of its day. The big sedan's immaculate black lacquer finish has been retouched only on the tops of the front fenders where slight fading had occurred.

When Hellstrom found the car, it was

I figured I couldn't possibly want to keep the '42 sedan, overchromed and bulbous as it was.

"But was I ever wrong! By the time I eased this big 98 sedan up onto the New Jersey Turnpike, less than a third of the way home, I was completely sold. What an incredible highway car! The Hydra-Matic shifted so smoothly at exactly the proper shift points, and the heavy old Straight 8 just whispered along without the slightest strain. Even though this is an early-run body (#1803), it has none of the misalignments and noises (except for one instrument panel squeak) that we've come to accept and expect in newer cars.

"Comparing this '42 with my 1941 Olds 98, I've found a number of changes. The dash-button starter was standard on the 1942 98 and optional ($7.50 extra) on other Oldses. On cars with the old-style floor starter (and the '41s), the Hydra-Matic lever got kicked up into neutral by mechanical linkage. In the '42 you have to shift

Bob Hellstrom bought this car to resell but fell in love with it. He also collects Olds literature.

With only 32,752 miles on the odometer, Hellstrom's 98 remains virtually new in every respect.

equipped with an optional left-foot accelerator, probably for the original owner. GM and other manufacturers had a number of driving accessories available for returning veterans who had become disabled in the war. In the 98, the installation of a left-foot accelerator required moving the headlight dimmer out of the way. Bob put back the conventional right-hand pedal and will gladly give the left accelerator and its linkage to any *SIA* reader who genuinely needs it. The brand name is "Variant," and it fits a number of makes and models of cars.

W E'LL LET Bob Hellstrom himself sum up the driving-impressions portion of this report. In his words:

"This 1942 is the only Olds I've ever bought with the original intention of reselling it immediately. From the first time I saw my first '42 Olds in grammar school, I've considered this model the ugliest ever built. When this car came up in *Hemmings* in 1969, though, I went down to Virginia to buy it. I needed money for a '41 Olds 98 convertible I was restoring, and

manually to neutral before you start the engine.

"After then moving the selector to Hi, the car takes off easily and keeps up with modern traffic. For passing, you plunge the accelerator to the floor, just as in today's cars.

"The '42 does sound as if it's going faster than it actually is, and actually the speedometer numerals are closer together on the high side of the dial. You get the distinct impression, though, that there must be a low axle in this car—and it is, at 3.63:1. Yet I managed 19.3 mpg on a 600-mile trip to Maryland and back.

"I've never had occasion to drive this car on winding back roads, so I can't comment on general handling, yet the soft 7.00 x 15 tires do tend to scuff the outer sidewalls if I take a corner faster than the posted speed limit. This keeps me from making maneuvers I shouldn't.

"Over the highway puts the 98 at its best. The four coil springs give a soft but controlled ride. There's absolutely no wheel hop on uneven surfaces and no strange suspension nor driveline noises. Steering feels remarkably light for a car of this weight.

OLDSMOBILE MODEL YEAR PRODUCTION 1942

Special Series (66 & 88)

Station wagon (Hercules)	795
Convertible coupe (423567)	848
Business coupe (423527B)	1,166
Club coupe (423527)	4,173
Club sedan (423507)	10,766
2-door sedan (423511)	3,688
4-door sedan (423519)	8,053
Town sedan (423569)	3,888

Dynamic Series (76 & 78)

Club sedan* (423607)	10,536
Deluxe club sedan** (423607D)	3,165
4-door sedan* (423609)	9,166
Deluxe 4-door sedan** (4236090)	3A00

Custom Series (98)

Convertible coupe (423967)	216
Club sedan (423907)	1,771
4-door sedan (423969)	4,672
Total	66,303

* Body has no rear center armrest
** Body has a rear center armrest

Coil springs all around plus stabilizer bars give B-44 an easy ride with good handling.

Above: Side and rear armrests, toe cavity make rear occupants happy. **Right:** Instrument clusters repeated shapes of taillights. The 98 had pushbutton starter.

Above: Spare stands upright; trunk is very spacious. **Below:** Rear fender panels, standard on Custom 8 Cruiser, cost $14 extra on Dynamics and Specials.

1942 Oldsmobile B-44 Line

Series	Wheelbase	No./cyl.	Displacement	Bhp @ rpm	Base-priced 4-dr sedan
Special 66	119 in.	6	238 cid	100 @ 3400	$1088
Special 68	119 in.	8	257 cid	110 @ 3600	1130
Dynamic Cruiser 76	125 in.	6	238 cid	100 @ 3400	1153
Dynamic Cruiser 78	125 in.	8	257 cid	110 @ 3600	1196
Custom Cruiser 98	127 in.	8	257 cid	110 @ 3600	1275

"As with all early Hydra-Matics, you have to wait a moment after putting the shift lever in gear before there's a decisive change in direction. And since there's no Park on the quadrant, reverse has a pawl that holds the car on slight inclines. In all, then, this car drives, rides, and feels like the best of the new ones, but better in the way it's put together and the ease with which I can work on it. Ugly it might still be, but it's a beauty when it comes to doing all those things a car is meant to do."

National Automotive History Collection, Detroit Public Library

OLDS PRODUCTION stopped on February 3, 1942. By that time, the last of the B44s had grey-painted trim, and some even had wooden 2 x 8 bumpers.

GM engineering vice-president Charles L. McCuen, who'd been Olds general manager from 1937 through 1940, was pretty certain in late 1941 that there'd be no 1943 models. "Whenever we are privileged to introduce our next new models, whether it will be 1944 or 1945, you will see many changes," McCuen told *Motor* magazine.

"You will see the use of plastics increased. You will see aluminum fighting it out with steel for position. You will see increased use of rubber, both natural and synthetic. One-hundred-octane fuel will be a general thing after the war, bringing more power with greater economy.... Synthetic materials will be in more general use. Nothing can stop progress. You may see it slowed up slightly, but you will not see it stopped.

"We will learn many things from this emergency," predicted McCuen, "both about materials and manufacturing; all of which should and will be reflected in a better product and better values."

A few lucky v.i.p.'s and bureaucrats got the last of the '42s. McCuen's predictions weren't wrong, and progress was indeed delayed a little. When production began again after the war, Olds dropped the double duty bumper/grille combination for a simplified and very influential "frown mouth" version. Olds customers for 1946 found substantially unchanged cars at their dealers when production resumed. Detroit, hard pressed to meet the postwar demand, was cranking out warmed-over '42s as fast as they could. Buyers were satisfied and Oldsmobile retained its traditional headlock on seventh place until 1949.

In that changeover year, restyling and the new Rocket V-8 moved the division into sixth place. The 1942 B-44's new Custom Cruiser bodies had served honorably for seven years. Their successors ushered in a performance image for Oldsmobile that continues today. ᛃ

Our thanks to James J. Bradley, National Automotive History Collection, Detroit Public Library, Detroit; The Oldsmobile Club of America, Inc., Box 1498, Samp Mortar Station, Fairfield, CT, 06430; The Oldsmobile Club of Canada, c/o Norman B. Horsfall, 107 Marlin Ave., Windsor, Ont., Canada N8W 2B2. Our special thanks to Bob Hellstrom, East Hampton, Connecticut.

Above: *B-44's front and upper grille bar was extensively reinforced by members attached to the frame:* **Below:** *Rugged Olds 8 got redesigned combustion chambers for 1942; it delivers 110 bhp. Owner Bob Hellstrom averaged 19.3 mpg on a recent 600-mile East Coast trip.*

specifications

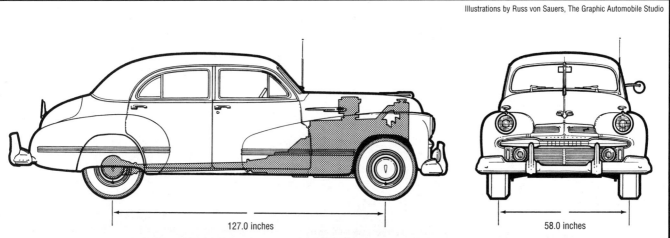

127.0 inches   58.0 inches

1942 Oldsmobile B-44 Custom Cruiser 98 sedan

Price when new ....$1,275 f.o.b. Lansing (1942).

Standard equipment .....Clock, rear center armrest, push-button starter, wheel trim rings, skirts, cigar lighter, vacuum booster pump.

Options ....Hydra-Matic, radio, heater, rear grille guard, trunk light, fog lights, exhaust deflector (delivered price $1,622.05).

ENGINE
Type ....L-head 8, cast-iron block, water-cooled, 5 mains, full pressure lubrication.
Bore & stroke ....3.25 x 3.875 in.
Displacement..............257.0 cid.
Max. bhp@rpm...........110 @ 3,600
Max torque @ rpm .....200 @ 1,800.
Compression ratio 6.5:1
Induction system.......Single 2-bbl. carburetor, mechanical fuel pump.
Exhaust system ....Cast-iron manifold, single exhaust.
Electrical system ....6-volt battery/coil.

CLUTCH
Type ....None.

TRANSMISSION
Type.........................Hydra-Matic 4-speed automatic, column shift.
Ratios: 1st 3.66:1
2nd 2.53:1
3rd............................1.44:1
4th............................1.00:1
Reverse 4.31:1

DIFFERENTIAL
Type..........................Hypoid.
Ratio.........................3.63:1
Drive axles.................Semi-floating.

STEERING
Type..........................Worm and double roller.
Turns lock to lock......4.5.
Ratio........................19:1 (geared 23:1)
Turn circle ....43.5 ft.

BRAKES
Type..........................4-wheel hydraulic drum internal expanding.
Drum diameter ....11.0 in.
Total lining area.........181.1 in.

CHASSIS & BODY
Frame ....Channel-section steel, double dropped, central X-member, 5 crossmembers.
Body construction ......All steel.
Body style.................4-door, 6-passenger sedan.

SUSPENSION
Front..........................Unequal length independent A-arms, coil springs, lever shocks. stabilizer bar.
Rear...........................Solid axle, coil springs, twin trailing arms, lever shocks, stabilizer bar.
Tires ....7.00 x 15, 4-ply
Wheels ....Pressed steel discs, drop-center rims, lug-bolted to brake drums.

WEIGHTS & MEASURES
Wheelbase.................127.0 in.
Overall length ....216.0 in.
Overall height ....64.2 in.
Overall width ....77.4 in.
Front tread................58.0 in.
Rear tread..................61.5 in.
Ground clearance ....8.0 in.
Curb weight...............3,715 lb.

CAPACITIES
Crankcase...................6.0 qt.
Cooling system...........20.5 qt.
Fuel tank....................19.0 gal.

FUEL CONSUMPTION
Best ....17-19 mpg.
Average ....14-16 mpg.

Oldsmobile pioneered Hydra-Matic transmission in 1940; it sold a good number in its 1942 models.

NO GEARS TO SHIFT!

NO CLUTCH TO PRESS!

This Is Not Your Grandpa's Oldsmobile!
1949 ROCKET 88

drive report

by Josiah Work
photos by Bud Juneau

THERE are those who can remember when the Oldsmobile was a staid, solid machine — durable, comfortable and a good value for the money — but totally un- exciting. It was the sort of car that would appeal to Grandpa, or perhaps to the upwardly mobile family, seeking a little more status than a Chevrolet could provide.

But all that changed with the introduction of the 1949 Rocket 88.

For several years, Oldsmobile had fielded five distinct series, two sixes and three eights, all with well seasoned in-line, side-valve engines. But when the 1949 models first appeared, on September 15, 1948, there were just two series to choose from, the 76 and the 98. The former was powered by Oldsmobile's hoary six-cylinder flathead, bored and stroked this time to 257.1 cubic inches, virtually the same displacement as the previous year's Olds straight-eight. Its 6.5:1 compression ratio enabled the 76 to operate satisfactorily on "regular" gasoline. Sharing with Chevrolet the new GM "A" body, it was a comparatively light car, weighing as little as 3,260 pounds. With 105 horsepower on tap, it offered more than adequate performance, by the standards of the time.

Originally published in Special Interest Autos #139, Jan.-Feb. 1994

The other Oldsmobile, the "Futuramic 98," offered quite a contrast. For under the hood of this big, C-bodied car was the brand new, overhead-valve Rocket V-8 engine. Of over-square dimensions — that is, the bore was greater than the stroke, a reversal of the customary practice in 1949 — it featured 7.25:1 heads, an unusually high compression ratio for 1949. About as high, in fact, as the premium fuels of the day would permit. Displacement was 303.7 cubic inches, and horsepower was rated, or perhaps underrated, at 135. The short, stout, rigid crankshaft was cradled in five main bearings, rather than the three used by competing V-8s. It was said that the engine was designed to accommodate compression ratios as high as 12.5:1, when suitable fuels became available.

Working under the direction of Gilbert Burrell, Oldsmobile engineers had been experimenting for some time with new engine layouts. Their research had led them to several conclusions:

● First, in order to permit the use of larger valves for improved breathing, as well as in the interest of reduced friction, a large-bore, short-stroke design was deemed to be critical.

● Second, even when fitted with the optional high-performance cylinder head, the L-head Oldsmobile straight-eight engine carried a compression ratio of just 7.00:1. Substantially higher ratios would lead to a loss of the smoothness for which Oldsmobiles were noted. Yet in the interest of both performance and economy, the numbers needed to go higher than that. Clearly, overhead valves were a must.

● Third, the V-8 configuration was called for, partly because a short crankshaft would eliminate the problem of "whip," and partly because a big-bore straight-eight would require an engine block that would be unacceptably heavy as well as excessively long.

Inspiration for Oldsmobile's high-compression V-8 came from "Boss Ket," Charles Franklin Kettering, research director and vice president of General Motors from 1920 to 1947. In the view of most automotive engineers during the early postwar period, compression ratios — which averaged no more than 6.5:1 in those days — had about reached their practical limit. Any substantial increase, the engineers said, would lead to unacceptably harsh and rough performance, high piston friction and insurmountable ignition problems. Furthermore, there would be little or no benefit in fuel economy. Or so they believed.

Kettering scoffed at this attitude. "To get high engine efficiency, explosion pressures have to be high," he declared. "There is no other way.... If you can get high economy with low explosion pressures, write me a letter about it. I would

Planets and rockets everywhere. **Above:** *Up front on the hood and,* **below,** *the hood ornament itself.* **Below left:** *Taillamp design is simpler than on '50 cars.* **Bottom:** *More planets on rocker trim.*

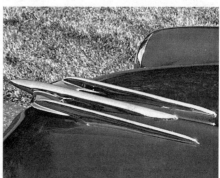
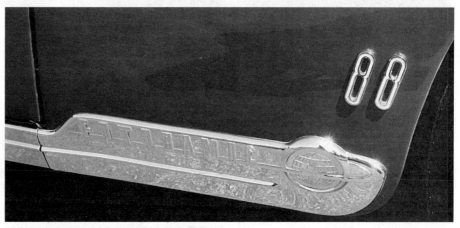

like to know how it is done."

Of course it couldn't be done. But neither, according to the critics, was it possible to build a practical, durable, smooth-running, high-compression passenger car engine. Not even if suitable fuels were to become available.

Kettering, never afraid of a challenge, set about to prove the critics wrong. He did so in the most convincing way possible: by building a prototype engine. This was not the Rocket V-8. Rather, it was a comparatively small (180-c.i.d.) in-line six. Fitted with seven main bearings and designed with the bore equal to the stroke, it carried a compression ratio of 12.5:1.

Intended strictly as a research exercise, the Kettering engine — which ran on an experimental fuel known as triptane — was installed in a 1947 Oldsmobile sedan. Available only in limited quantities, triptane carried an octane rating of 99, compared to about 80 in the premium fuels then available to the public. Which, of course, meant that the Kettering engine was quite unsuitable for general use.

But with his prototype, Kettering proved his point very convincingly: It was possible to design a gasoline engine with a very high compression ratio without sacrificing the smoothness associated with conventional powerplants. Its fuel economy was very nearly equal to that of a diesel, 35 to 40 percent higher than that of a comparable standard-compression gasoline engine. Its mechanical efficiency was higher; its heat loss to the cooling water was 30

*Above: Simple but effective double bar grille gives Olds a distinct appearance. **Below:** "Airscoops" under headlamps were inspired by jet fighter design, then a new phenomenon.*

Optional Equipment, 1949 Oldsmobile
(partial list)

Radio, standard	$88.00
Radio, super deluxe	$96.00
Heater/defroster	$67.00
Auxiliary driving/fog lights	$19.00
Cadet visor	$30.00
Traffic light viewer	$5.00
Spotlight	$26.00
Turn signals	$21.00
Glovebox light	$2.00
Backup lights	$15.00
Underhood light	$2.00
Trunk light	$2.00
Windshield washer	$9.00
Stainless steel wheel rings	$10.00
Exhaust extension	$2.00
Vanity visor mirror	$2.00
Hood ornament	$5.00

1949 OLDSMOBILE

percent lower. And drivers found the demonstration car to operate no less smoothly than the standard production Oldsmobiles with which it was compared.

Nearly six months after the arrival of the first 1949 Oldsmobiles, the really sensational new Olds was introduced: the Rocket 88. Apparently it was Sherrod E. Skinner, Oldsmobile's canny general manager, who conceived the idea of dropping the hot new V-8 into the chassis of the 87, thus creating an automobile with the phenomenal (for 1949) power-to-weight ratio of 26.3 pounds per horsepower. (By way of comparison, the Ford V-8, itself a rapid piece of machinery, had a weight-to-horsepower ratio of 29.6:1. Calculations are based on the weight of club coupes in the bottom trim line.)

There was evidently some resistance coming from the corporate board room, but finally the green light was given, and during February 1949 the Rocket 88 appeared.

Perhaps Skinner had his eye on the publicity his hot little car might generate in competitive events, such as those sponsored by NASCAR (the National Association of Stock Car Auto Racing). Or again, maybe not; in any event the factory did not immediately undertake to sponsor or promote the contests. But factory participation or no, Olds won six of the nine stock car races staged during 1949 by NASCAR's Grand National division. Of course, it was a publicity bonanza for Oldsmobile. Further recognition came from the famed Indianapolis 500, when an Oldsmobile 88 convertible was selected to pace the 1949 race, and the following year a fleet of Rocket 88 two-door sedans was purchased by the California Highway Patrol.

Six body styles were offered for 1949, four of them in a choice of either Standard or Deluxe trim. The two-door club sedans and the four-door town sedans featured sporty fastback styling, while the four-door sedans and the club coupes were "notchback" types. Fastbacks had been quite popular for a time and the club sedans did rather well during the 1949 model year, though their popularity faded quickly after a notchback two-door sedan was introduced for 1950 (see *SIA* #1). The town sedans, however, attracted only 5,833 buyers during 1949, about evenly divided between Standard and Deluxe models. By 1950 the notchback version was the only four-door sedan in the line. And for 1950, also, a hardtop Holiday coupe was added to the 88 roster.

Convertibles and station wagons were

offered only in Deluxe trim. Early in the 1949 model year the wagons were fitted with wooden bodies, but later on an all-steel version (complete with ersatz wood paneling, of course) was substituted. The steel-bodied haulers were much cheaper to manufacture, and by 1950 the price of the wagon had been reduced by several hundred dollars.

Incidentally, the six-cylinder Series 76 was offered in the same body styles and trim levels as the 88. The larger 98, on the other hand, was available initially only in sedan, club sedan and convertible form, the first two coming in a choice of Standard or Deluxe trim. Then at mid-year Olds offered a smart Holiday (hardtop) coupe on the 98 chassis, bringing the total to 26 distinct Oldsmobile models for 1949. Thirteen standard colors and eight two-tone combinations were catalogued, as well as several upholstery combinations.

Those first-generation Rocket 88s came with the HydraMatic transmission as standard issue, but when the nearly identical 1950 models were introduced, the automatic cost $185 extra. This change enabled Olds to advertise a much lower list price, although apparently few units were delivered with the column-mounted, three-speed manual shift.

Perhaps a more important reason for listing the stick shift as standard equipment had to do with NASCAR, and other competitive events. The term "Stock Car," in those days, meant exactly that. Cars seen on the nation's tracks were the same as you would find in the showrooms, though admittedly they were tuned to perfection. And according to test runs conducted for *Mechanix Illustrated* by Tom McCahill, the stick-shift Oldsmobiles were about a second and a half faster in the standing half-mile than the HydraMatic-equipped cars.

By the bye, Oldsmobile's advertising people liked to compare their three-speed manual gearbox to the legendary pre-war LaSalle transmission, so beloved by hot-rodders. But McCahill, who was generally enthusiastic about the 88, called the transmission "rough," and "balky." Nevertheless, he concluded that "if you want to get there in a hurry and know when to shift with a conventional transmission, you can tear the ears off the finest automatic rig ever built so far as performance is concerned."

Once again, the Olds 88 was the car to beat on the stock car circuit. Of 19 NASCAR races that year, Oldsmobiles took the checkered flag in ten of them. Hershell McGriff and Ray Elliott won the Carrera Panamericana — the Mexican road race — in an 88 that year, though they were driving a 1951 model, one of 13 Oldsmobiles in the contest.

But Olds was moving upscale. The six-

Above: Olds handles well, but non-assisted steering's quite heavy. **Below left:** *Wheel cover design was carried over from 1948 cars.* **Below right:** *Automatic tranny was advertised on trunk handle.*

1949 Oldsmobile Prices, Weights and Production

	Price	Weight	Production
Series 76			
Club Coupe 5-passenger	$1,748	3,260	12,683
Club Sedan, 5-passenger	$1,774	3,290	23,059
Town Sedan, 5-passenger	$1,837	3,335	3,741
Sedan, 5-passenger	$2,265	3,340	23,631
Deluxe Club Coupe	$1,889	3,315	3,280
Deluxe Club Sedan	$2,322	3,355	8,960
Deluxe Town Sedan	$2,385	3,400	2,325
Deluxe Sedan	$1,990	3,375	13,874
Convertible Coupe	$2,164	3,580	5,338
Station Wagon, Deluxe	$2,911	3,680	1,545
Total Production, Series 76			98,436
Series 88			
Club Coupe, 5-passenger	$2,164	3,550	6,562
Club Sedan, 5-passenger	$2,191	3,585	16,887
Town Sedan, 5-passenger	$2,254	3,625	2,859
Sedan, 5-passenger	$2,265	3,615	23,342
Deluxe Club Coupe	$2,295	3,590	4,999
Deluxe Club Sedan	$2,322	3,615	11,820
Deluxe Town Sedan	$2,385	3,665	2,974
Deluxe Sedan	$2,396	3,645	23,044
Convertible Coupe	$2,580	3,845	5,434
Station Wagon, Deluxe	$3,317	3,945	1,355
Total Production, Series 88			99,276
Series 98			
Club Sedan	$2,447	3,835	2,311
Sedan	$2,521	3,890	8,820
Deluxe Club Sedan	$2,541	3,840	16,200
Deluxe Sedan	$2,615	3,925	49,001
Convertible Coupe	$2,994	4,200	12,602
Holiday (hardtop) Coupe	$2,973	3,945	3,006
Total Production, Series 98			91,940
Grand Total, 1949 Model Year Production			289,652
Grand Total, 1949 Calendar Year Production			282,887

specifications

illustrations by Russell von Sauers, The Graphic Automobile Studio

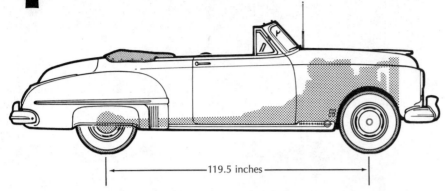

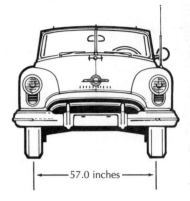

←———— 119.5 inches ————→

←— 57.0 inches —→

1949 Oldsmobile 88

Original price	$2,580 f.o.b. factory, with standard equipment; federal taxes included
Standard equipment	HydraMatic transmission, power top, clock, deluxe steering wheel with horn ring, wheel trim rings, fender panels, directional signals
Options on dR car	Radio, heater, white sidewall tires
Aftermarket equip.	Auxiliary gauges

ENGINE

Type	Overhead-valve V-8
Bore x stroke	3.75 inches x 3.4375 inches
Displacement	303.7 cubic inches
Compression ratio	7.25:1
Horsepower @ rpm	135 @ 3,600
Torque @ rpm	263 @ 1,800
Taxable horsepower	45.0
Valve lifters	Hydraulic
Main bearings	5; crankshaft with 6 counter-weights
Fuel system	Carter 1.4375-inch dual down-draft carburetor, camshaft pump
Lubrication system	Pressure
Cooling system	Centrifugal pump
Exhaust system	Single
Electrical system	6-volt battery/coil

TRANSMISSION

Type	HydraMatic 4-speed automatic planetary
Ratios: 1st	3.82:1
2nd	2.63:1
3rd	1.45:1
4th	1.00:1
Reverse	4.31:1

DIFFERENTIAL

Type	Hypoid
Ratio	3.2:1
Drive axles	Semi-floating

Torque medium	Stabilizing arms

STEERING

Type	Saginaw worm-and-roller
Turns lock-to-lock	4.5
Ratio	19:1
Turning diameter	40 feet

BRAKES

Type	4-wheel hydraulic, drum type
Drum diameter	11 inches
Effective area	191.7 square inches

CHASSIS & BODY

Construction	Body-on-frame
Frame	Double-drop, extra heavy channel section steel with X-member
Body construction	All steel
Body style	Convertible coupe

SUSPENSION

Front	Unequal A-arms, coil springs, anti-roll bar
Rear	Rigid axle, coil springs, anti-roll bar
Shock absorbers	Double-acting lever type
Tires	7.60/15 4-ply tube type
Wheels	Pressed steel, drop-center rims

WEIGHTS AND MEASURES

Wheelbase	119.5 inches
Overall length	202 inches
Overall width	75.19 inches
Overall height	63.344 inches
Front track	57 inches
Rear track	59 inches

Min. road clearance	8.281 inches
Shipping weight	3,845 pounds

INTERIOR MEASUREMENTS (front seat)

Hip room	59.94 inches
Head room	36 inches
Leg room	42.69

CAPACITIES

Crankcase	5 quarts
Cooling system	21.5 quarts
Fuel tank	18 gallons
Auto transmission	11.5 quarts (dry)
Rear axle	3.75 pints

CALCULATED DATA

Horsepower per c.i.d.	.445
Weight per hp	28.5 pounds
Weight per c.i.d.	12.7 pounds
P.S.I. (brakes)	20.1 pounds

PERFORMANCE

Top speed.	91.74 mph (average)
Standing 1/4 mile	19.86 seconds
0-30	4.6 seconds (trans. in "Drive")
0-60	12.44 seconds
Braking from 30 mph	27 feet, 2 inches
Braking from 60 mph	164 feet, 9 inches
Fuel consumption	20.19 mpg (Mobilgas Grand Canyon Run)
At steady 50 mph	18.75 mpg

(from a *Motor Trend* road test of a 1950 Olds 88 sedan equipped with HydraMatic transmission)

PERFORMANCE

Top speed	96-97 mph
Standing 1/2 mile	30 seconds (through gears)
0-30 mph	4.4 seconds
0-60 mph	12.0 seconds
0-70 mph	16.8 seconds

Right: Stainless splash shields were standard on all '49 Oldsmobiles. *Far right:* Split windshield looks slightly old-fashioned on sleek '49 styling.

1949 OLDSMOBILE

cylinder line was dropped for 1951. Meanwhile a new series, the Super 88, had been introduced. Sales of these slightly larger, marginally heavier (and about $125 costlier) cars immediately eclipsed those of the original 88, which were phased out before the end of the model year. Meanwhile there was competition from an unexpected quarter as NASCAR crowned a new champion that season: the Hudson Hornet.

Driving Impressions

Supposedly, our driveReport car had been restored to "new" condition before it was purchased by its present owners, Mark and Kay Barchas, of Los Altos Hills, California. A thick file of receipts attests to the fact that the previous owner had indeed paid for a total, ground-up restoration, but in some respects the quality of the job was not what it should have been, and in a number of areas it had to be done over. Body and paint, upholstery and top represented very good work, but the transmission, rear axle, steering, brakes, front end — virtually all mechanical components except the engine — were found to be faulty.

Nothing is known about the prior history of this car, except that in 1986, following the original restoration, it was taken to the national meet of the Oldsmobile Club of America, where it took first-in-class honors. Given the problems that later surfaced, one presumes that it was judged primarily on its cosmetic condition; yet there is nothing about the car to suggest that it has ever been abused. It should have been, in fact, an ideal subject for a complete but relatively easy restoration.

Top: Rocket ohv V-8 made all the difference in Olds's performance image. It became the car to beat. *Above:* Dash is almost severely plain. *Below:* Clock and radio dominate center of dash. Steering wheel design is particularly attractive. *Bottom:* Half-round instrument housing is easy to read.

1949 OLDSMOBILE

Above: *Slab-side styling was introduced on 98 series in '48, extended to entire model lines in '49.* **Below:** *303 V-8 gives 88 jackrabbit acceleration thanks to high torque at low rpm.*

Olds Versus the Competition

	Olds 88	Buick Super	DeSoto	Mercury
Price, convertible	$2,580	$2,603	$2,578	$2,410
Wheelbase	119.5″	121″	125.5″	118″
Overall length	202″	207.5″	206.25″	206.75″
Shipping weight	3,845 lb.	3,985 lb.	3,785 lb.	3,591 lb.
Engine	V-8	Straight 8	6-cyl.	V-8
Valve configuration	Ohv	Ohv	L-head	L-head
Displacement (cu. in.)	303.7	248.1	236.7	255.4
Compression ratio	7.25:1	6.60:1	7.00:1	6.80:1
Horsepower/rpm	135/3,600	115/3,600	112/3,600	110/3,600
Torque/rpm	263/1,800	212/2,000	195/1,600	200/2,000
Automatic transmission*	HydraMatic	Dynaflow	Tip-Toe**	None
Final drive ratio	3.2:1	4.1:1	3.73:1	3.91:1
Steering	Worm/roller	Worm/nut	Worm/roller	Worm/roller
Ratio	19:1	19.8:1	18.2:1	18.2:1
Turning diameter	40′	43′	N/A	43′ 8″
Braking area (sq. in.)	191.7	161.5	173.5	179.0
Drum diameter	11″	12″	11″	11″
Tire size	7.60/15	7.60/15	7.60/15	7.10/15
Horsepower/c.i.d.	.445	.464	.473	.431
Weight (lb.)/hp	28.5	34.7	33.8	32.6
Weight/c.i.d.	12.7	16.1	16.0	14.1
P.S.I. (brakes)	20.1	23.5	21.8	20.1

* Optional, extra cost
** Semi-automatic

We knew in advance, of course, that this would be a fast, lively car. Mark Barchas speaks of its "hair-trigger" accelerator, and indeed, we found that the Olds fairly jumps away at the slightest pressure on the accelerator. It takes some getting used to.

The seating position is good; seats are comfortable and supportive. Space utilization is excellent, and the body is solidly constructed. Front leg room is generous, while the rear seat provides more space than many cars of this type. The moderately firm ride is very comfortable, as well, and cornering ability is excellent for a car of this character. And we love the powerful sound of that Rocket engine.

Steering is heavy, which is hardly surprising. Not for another three years would Olds offer a power-assist; meanwhile, the 88 outweighed the comparable 76 by about 160 pounds, with the front wheels carrying the additional heft. Even so, the car handles well. We've driven — and in fact we've owned — automobiles whose heavy engines created a serious imbalance, giving them a tendency to plow straight ahead when the car enters a high-speed turn. No such problem here.

The HydraMatic, in our view, was by far the best available automatic transmission in 1949. Greeted with some skepticism when it was first introduced back in 1940, by 1949 it had proven itself in both military and civilian service to be a durable, remarkably efficient unit. There is something of a surge as it shifts from gear to gear, but we've never found it to be disconcerting.

For 1949 Olds advertised the "Whirlaway" HydraMatic, in reference to an automatic downshift for extra acceleration during passing, similar to that of the Borg-Warner overdrive of that period. It's a desirable improvement over the original unit. We still have our reservations, however, about the placement of Reverse at the bottom of the quadrant, where stick-shift drivers — whose names were legion in 1949 — were accustomed to finding low gear.

But of course, the characteristic for which the original Olds 88 was best known was its performance. Walt Woron, writing in *Motor Trend*, commented that, "For its price, it would be difficult to obtain a car equal in performance to the Oldsmobile 88." Did Walt say "difficult"? Try impossible.

Tom McCahill, in his customary, colorful fashion, summed it up: "The 88 looks like a well fed Chevy. It is fast, comfortable and has good road-holding quality by American standards. It has the best engine of any American car sell ing for under $2,500, and is a real thrill to drive. I highly recommend the 88 for the grandsons of the old fogies who used to admire the Olds before the Rocket. And, Gramp, you ought to try it, too — it will give that weary old frame of yours a new charge of vitamins."

❏

Acknowledgments and Bibliography

Automotive Industries, *March 15, 1949, and June 1, 1949;* Boyd, T.A., *Professional Amateur;* Casteele, Dennis, *The Cars of Oldsmobile;* Gunnell, John (ed.); *Standard Catalog of American Cars, 1946-1975;* Heasley, Jerry, *The Production Figure Book for US Cars;* Kimes, Beverly Rae and Richard M. Langworth, *Oldsmobile: The First Seventy-Five Years;* Leslie, Stuart W., *"Charles Franklin Kettering,"* Encyclopedia of American Business History and Biography; McCahill, Tom, *"88,"* Mechanix Illustrated, *July 1950; Oldsmobile factory literature;* Woron, Walter A., *"Motor Trials: 1950 Oldsmobile,"* Motor Trend, *July 1950.*

Our thanks to Tom Behring, vice president and Skip Marketti, curator, The Behring Museum, Blackhawk, California; Bud Juneau, Brentwood, California. Special thanks to Mark and Kay Barchas, Los Altos Hills, California.

Above: *Horizontal trim makes car appear quite long and low.* **Below:** *There's excellent trunk room;* **Bottom:** *And a clean appearance in the rear aspect, especially with the top down.*

1949 Cadillac vs. 1949 Oldsmobile 98

Similar But Different

by Arch Brown
photos by Bud Juneau

BY 1949 the entire American automobile industry was sporting a new look. Warmed-over pre-war stylings were gone at last, and we had fresh designs to admire. But beneath the hoods it was, in most instances, the same-old same-old. Straight-eights, for instance, were still employed by Buick, Packard, Pontiac, Chrysler and Hudson. Of that group, all but Buick clung to the outmoded L-head configuration, and in every case the stroke was greater than the bore.

There were two exceptions to all this: Two, and only two, brand new state-of-the-art powerplants were offered, one featured by Cadillac, the other by Oldsmobile. Those two engines were similar, yet neither was a carbon-copy of the other, and for the most part — though not quite entirely — they were developed independently. Gilbert Burrell, chief engineer at Olds in those days, insisted that his engine was "strictly an Oldsmobile project," a claim disputed to some degree by Harry Barr, motor-engineer at Cadillac (and, later, General Motors' engineering vice president).

Prior to World War II, experimental work had gone on in the engineering departments at both Cadillac and Olds. Oldsmobile engineers, under Burrell's leadership, had tried various layouts: L-head versus overhead-valves; straight-eight versus V-8; long- versus short-stroke. They concluded, first, that the practical limit of the side-valve design was a compression ratio of about 8.00:1. Beyond that figure, the familiar "flathead" tended to become rough and noisy. Looking toward the time when high-octane fuels would become available, Burrell and his group were aiming higher, with ratios running perhaps as high as 12.5:1. So overhead valves were clearly the way to go.

At the same time, the large bore, short stroke design was believed to be the wave of the future, partly because valves could be larger, resulting in improved breathing, but mostly because by reducing piston travel by 20 percent or so, the short stroke substantially decreased friction. A big-bore straight-eight was found to require an engine block that would be unacceptably heavy, as well as excessively long; so the eight-in-line was dropped from contention. Thus, in the end a short-stroke overhead valve V-8 with a relatively high compression ratio became Gilbert Burrell's goal.

Meanwhile, commencing as early as 1937, Cadillac had been conducting more or less parallel experiments, and coming to essentially the same conclusions as Oldsmobile. In a 1985 telephone interview with this writer, Harry Barr gave his version of the story, explaining that development of the new Cadillac V-8 had begun under the leadership of John F. "Jack" Gordon, who in later years would become president of General Motors. But then Gordon was transferred to the Allison Division, where problems were being encountered with a new aircraft engine.

"This was just before we got into the war," Barr recalled. "'39 or '40. Then I took [Gordon's] job as motor engineer [at Cadillac] and we were developing both an L-head and an overhead-valve engine, with the concept of a short stroke and a big bore. And we were going to see, by comparing these two engines that were identical in every [other] way, whether the L-head had a place with the higher compression ratios that we were going to have.... We had those two engines just ready to go in dynamometer testing on December 7, 1941. Through the war years we got a lot of high-octane fuel, and we knew that the L-head could not make it, so we concentrated our efforts on the overhead valve. That was the genesis of the 1949 Cadillac. I was motor engineer on that, and Jack Gordon came back as chief engineer....

"Byron [Ellis] had gone to work on a better hydraulic [valve] lash adjuster for this new engine. We had a devil of a time with hydraulic lash adjusters on the tanks during the war. There were 16 of those things in a tank, under armor plate, and we couldn't get by the Army

Cadillac's traditional "V" took on more significance than ever with the new ohv engine. Oldsmobile, meanwhile, eschewed all symbols of the new powerplant lurking under the hood.

inspector if just one hydraulic tappet made a noise. They'd make a noise because a little chip of dirt got between the ball and the seat.... So Byron went to work to get a better hydraulic tappet. This was his assignment during the war. He came up with a very sharp radius and a hardened radius-seat to this ball. And that's the way all hydraulic lash adjusters are made, post-war.

"So these things came together on the 1949 Cadillac engine, and we had a year's jump on anybody else. There was a guy named C. L. McCuen, who had been general manager of Oldsmobile. He was vice president of the [GM] engineering staff, and knew all about our Cadillac engine because of his position. He convinced Jack [Gordon] that we should show this design to the Oldsmobile engineers. I well remember a guy by the name of Tony Waters, who was their engine-engineer, working with Jack Wilson. [He] came down and we showed him our entire design. And that's where Oldsmobile got started on what they tried to call the 'Kettering'

engine. But Alfred Sloan said 'You can't name an engine after a living individual,' so they changed it and called it the 'Rocket' engine.

"So Cadillac led that thing, I don't care what anybody says. We got into a cooperative program. We had some difficulty with tappet faces scoring the camshaft and...that's the one big contribution Oldsmobile made. They helped a lot in getting a durable tappet face, and got us out of that trouble."

Hydraulic valve lifters were employed by both divisions in the interest of quieter operation. And in both instances one of the secrets behind the new engines' lively performance had to do with their use of "slipper" pistons. Another development pioneered by Byron Ellis, these pistons featured a half-moon section cut from either side of the lower skirt. This permitted the pistons to drop between the crankshaft counterweights, which in turn facilitated the use of short, relatively light connecting rods, and a much lighter crankshaft. Block and heads were also reduced in weight, and the re-

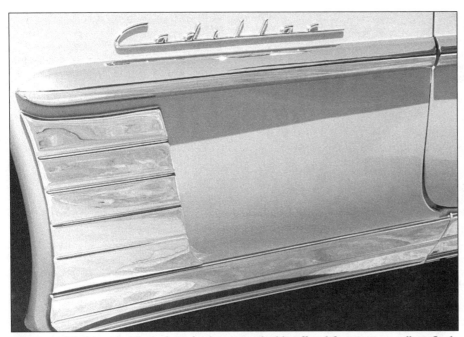

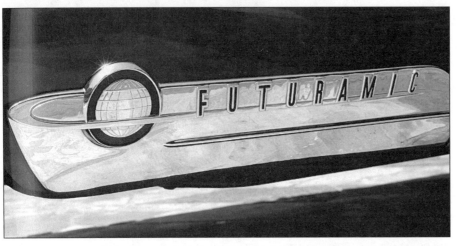

*Above and below: Cadillac's front fender stone shields offered function as well as flash. Oldsmobile caried its Futuramic theme into the front fender trim. **Right:** Cadillac's famous "sombrero" wheel covers look much posher than Olds's simple discs.*

1949 Cadillac Prices, Weights and Production

	Price	Weight (lb.)	Production
Series 61, 126-inch wheelbase			
Sedan, 4-door, 5-passenger	$2,893	3,915	15,738
Club coupe (fastback), 5-pass.	2,788	3,838	6,409
Chassis only	n/a	n/a	1
Series 62, 126-inch wheelbase			
Sedan, 4-door, 5-passenger	3,050	3,956	37,617
Club coupe (fastback), 5-pass.	2,966	3,862	7,515
Coupe DeVille, 5-passenger	3,496	4,033	2,150
Convertible coupe, 5-pass.	3,523	4,218	8,000
Export sedan	3,050	3,956	360
Chassis only	n/a	n/a	1
Series 60-Special Fleetwood, 133-inch w/b			
Sedan, 4-door, 5-passenger	3,828	4,129	11,399
Special Coupe DeVille	n/a	n/a	1
Series 75 Fleetwood, 136-inch w/b			
Sedan, 5-passenger	4,750	4,579	220
Sedan, 7-passenger	4,970	4,626	595
Business sedan, 9-passenger	4,650	4,522	35
Imperial sedan, 7-passenger	5,170	4,648	626
Business Imperial, 9-passenger	4,839	4,573	25
Chassis only	n/a	n/a	1
Commercial chassis (163-inch w/b)	n/a	n/a	1,861
Total Cadillac production, 1949 model year:			92,554
Total Cadillac production, calendar 1949:			81,545

quired cooling capacity was less. In the case of the Cadillac, the new engine was five inches shorter and four inches lower than the L-head V-8 that it replaced, and its "wet" weight (including the radiator) was reduced by 220 pounds.

In both instances — Cadillac and Oldsmobile — both horsepower and torque were increased. The flathead Cadillac of 1948, for instance, had produced 150 horsepower and 283 foot pounds of torque. Horsepower and torque ratings of 1949's overhead-valve job, in contrast, came in at 160 and 312, respectively. That's a 6.7 percent increase in horsepower and a 10.2 percent increase in torque, despite a 4.3 percent reduction in displacement.

The record at Oldsmobile was almost as impressive, although in that case engine displacement had grown by 18 percent. The flathead straight-eight of 1948 had been rated at 115 horsepower, with 213 foot pounds of torque, compared to 135 horsepower and 255 foot pounds for its ohv V-8 replacement, increases amounting to 17.4 and 19.7 percent, respectively. Performance of both the Cadillac and the Oldsmobile was substantially enhanced, while economy was improved by at least two miles per gallon.

Initially, it had been Olds's intention to use the new engine only in its big "98" series. But Sherrod E. Skinner, the Oldsmobile Division's canny general manager, conceived the idea of stuffing the new V-8 into the chassis of the "A"-bodied six-cylinder Olds. The result, introduced a couple of months into the model year, was the original "Rocket 88." Nearly 300 pounds lighter than the "98," it quickly became the nation's stock-car champion, winning six of the nine races staged that year by the NASCAR grand national division. But that's another story.

(Incidentally, as between the Cadillac and Oldsmobile powerplants, John Bond, writing in *Motor Trend*, noted that "the engines are not by any means the same. The Cadillac, with ten percent more piston displacement, develops 18.5 percent more bhp and weighs a few pounds less.")

Styling was carried over from 1948, when a new General Motors "C" body had been introduced in both the biggest Olds and the smaller Cadillacs. Olds referred to its version as "Futuramic," extending that name to the smaller models when they adopted a similar styling theme for 1949. There was no such catchy title for the Cadillac, but the Cad's fin-like taillamps were clearly the styling sensation of the time. Frankly inspired by the P-38 fighter planes of World War II, they would establish a trend to be followed by virtually the entire industry for more than a decade to come.

Both makes featured two-piece, curved glass windshields, and initially, three body types were offered: four-door sedan, two-door "fastback" coupe and convertible. In mid-1949, these were joined by a pair of handsome newcomers, the Cadillac Coupe deVille and the Oldsmobile Holiday. Along with the Buick Roadmaster Riviera, these were the industry's first series-produced pillarless "hardtop" coupes. They, too, would set the trend for the industry for years to come.

Unlike Cadillac, Olds offered its sedans and coupes in two levels of trim. The deluxe package, for which buyers paid an extra $94.00, included upgraded, two-tone upholstery, rear seat center armrest, deluxe instrument cluster, deluxe carpeting, deluxe steering wheel, aluminum sill plates and an electric clock. Evidently, buyers found these amenities to be worth the extra money, for the deluxe cars outsold their plainjane counterparts by better than five-to-one.

There's an interesting sidelight regarding that 1948-49 GM C-body. In a recent letter to this writer, retired General Motors stylist Richard H. Stout explained that "this 1948 C-body series was originally designated the 1948 B-body. This is why wheelbases on the new jobs were the same as the old B-body and three inches shorter than the previous ones. GM simply did not have time to get a C-body done, so this was rechristened C from B. Cadillac had to be first with some all-new stuff." A quick comparison of specifications bears out Dick Stout's statement, for the 1947 Cadillac "62" had a wheelbase of 129 inches, against 126 for the 1948-49 models.

Among the more significant differences between our comparisonReport cars was the matter of cost. The base

Neither car spared the shiny stuff on rear fender accents. Stainless steel rather than chrome plate was used for ease of upkeep and stamping of shapes.

price of the Cadillac 62 was $3,050, compared to $2,594 for the Oldsmobile, a difference of 17.6 percent. In truth, however, the spread was greater than that, for it cost the Cadillac buyer $174 extra to go "shiftless," though 98 percent of the 1949 cars left the factory equipped with the automatic. Meanwhile, Olds included the HydraMatic transmission at no extra cost with its eight-cylinder cars. Not until 1950 would the HydraMatic be supplied as standard equipment on the Cadillac Series 62.

This suggests that the big Olds was really an excellent value. Even so, a lot of buyers were willing to pay the premium for the extra power and prestige of the Cadillac, for despite its substantial price advantage, sales of the Olds 98 were only about 17 percent ahead of the combined total for the Cadillac Series 62 and its slightly less costly near-twin, the Series 61.

Driving Impressions

We found our comparisonReport cars at the 1995 Hillsborough Concours d'Elegance. They made a perfect pair for our purposes, for both cars are in superb condition, both cosmetically and mechanically.

The Oldsmobile, owned by Dr. John D'Attilio, a Carmel ophthalmologist, was originally the property of his father, John D'Attilio Sr., who purchased it in New Jersey. As a teenager, one of Dr. D'Attilio's regular chores was taking care of the car; so of course he developed a great affection for it. For 40 years the Olds served as the elder D'Attilio's family car, logging a modest 86,000 miles over that period of time. At that point Mr. D'Attilio gave up driving, shipped the Olds to California and gave it to his son. ("Who says this is not my father's Oldsmobile?" asks John, rhetorically.)

Dr. D'Attilio had the car restored to

1949 Oldsmobile Prices, Weights and Production

	Price	Weight	Production
Series 76, 6-cylinder, 119-inch w/b			
Club coupe	$1,748	3,260	9,403
Club coupe, Deluxe	1,889	3,315	3,280
Club sedan	1,774	3,290	23,059
Club sedan, Deluxe	1,916	3,355	8,960
Sedan, 4-door	1,848	3,340	23,631
Sedan, 4-door Deluxe	1,990	3,375	13,874
Town sedan, 4-door	1,837	3,335	3,741
Town sedan, 4-door Deluxe	1,979	3,400	2,725
Convertible coupe, Deluxe	2,184	3,580	5,338
Station wagon, Deluxe	2,911	3,680	1,545
Series 88, 8-cylinder, 119-inch w/b			
Club coupe	2,164	3,550	6,562
Club coupe, Deluxe	2,295	3,590	4,999
Club sedan	2,191	3,585	16,887
Club sedan, Deluxe	2,322	3,615	11,820
Sedan, 4-door	2,265	3,615	23,342
Sedan, 4-door Deluxe	2,396	3,645	23,044
Town sedan, 4-door	2,254	3,625	2,859
Town sedan, 4-door Deluxe	2,385	3,665	2,974
Convertible coupe, Deluxe	2,580	3,845	5,434
Station wagon, Deluxe	3,317	3,945	1,355
Series 98, 8-cylinder, 125-inch w/b			
Club sedan	2,426	3,835	3,849
Club sedan, Deluxe	2,520	3,840	16,200
Sedan, 4-door	2,500	3,890	8,820
Sedan, 4-4oor Deluxe	2,594	3,925	49,001
Convertible, Deluxe	2,973	4,200	12,602
Holiday Coupe, Deluxe	2,973	4,000	3,006
Total Oldsmobile production, 1949 model year			291,310
Total Oldsmobile production, calendar 1949			282,887

Above and below: Both cars corner competently at moderate speeds. **Bottom:** 1949 marked the second year for Caddy's tailfin taillamps. Olds taillamp design, like rest of car, was new for '49. **Facing page:** Cadillac lamps double as fuel filler doors. Olds goes the more traditional route for gas pump access. Caddy's parking lamps integrate nicely into grille design, Oldsmobile's are part of "airscoops."

perfection. The engine was rebuilt by Ryan Falconer, of Salinas, and the HydraMatic by Uyeda Transmission, Monterey. Paint, in the original black, was flawlessly applied by Jerry Graham, of Del Rey Oaks, and upholstery was by Rick's, of Sand City. (John was able to find a piece of the original cloth, only to discover that there wasn't enough material to do the job. He settled for the closest match he could find.)

John D'Attilio has added another couple of thousand miles to the Oldsmobile's odometer, using it on weekends, mostly locally. He has shown it a few times, taking a First and a Third at Hillsborough, and Best of Show at the 1994 Oldsmobile Club of California meet, held at Cambria.

We asked about cruising speed. John had driven the Olds from his home in Carmel to our photo location in East Los Gatos, a distance of about 75 miles, and he reported that for a part of that distance he was traveling 70 miles an hour, "with no strain," he tells us. As a rule, however, he holds it to about 60.

Evidently the family shares John's enthusiasm for the car. "I have five children," John tells us, "and they're all fighting over who's going to get it next"

Our Cadillac, in contrast, has been a California car all its life, having been sold originally by the Paddleford dealership in Palo Alto, to a Saratoga owner. In 1951, for some undetermined reason, the Cad was stored under cover, loaded — fortunately — with moth balls. The clock showed about 38,000 miles at that point. It remained in storage until 1983, when it was acquired by a collector named Doug Burnell.

Burnell owned the car for some eight

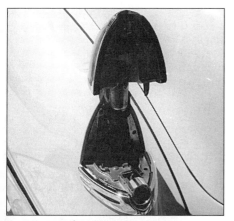

Specifications: 1949 Cadillac 62 vs. 1949 Oldsmobile 98

	1949 Cadillac	1949 Oldsmobile
Base price, 4-door sedan	$3,078	$2,594
Engine	Ohv V-8	Ohv V-8
Bore x stroke	3.69 x 3.625 inches	3.75 x 3.44 inches
Displacement	331.0 cubic inches	303.7 cubic inches
Compression ratio	7.5:1	7.25:1
Horsepower @ rpm	160 @ 3,800 rpm	135 @ 3,600 rpm
Torque @ rpm	312 @ 1,800	263 @ 1,800
Taxable horsepower	46.5	45.0
Valve lifters	Hydraulic	Hydraulic
Main bearings	5	5
Fuel system	1.25-inch dual downdraft, camshaft pump	1.44-inch dual downdraft, camshaft pump
Lubrication system	Pressure	Pressure
Electrical system	6-volt	6-volt
Cooling system	Centrifugal pump	Centrifugal pump
Exhaust system	Single	Single
Transmission	HydraMatic* * Optional @ $124	HydraMatic
Ratios	1st: 3.97; 2nd: 2.55; 3rd: 1.55; 4th: 1.00; Reverse: 3.74	1st: 3.82; 2nd: 2.63 3rd: 1.45; 4th: 1.00; Reverse: 4.31
Differential	Hypoid	Hypoid
Ratio	3.36:1	3.64:1
Drive axles	Semi-floating	Semi-floating
Steering	Recirculating ball	Worm/roller gear
Turns, lock-to-lock	4	4.25
Ratio	21.3:1	19.0:1
Turning diameter	46 feet, 8 inches	42 feet, 0 inches
Brakes	4-wheel hydraulic	4-wheel hydraulic
Drum diameter	12 inches	11 inches
Total swept area	220.0 square inches	191.7 square inches
Construction	Body-on-frame	Body-on-frame
Frame	Channel section w/X-member	Channel section w/X-member
Body construction	All steel	All steel
Body type	4-door sedan	4-door sedan
Front suspension	Independent, coil springs	Independent, coil springs
Rear suspension	Rigid axle, longitudinal leaf springs	Rigid axle, coil springs
Shock absorbers	Lever hydraulic	Lever hydraulic
Wheels	Pressed steel	Pressed steel
Tires	8.20/15 4-ply	7.60/15 4-ply
Wheelbase	126 inches	125 inches
Overall length	215.0625 inches	213 inches
Overall width	78.8125 inches	78.75 inches
Overall height	63.44 inches	63.844 inches
Front track	59 inches	58 inches
Rear track	63 inches	61.5 inches
Min. road clearance	8 inches	8.28 inches
Shipping weight	3,980 lb.	3,925 lb.
Crankcase capacity	5 quarts (less filter)	5 quarts (less filter)
Cooling system capacity	18 quarts	21.5 quarts
Fuel tank	20 gallons	18 gallons
Transmission	24 pints	21 pints
Rear axle	5 pints	3.75 pints
Horsepower per c.i.d.	.483	.445
Lb. per hp	24.9	29.1
Lb. per c.i.d.	12.0	12.0
P.S.I. (brakes)	18.1	20.5
Performance: 0-60 mph	13.4 seconds	13.5 seconds
Top speed	99.6 mph	96 mph

Options on comparisonReport Oldsmobile: Deluxe package, radio, white sidewall tires, left outside mirror, hydraulic windows

Options on comparisonReport Cadillac: HydraMatic transmission, "Sombrero" wheel covers, white sidewall tires, spotlight with mirror, outside visor, side window rain shields, radio, heater, twin backup lights, day/night mirror, vanity mirror, two-tone paint

years, and although he drove it to points as far away as the East Coast and the Canadian Rockies, he logged only about 10,000 miles with it before selling it to the present owner, Richard Lovejoy, of Santa Clara. Richard, by his own statement, drives it "everywhere," having covered about 14,000 miles in three and a half years of ownership. In a sense, Richard has accomplished the impossible, for although the Cadillac is treated as a "driver," Richard also shows it, and he tells us he has garnered 23 First Place trophies in 25 shows.

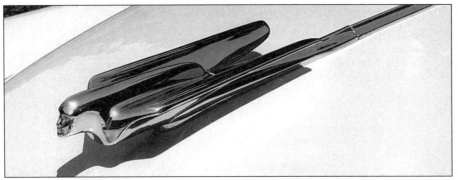

Cadillac continually evolved their flying lady starting from the original design in 1930. Oldsmobile, not unexpectedly, uses a rocket for their hood ornament.

Another fine distinction between the two cars: a buyer couldn't get a Fleetwood interior on an Oldsmobile for any price.

Both instrument groups contain full set of gauges surrounded by lots of chrome.

The most remarkable thing about Richard Lovejoy's Cadillac is its nearly flawless, original interior. Only the carpeting has been replaced. Engine and transmission are also original, though new U-joints have been installed, carburetor, generator and distributor have been overhauled, and just recently Richard overhauled the brakes. A new paint job, in the original Vista Gray Metallic over French Gray, was applied by Jack Williams, of Auto Specialty Painting in nearby Campbell.

We asked Richard about the Cadillac's cruising speed. "I've had it up to 75," he replied, "but I'm afraid that visor will take the windshield with it and go." (The exterior visor, a rather popular accessory in the late 1940s and early fifties, was added by Doug Burnell. It has its advan-tages, but it does indeed trap air, with potentially disastrous results.)

In driving the two cars, we found more differences than we expected:

● The HydraMatic in the Olds shifts with a pronounced surge, while the Cadillac moves smoothly from gear to gear. On the other hand, the Olds is markedly quicker off-the-line. Road tests when these cars were new confirm this observation: The Cad has a higher top speed, but the Olds has the advantage in acceleration. (We should confess at this point that we've always suspected that the Rocket engine may have been under-rated at 135 horsepower.)

● Cruising down the highway, the Cadillac is noticeably quieter than the Oldsmobile, suggesting that its sound insulation is superior.

Similar cars, perhaps, but Cadillac based at 20 percent higher price than big Oldsmobiles.

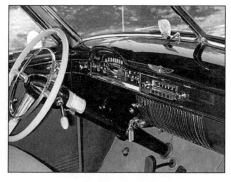

• By modern standards, steering is heavy in both cars, but in this respect the Olds takes slightly less effort than the Cad, though the latter has a slightly slower ratio. Perhaps the difference has to do with the fatter tires on the Cadillac, or possibly it reflects the fact that the Cadillac uses the recirculating ball system, while the Oldsmobile is fitted with worm and roller gear mechanism.

• Both cars, as far as we could tell in our limited test drive, have excellent brakes. Pedal pressure is surprisingly light, and the binders haul these heavy cars quickly to a straight, even stop.

• In both cars, the seats would do credit to anybody's living room. In this writer's view, however, for long-distance travel they would leave something to be desired in terms of back support. To be fair, we must add that this criticism would hold true of most American cars in 1949.

• Given their fairly generous size, the trunks in both of these automobiles are downright skimpy. But again, the 1949 buyer was accustomed to that deficiency.

So, in the end, which to choose: Olds 98 or Cad 62? The answer, in 1949, would have depended upon the buyer's circumstances, we believe. It boils down to this: The Cadillac was the better car, over-all, but the Oldsmobile was clearly the better buy. Throw in a HydraMatic transmission for the Cad and the difference in cost comes to $658, a hefty piece of change by 1949 standards. But as we've noted, to a lot of people it was money well spent. ❧

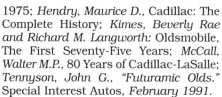

1975; *Hendry, Maurice D.*, Cadillac: The Complete History; *Kimes, Beverly Rae and Richard M. Langworth:* Oldsmobile, The First Seventy-Five Years; *McCall, Walter M.P.*, 80 Years of Cadillac-LaSalle; *Tennyson, John G.*, "Futuramic Olds." Special Interest Autos, *February 1991.*

Our thanks to Ken Gimelli, East Los Gatos, California; Richard H. Stout, Delray Beach, Florida. Special thanks to John D'Attilio, Carmel, California; Richard Lovejoy, Santa Clara, California.

Top left and below: *Cadillac dash design is more conservative than future-oriented Olds.* **Above and left:** *Cadillac V-8 has a 35 bhp rating over Olds.* **Below:** *Trunks may look big, but they're not.*

Acknowledgments and Bibliography

Automotive Industries, *March 15, 1949; Casteel, Dennis,* The Cars of Oldsmobile; *Gunnell, John (ed.),* Standard Catalog of American Cars 1946-

1953 OLDSMOBILE FIESTA

by John Lee
photos by the author

WHEN THE DREAM CAME ALIVE....

A few decades ago the General — General Motors — had a flair for showmanship. It wasn't enough to make up a display of some extra-flashy, maybe slightly customized new models for shows in New York, Chicago, Los Angeles, and a few other major cities. No, GM also assembled its very own show with those attractions, plus a few dream cars to test public reaction and, like a traveling circus, took it on the road.

First tried in 1949, the extravaganza which came to be known as the GM Motorama was then staged in eight of the 13 years through 1961 (see *SIA* #21). It was held early in the model year, thus getting a jump on the other shows and resulting in a tremendous publicity advantage for GM. Always opening in New York at the Waldorf-Astoria Hotel, the Motorama attracted not only the automotive press, but business, news, and general interest periodicals like *Colliers* and *The New Yorker*, too.

GM didn't have to share the spotlight with other manufacturers at these affairs. The publicity was generated in time to pique the interest of consumers and bring them out to see the latest dream models at new car shows in their cities later on.

Driving Impressions

Originally published in Special Interest Autos #106, Jul.-Aug. 1988

General Motors' first show in 1949 went to Boston after the New York engagement. The second was presented only at the Waldorf in 1950. There were no Motoramas in 1951 and 1952, as auto manufacturers were busy filling defense contracts for the Korean conflict. Given that and what was felt to be a "flush market," with unmet demand for models that had received wholesale restyling in 1949, GM brass felt the costly Motorama promotion was unnecessary.

By the summer of 1952, however, new car sales were in need of stimulation once again. While Chevrolet and Pontiac were due for new bodies in 1953, they were not radically different, and the corporation's other lines would be getting only facelifts. To give the line a boost, plans were made to revive the GM Motorama for presentation in January of 1953. It would be a spectacular production, and following its New York run would tour five additional US cities, a pattern that was to be continued in subsequent years.

The show that opened at the Waldorf in January 1953 was possibly the greatest collection of new styling and ideas GM had ever put together under one roof. As *Business Week* reported, "Four of the five divisions unveiled sports-type experimental cars at New York. All had sweeping horizontal lines and advanced mechanical treatment. Their body shells were plastic, an area in which recent developments have started GM on some significant long-term thinking." The magazine also stated, "Each GM division is making a sports car for limited 1953 marketing."

The latter statement was slightly in error. Pontiac never did enter that market. But there must have been some confusion in the Waldorf ballroom over which were the dream cars and which were slated for limited production:

• Cadillac showed the Le Mans, a two-passenger roadster of fiberglass, as well as the Eldorado, a full-sized steel convertible.

• Buick's entries were the Wildcat, a plastic two-seater on a shorter 114-inch wheelbase, and the standard-length Skylark.

• Carrying the Oldsmobile banner were the fiberglass Starfire, which seated four but was smaller than production models, and the Fiesta Coupe, a convertible based on the 98 chassis.

• LaParisienne, from Pontiac, was the only non-convertible and the only steel dream car in the line-up. It had a cantilever rear roof section without quarter windows and a removable front roof section.

• Chevrolet's presentation at the Motorama was the Corvette sports roadster, for which GM had already announced plans for limited production.

As it turned out, the Corvette did appear later in the spring in limited numbers. Pontiac never did field a special model for 1953. Olds, Buick, and Cadillac each went into production with their more-or-less conventional show cars, while bits and pieces of the dream cars continued to appear on production models during the following years.

The Cadillac Eldorado, Buick Skylark, and Oldsmobile Fiesta shared several characteristics, besides the fact that each was priced from $1,500 to $3,600 above the regular production convertible. All had a characteristic dip in the

Seeing Larry Schefcik's 1953 Fiesta was a case of *déjà vu*. It was parked in the same driveway where it had often sat when new, 35 years ago (see sidebar, page 45); Larry's mother now lives in the house where his grandparents lived then.

Larry has elected to keep the Fiesta in unrestored condition, believing it has greater value as an original car. The factory white and red-orange paint job is still shiny, but repeated polishing has nearly worn through the finish on the tops of the fenders. The red and white leather upholstery is still quite good, but some of the seams are beginning to split, and the red carpeting shows its age.

As we prepared to take the aging beauty out for the photo session, Larry pushed the control lever and the top folded itself away as neatly as it might have in 1953. All the hydraulic servo-assisted windows also did their disappearing act on cue. The big (for the period) V-8 jumped to life and idled with a minimum of the lifter clatter characteristic of early Olds Rockets.

Driving a big 1950s convertible with the top down is a thrill all its own that can't be matched in a Mustang or Camaro or a K-car. You're sitting high above the blacktop on a firm, leather-covered seat, gripping a large steering wheel in one hand and with theother toying with the unique windwings that Olds revived on this model. They fit outside the front door glass and take the place of the normal vent windows.

Some distortion from the steeply sloped wraparound windshield may contribute to the feeling of riding up in the air in the Olds. Its ride is also soft, with a floating feel. The acceleration is adequate, but not extremely swift. Shifts in the Hydra-Matic are somewhat harsh, which may be a result of this car's infrequent use. Once up to speed, the Olds cruises effortlessly at 60. The engine is quiet, and the windwings effectively limit the wind's buffeting. This particular car seems exceptionally tight and rattle-free, considering its 35-year age and 115,000 miles of travel.

Oldsmobile called its first two-door hardtops "Holiday." When they came out with this special convertible model for 1953, they turned to the Spanish for the name, "Fiesta," which means a day or time of celebration.

Driving this Olds Fiesta is certainly a "celebration" of the big, "overstuffed" dreamboats of the 1950s.

Above: *It's all stock Olds up front, and that's flashy enough.* **Below:** *Leather two-toning and design gives car a four-seater appearance.*

Above: Perhaps the most prominent GM dream car aspect which carried over into the Fiesta was the wraparound windshield, which became a stock item throughout the entire 1954 Oldsmobile lineup.
Above right: It wouldn't be an Oldsmobile without a rocket ship for a hood ornament.
Right: Pillarless vent windows are another distinctive Fiesta touch. Below: Stock '53 taillamps were used on Fiestas.

beltline behind the front door, a styling element that would show up in production models the following year. The Eldorado and Fiesta shared another new GM feature, the wraparound windshield that was also slated for full production. Their top height was three inches shorter than a regular convertible. Although Buick didn't use the new windshield, the Skylark was still "chopped" two inches.

All three cars used the Ohv V-8s of their respective lines with modifications for greater horsepower output. Leather upholstery and many otherwise optional accessories were made standard.

Of the three, the Olds was the most poorly received and was the only GM "special" that failed to make it into a second year of production. Instead, 1954's 98 convertible incorporated some of the Fiesta's special features, although the accessories were optional rather than standard as they had been on the Fiesta. The '54 98 convertible carried the name of Olds's 1953 Motorama dream car, the Starfire (see SIA #55, page 48).

There were only 458 Oldsmobile Fiestas built in 1953. Cadillac fared only slightly better, building 532 Eldorados, while Buick sold 1,690 Skylarks. Price was a factor, even in this ultra-upper class. The Buick sold for $5,000, while the Olds listed at $5,715, and the Cad a healthy $7,750.

As the rarest of this rare trio, the Olds Fiesta is almost impossible to put a value on. There are so few, and they so rarely change hands, that there is no "market" in them. Their owners treasure them highly and tend to hang onto them. Scarcity of the parts that distinguish the Fiesta from other Oldsmobiles makes a very extensive restoration next to impossible.

In the Olds, that premium of $2,752 over the 98 convertible got you more than the satisfaction of having the only one in town. Special manifolding from the four-barrel carburetor and a com-

The Schefcik Fiesta

The story that is told around western Nebraska about how the 1953 Oldsmobile Fiesta joined the Schefeik family goes something like this:

Farmer Eugene Schefcik's tractor was broken down that spring day in 1953. Schefcik raised wheat and some hay on the dryland out north of Alliance.

He drove the 15 miles into Alliance to the International Harvester dealer, who didn't have the necessary part, so Eugene had to drive 60 miles further to the next IH dealer in Scottsbluff. As was often the case in those days, the International dealer was also an automobile dealer, in this case S&T Olds.

When Eugene walked in and headed for the parts counter, he was stopped short by the flashy convertible occupying the show-room. Long and low with a bright two-tone-job of white and red-orange with a matching leather interior, it was the most beautiful car he'd ever seen! He spent more time than his cultivating work would permit looking over every detail of the convertible, from the low, wraparound windshield to the three-bar flipper wheel covers.

He got the tractor part, and before he left told the salesman, "Don't sell that car. I'll be back for it." Noticing Eugene's farmer clothes, which he hadn't bothered to change just to run to town for a tractor part, the salesman is said to have laughed and replied, "Ha, you don't have enough money to buy that car!" After all, this was a special, limited-production model with a factory price tag of $5,715. With transportation charges to western Nebraska, the sticker was right at $6,000, nearly twice that of a regular Olds 98 convertible.

Well, you can't judge a book by its cover. It seems the Schefcik family spread of wheat land was considerable, and prices for the commodity were quite good in 1953.

The upshot was that Eugene did, indeed, return to S&T Olds before the end of the day, better dressed this time, and he had the $6,000 required to buy the Olds Fiesta — in cash!

The S&T people might have had visions of selling the unique Fiesta to a banker or some other prominent local citizen, but those vanished when they saw the color of Eugene's money. They even had a photographer shoot a picture of Eugene taking the wheel and sent him an 8x10 glossy print which is reproduced here.

This writer was a car-crazed teenager in Alliance when the Fiesta showed up on the streets. I'd seen the car pictured in *Motor Trend* and was excited to have "one of those" in our little town. We already had a green 1953 Buick Skylark, the property of the hotel owner. I didn't know the Schefcik family at the time, but often saw the Fiesta parked on the street a few blocks from our house. It was sometimes covered with mud, so I surmised that the owner lived somewhere in the country, which was the case. Eugene's parents lived in the house up the street, which explained the car's appearance there.

Though gone from there for more than 30 years, I still pictured that car in my mind whenever I thought of Olds's Fiesta. A couple of years ago I heard that the car was still in the area, and I eventually managed an introduction to its current owner, Larry Schefcik, youngest son of the original

purchaser. I was able to photograph the Olds and take it for a short spin.

Larry talked of family vacations in the car when he was a tiny tyke. One can imagine the thrill of top-down touring through the Black Hills to Mt. Rushmore, and to Rocky Mountain National Park and Estes Park in such a vehicle! Larry said that even when new, the Fiesta was the focus of admiration and the curiosity of other tourists who had never seen one.

When he came of age, Larry's older brother was permitted to use the convertible for dates, as were a sister and Larry himself when their turns came. "I think we all thrashed it pretty bad on occasion," he smiles.

But the Olds survived. Eugene Schefcik has since passed away, and responsibility for the treasured car, and the family wheat farm, has fallen to Larry. The Fiesta is kept in town now and driven only rarely, in nice weather, to exercise her systems. With 115,000 miles, the car is being kept as original as possible. The top, tires, and exhaust have been the major replacements in its 35-year life. But Larry would like to replace the windshield if he could ever find a new one. Chips from those gravel roads, you know.

45

specifications

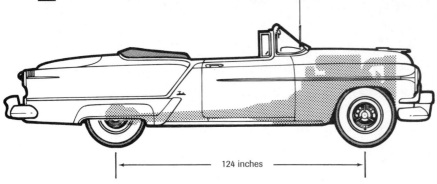
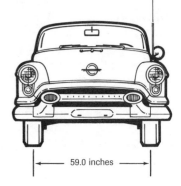

124 inches

59.0 inches

1953 Oldsmobile Fiesta

Price when new	$5,715 f.o.b. factory
Standard equipment	Dual-range Hydra-Matic, power steering, power brakes, power windows, power seat, power antenna, electric clock, Signal-Seeker AM radio, pre-heat heater, 120-mph speedometer, power top, dual outside mirrors, oil filter, leather upholstery, heavy duty air cleaner

ENGINE
Type	90-degree V-8, overhead valves, five main bearings, full pressure lubrication
Bore & stroke	3¾ inches x 3 7/16 inches
Displacement	303 cubic inches
Max bhp @ rpm	170 @ 3,600
Compression ratio	8.3:1
Induction system	Four-barrel downdraft carburetor, automatic choke, mechanical fuel pump
Exhaust system	Cast-iron manifolds, single muffler and tailpipe
Electrical system	12-volt battery, coil

TRANSMISSION
Type	Hydra-Matic four-speed automatic, column lever

Ratios: 1st 3.82:1
2nd 2.63:1
3rd 1.45:1
4th 1:1

DIFFERENTIAL
Type	Spiral bevel gears
Ratio	N/a

STEERING
Type	Recirculating ball and nut, hydraulic power booster
Turns lock to lock	5.5
Turning circle	43 feet

BRAKES
Type	Four-wheel hydraulic, internal expanding shoe and drum, cast iron
Drum diameter	11 inches (inside)
Total swept area	191.7 square inches

CHASSIS & BODY
Frame	Rigid girder, I-beam X-member construction, five crossmembers
Body construction	Steel

Body style	Two-door convertible coupe, five-passenger

SUSPENSION
Front	Independent, coil springs, cam and lever double action shock absorbers
Rear	Semi-elliptic leaf springs, solid axle, direct action shock absorbers
Tires	8.00 x 15
Wheels	Pressed steel

WEIGHTS AND MEASURES
Wheelbase	124 inches
Overall length	215 inches
Overall height	N/a
Overall width	N/a
Front track	59 inches
Rear track	59 inches
Shipping weight	4,459 pounds

CAPACITIES
Crankcase	6 quarts (with filter)
Cooling system	22½ quarts
Fuel tank	18 gallons

Robust Rocket V-8 provided 170 healthy horses to propel Fiesta down the road.

pression ratio boost to 8.3:1 from 8.0:1 gave the Fiesta's 303-cubic-inch V-8 a slight edge, 170 horsepower vs. 165, over the version used in the 98 and Super 88. Dual-range Hydra-Matic was standard, and a different rear axle was supposed to give the nearly 4,500-pound car better performance.

Power steering and brakes, top, windows, and seat were all standard on the Fiesta. So was the Signal-Seeker AM radio activated by a bar on the radio or a button on the floor, windshield washers, electric clock, power antenna, dual outside mirrors, 120-mph speedometer, and electric coils in the heater that produce instant heat while the engine is warming up. Fiestas were also equipped with the special three-bar flipper hubcaps that became a popular Olds and aftermarket accessory (see sidebar, this page). ☞

Acknowledgements and Bibliography
John A. Gunnell, editor, Standard Catalog of American Cars 1946-1975; *Dennis Casteele,* The Cars of Oldsmobile; *Richard M. Langworth and the editors of Consumer Guide,* Encyclopedia of American Cars 1940-1970; *Terry Boyce,* "1954 Oldsmobile 98: Substance Beneath the Glitter," SIA #55; "GM's Motoramas," SIA #21; Business Week, *January 24, 1953;* Popular Mechanics, *March 1953;* Newsweek, *various issues;* "Spotlight on Detroit" and "Detroit Tackles the Sports Car Market," Motor Trend, *March 1953.*

Special thanks to Larry Schefcik, Alliance, Nebraska.

Above: Slight dip in side window area also helped to set Fiesta apart from fellow Olds convertibles. Below left: Hydroelectric window controls are set into leading edge of driver's door armrest. Below right: Big, round, easy-reading instruments face directly in front of driver.

The Fiesta Wheel Cover

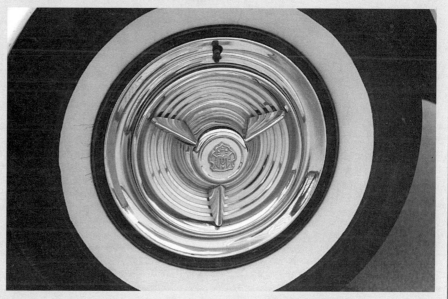

While it's easy enough to forget the Fiesta car, it's not easy to forget the Fiesta hubcap. Oldsmobile started a new trend with the introduction of this beautiful wheel cover on the 1953 Fiesta and also on the Motorama dream car, the Starfire. The unique design had a deeply dished center section with flipper bars forming a three-point star. The whirling bars provide additional action when the car is in motion, drawing attention to the wheels, and lending a sporty flair suggestive of the knock-off wheel caps of the European sports cars.

The wheel covers gained popularity as they were offered optionally on all Oldsmobiles in 1954 and 1955. Interestingly, although the Fiesta coupe (Olds called it a coupe, not a convertible) was dropped after 1953, and the name was not revived until 1957 for the station wagons, the wheel covers continued to be known as Fiestas. The Starfire dream car also had them, as did most of the 1954 and 1955 98 convertibles, which picked up the Fiesta name, but the caps were seldom called Starfire caps.

Other car makers were quick to pick up on the trend, offering their own flipper-bar wheel cover designs. The aftermarket industry went for them in a big way, too,

turning out reproductions of the originals and cheaper spinoffs to offer hot rodders and customizers — those who elected to buy them rather than "lift" a set off the neighbor's new Oldsmobile.

For 1956 Olds styled a new, three-bar flipper wheel cover, similar in design, which became even more popular as an aftermarket item than the original. And it was also known as a Fiesta.

1955 Dodge, Mercury and Oldsmobile

by Arch Brown
photos by Vince Manocchi

LOOKING back on It, 1955 was really the best of times. The Korean War was behind us and the world was at peace. Well, most of the world, anyway.

The paterfamilias was in the White House, and there was the feeling that all was well. A chill ran through us on September 24 when it was announced that President Eisenhower had suffered a heart attack, but it soon became apparent that the tough old general was on the road to recovery, and our fears were allayed.

Dr. Jonas Salk perfected his vaccine against polio, and another of our fears was put to rest

With Mary Martin in the title role, NBC telecast *Peter Pan* in compatible color—a landmark event in the development of color television.

Marian Anderson sang at the Metropolitan Opera, the first black person to be engaged as a regular member of the company. One more barrier down!

Hollywood gave us such notable films as *Mister Roberts* (Henry Fonda), *The Seven Year Itch* (Marilyn Monroe) and *East of Eden* (James Dean).

And on Broadway, audiences were captivated by the likes of *Bus Stop, Cat on a Hot Tin Roof, The Diary of Anne*

Frank and the Cole Porter musical smash, *Silk Stockings*.

It was a record-breaking year for the American automobile industry. Business had literally never been so good— at least for General Motors, Ford, and Chrysler. It was a prosperity in which the independent firms did not share, however. Most of them were sinking fast.

Nineteen-fifty-five was a particularly felicitous time for cars of the medium-priced field. Their customary share of the market had faltered a bit in recent years, but in '55 they scored a resounding comeback. (Seeing this as a portent of what was to come, the folks at Ford began to plan a new entry for this already crowded field. But that's another story.)

If the somber hues in which so many of today's cars are finished can be said to reflect the tenor of the times, the same was no less true of the bright colors that characterized the equipage of the Eisenhower era. The economy was booming; it was a happy time, and

America enjoyed its expression in brightly painted automobiles. Even pink was popular, for heaven's sake, prompting the speculation that somebody in Detroit may have been inspired by his wife's false teeth! Dodge, among others, actually offered three-tone color schemes, combining yellow or pink with black and white. It was all a bit much, and mercifully the fad died a rapid death.

Important changes had been made by the major manufacturers in nearly all of their product lines: new developments in engineering, and especially in styling. The most obvious differences in the latter respect were to be found in the cars from the Chrysler Corporation.

Take, for instance, the Dodge. The division's 1953-54 models had been stubby and stodgy, not to say downright ugly. Corporation President K.T. Keller, a practical-minded, man, had decreed that they should be "smaller on the outside, larger on the inside." And so they were, but at what a cost!

Dodge's 1955 line, however, was a totally different story. Wearing a completely redesigned body shell, based on but attractively differentiated from that of the Plymouth, the new Dodge in sedan form was nearly seven inches longer than its predecessor. And in convertible, hardtop, and station wagon configurations the stretch came to no less than sixteen inches! Less curvaceous than the General Motors products, the new Dodge presented a lean, trim appearance that stood in marked contrast to its dumpy predecessor. And its windshield, wide enough to provide maximum visibility, managed to avoid the knee-rapping, distortion-producing "dogleg" so common at the time.

Three trim lines were offered by Dodge, all on the same chassis. The Coronet name, which only a couple of years earlier had designated the top trimline, was now applied to the base car. Gussied up a little, it was known as the Royal, while the top series was called the Custom Royal.

Dodge's familiar hemi V-8, bored for an additional 29 cubic inches of displacement, was retained for the Custom Royal models, while the same block, fitted with conventional heads, was used in the less expensive Royal and Coronet series. The latter could also be ordered with Chrysler Corporation's hoary L-head six, but fewer than one out of every eight 1955 Dodges was so equipped.

The public's reaction to the new car was almost overwhelming. A former Dodge dealer told *SIA* that the reception accorded the 1955 model was "by far the most enthusiastic I ever saw, in more than 20 years in the business!"

Dodge sales shot up by an astonishing 106 percent!

At Mercury the changes were less dramatic. The new, overhead-valve V-8, introduced just the year before, was bored and stroked, raising its horsepower rating from 162 to 188. The horsepower race, most visible among cars of the luxury class, was making itself felt even among the more modest automobiles of the day.

Like the Dodge, the Mercury came in three series, all sharing the same 119-inch wheelbase. The base car was called the Custom. With upscale trim, the same automobile became the Monterey. And at the top of the heap rode the Montclair, a slinky number standing two-and-a-half inches lower than the less expensive cars.

Sheet metal, derived from that of the Ford, was brand new for 1955, though there was enough resemblance to the 1954 model to make the new Mercury readily identifiable. A wraparound windshield similar to that of the GM cars was featured. Dimensions, apart from the Montclair's lowered roof line, were nearly the same as those of the previous year's Merc, yet the new car's lines somehow contrived to make it appear longer and lower than before.

Buyers responded on cue; Mercury scored an impressive 69 percent sales increase.

Meanwhile, over at GM the price dis-

All three cars were styled with trim which encouraged two-tone paint schemes. Mercury had most conservative trim, Dodge the wildest.

tinctions between the various divisions had become blurred. For years it had been the Pontiac that had slugged it out with Dodge (and later with Mercury as well) for leadership in the lower-medium-priced field. But with the 1939 introduction of the "60" series, Oldsmobile had invaded Pontiac's territory. and by 1954 Olds sales had surpassed those of Pontiac. (Buick, its somewhat higher price structure notwithstanding, was still ahead of both of its sister divisions.)

Olds, along with Buick, had been rebodied for 1954; for 1955 there was only a minor facelift to distinguish the new car from its predecessor. There were

some mechanical refinements such as recalibrated front springs and a new front stabilizer, but essentially the people at lansing had refrained from messing with what was obviously a very good thing.

The policy paid off. Olds set a sales record that year that would stand for a decade.

Three distinct Oldsmobiles were offered for 1955. Flagship of the line was the 98, a sumptuously trimmed automobile built on an extended wheelbase. The division's bread and butter came, however, from the more modest 88 and Super 88 lines. Sharing the mechanical

Comparison Chart: 1955 Dodge, Mercury, Oldsmobile—And Pontiac

	Dodge Custom Royal	Mercury Montclair	Oldsmobile Super 88	Pontiac Star Chief
Series tested				
Body style	Convertible	Convertible	Convertible	Convertible
Price, model tested**	$2,723	$2,712	$2,894	$2,681
Price, base V-8 sedan**	$2,171	$2,277	$2,362	$2,164
Engine	ohv V-8	ohv V-8	ohv V-8	ohv V-8
Bore/stroke (inches)	3.63/3.25	3.75/3.30	3.875/3.4375	3.75/3.25
Displacement (cubic inches)	270.0	292.0	324.3	287.2
Compression ratio (model tested)	7.6:1	8.5:1	8.5:1	8.0:1
Compression ratio (base engine)	same	7.6:1	same	7.4:1
Bhp @ rpm (model tested)	183 @ 4,400	198 @ 4,400	202 @ 4,000	180 @ 4,600
Bhp @ rpm (base engine)	175 @ 4,400	188 @ 4,400	185 @ 4,000	173 @ 4,400
Bhp per c.i.d. (model tested)	.678	.702	.623	.627
Bhp per c.i.d. (base engine)	.648	.644	.570	.602
Torque @ rpm (model tested)	245 @ 2,400	286 @ 2,500	332 @ 2,400	264 @ 2,400
Torque @ rpm (base engine)	240 @ 2,400	274 @ 2,500	320 @ 2,000	256 @ 2,400
Carburetor	Dual downdraft	4-barrel	4-barrel	Dual downdraft
Electrical system	6-volt	6-volt	12-volt	12-volt
Automatic transmission	Powerflite	Merc-o-Matic	Hydra-Matic	Hydra-Matic
				No
Torque converter?	Yes	Yes	No	
Number of speeds	2	3	4	4
Ratios (:1)	1.72/1.00	2.40/1.47/1.00	3.82/2.63/1.45/1.00	4.10/2.63/1.55/1.00
Differential	Hypoid	Hypoid	Hypoid	Hypoid
Drive axles	Semi-floating	Semi-floating	Semi-floating	Semi-floating
Ratio	3.54:1	3.15:1	3.23:1	3.08:1
Front suspension	Ind. coil spring	Ind. coil spring	Ind. coil spring	Ind. coil spring
Steering (power, type)	Recirc. ball nut***	Worm and roller	Ball nut	Recirc. ball brg.
Ratio (:1, gear)	16.2	20.1	19.1	21.3
Turn circle (curb/curb)	42' 3"	42' 4"	42' 0"	42' 11"
Brakes (type)	Hydraulic, drum	Hydraulic, drum	Hydraulic, drum	Hydraulic, drum
Drum diameter	11"	11"	11"	12"
Effective area (sq. in.)	173.5	190.9	191.7	178.0
Tread, front	58.9"	58"	59"	58.7"
Tread, rear	59.1"	59"	59"	59.1"
Capacities:				
Cooling system (qts, w/heater)	20	20	21.5	26
Fuel tank (gallons)	17	18	20	20
Shipping wgt, car tested (lbs)	3,610	3,490	3,989	3791
Shipping wgt, base sedan	3,395	3,450	3,707	3511
Measurements:				
Wheelbase	120"	119"	122"	124"
Overall length	212.1"	206.3"****	203.4"	210.2"
Overall width	74.5"	76.4"	77.8"	75.4"
Overall height (sedan)	62.6"	60.5"	62.2"	62.5"
Minimum road clearance	5.0"	6.6"	6.3"	6.7"
Tire size	7.10 x15	7.10 x 15	7.60 x 15	7.10 x 15
Front leg room	44.5"	43.8"	42.9"	42.7"
Rear leg room (sedan)	35.5"	35.4"	35.6"	35.6"
Front head room (sedan)	35.5"	33.5"	35.6"	35.6"
Rear head room (sedan)	34.9"	32.2"	34.6"	35.9"
Front hip room	62.5"	60.6"	62.3"	61.8"
Rear hip room (sedan)	62.8"	60.3"	62.4"	63.1"
Front shoulder room	58.0"	57.0"	58.2"	56.6"
Rear shoulder room (sedan)	57.8"	56.8"	56.7"	56.4"
Front seat adjustment	5.0"	4.9"	4.4"	4.4"
Front seat height	13.4"	12.0"	13.2"	13.7"
Rear seat height (sedan)	12.8"	13.1"	12.4"	12.0"
Registrations (calendar year)	284,323	371,837	589,515	530,007
Production (calendar year)	313,088	434,911	643,459	581,860
Production (model year)	276,936	329,808	583,179	553,808
Production, this body style	3,302	10,668	9,007	19,762
Performance factors				
Lbs per bhp (car tested)	19.73	17.63	19.75	21.06
Lbs per bhp (base sedan)	19.40	18.35	20.00	20.20
Lbs per c.i.d. (car tested)	13.37	11.95	12.30	13.20
Lbs per c.i.d. (base sedan)	12.57	11.82	11.40	12.22

*The Pontiac was not tested. Figures are shown here for comparative purposes.

**Price f.o.b. factory, including federal excise tax.

***Test car was equipped with worm-and-roller manual steering, ratio 18.2:1.

****Length shown does not include optional continental kit.

Primary source: *Automotive Industries*, March 15, 1955.

Below: *Dodge taillamp treatment was very space-age, while Olds,* **far left,** *stayed with its traditional bullet treatment. Merc,* **left,** *opted for busy vertical effect.* **Below center and bottom:** *All three cars present a pleasant rear appearance, with Olds having the cleanest styling of the lot.*

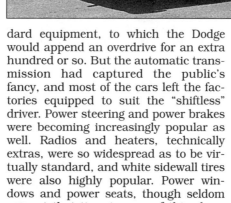

components of the larger car, they were priced within the reach of the Pontiac (or Dodge or Mercury) buyer. (See comparison chart, page 50.)

Statistically, the Dodge-Mercury-Oldsmobile trio of 1955 have much in common, though the Olds is a little heavier and more powerful than the other two—as well as marginally more expensive.

The Dodge, though a bit narrower overall than its competition, furnished a little extra shoulder and hip room, and for the tall driver it had a substantial advantage in leg room.

But perhaps the most obvious difference among the three cars, appearance aside, lay in their optional automatic transmissions. Oldsmobile used, as it had since 1940, the venerable four-speed Hydra-Matic. Mercury employed, for the fifth straight year, the Merc-o-Matic, a three-speed unit tied to a torque converter. Dodge, whose first fully automatic transmission had been introduced only two years earlier, stayed with the Powerflite, a two-speed planetary arrangement coupled to a torque con-verter. All three transmissions had excellent records in terms of durability.

Options abounded. Dodge, Mercury and Oldsmobile all came with three-speed manual transmissions as stan-dard equipment, to which the Dodge would append an overdrive for an extra hundred or so. But the automatic transmission had captured the public's fancy, and most of the cars left the factories equipped to suit the "shiftless" driver. Power steering and power brakes were becoming increasingly popular as well. Radios and heaters, technically extras, were so widespread as to be virtually standard, and white sidewall tires were also highly popular. Power windows and power seats, though seldom seen at that time in cars of this class, were available to buyers who wanted them; and Dodge was beginning to push its Chrysler Air-Temp air-conditioner, at $567 the most costly of all options. At that price there were few takers.

Thanks to some vigorous legwork on the part of photographer Vince Manocchi, *SIA* was able to bring together three particularly choice convertibles for this comparisonReport—one from each of the major US manufacturers.

• Representing the Chrysler Corporation was Nick Dezmura's Dodge Custom Royal Lancer.

• Carrying the flag for the Ford Motor Company was Cindy Keetch's Mercury Montclair.

• And upholding the honor of General Motors was an Oldsmobile Super 88 belonging to Norb Kopchinsky.

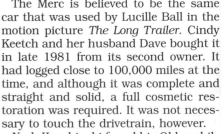

Above: Dodge rolls on factory-option Kelsey-Hayes wires, while Merc and Olds hubcaps are quite restrained in design: ***Right and below:*** Model ID appears on Merc's continental kit. Olds need only say "88" for instant recognition, but Dodge spells it out. ***Bottom, left to right:*** '55 was first year for Mercury's full wraparound windshield. Dodge opted for semiwraparound and Olds continued its raked wraparound, introduced in 1954.

We drove them all—and we loved them! Our Dodge's early history is shrouded in mystery, since Nick bought it in 1979 off a consignment lot. But there is every indication that the 77,000-mile odometer reading is probably correct. The car even has its original Coodyear widewhitewall spare tire.

The Merc is believed to be the same car that was used by Lucille Ball in the motion picture *The Long Trailer.* Cindy Keetch and her husband Dave bought it in late 1981 from its second owner. It had logged close to 100,000 miles at the time, and although it was complete and straight and solid, a full cosmetic restoration was required. It was not necessary to touch the drivetrain, however.

Norb Kopchinski found his Oldsmobile in 1982, in a Pennsylvania barn where it had been stored for many years, forgotten and neglected. A 36,000-mile original car in generally sound mechanical condition, it was suffering from rusted-out front fenders and quarter panels. Without laying a wrench on it, Norb was able to drive the Olds home to California at speeds that he would be reluctant to discuss with the Highway Patrol. The original leather interior is still in good condition, but of course the car's exterior needed extensive attention.

We have owned Chrysler Corporation

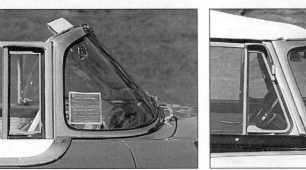

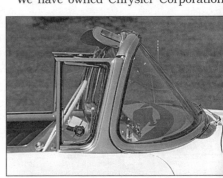

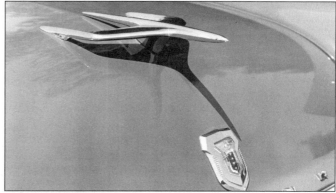

cars of 1953 and 1958 vintage in years gone by, and we were not impressed with the body structure of either of them. So it came as something of a surprise when we found the Dodge to be—seemingly, at least—the most solidly constructed of the three ragtops used for this report. Leg room is ample, front and rear—the best of the lot in that respect. Seating is comfortable, too, though the edge in that department would have to go to the Olds.

We appreciate the absence of a dogleg in the Dodge's panoramic windshield. Not only is this design kinder to the knees of a long-legged occupant, but it produces almost no distortion.

A full set of dashboard instruments characterizes all three of these cars. We like that. The people who invented and promoted idiot lights have a lot of penance to do.

The Mercury's front seat is wide and comfortable, if a bit low for our taste. Leg room is ample in the driver's compartment. Seated in the rear, however, we found our knees tucked up under our chin. The back seat is wide enough for two, but for three people it would be an impossibly tight squeeze. And the head room, thanks to the Montclair's low profile, is limited.

Boarding the Oldsmobile, we found the best seating accommodations of the lot—in front. Rear knee room is nonexistent for a six-footer, however. The seat cushions seem more supportive than those of the other two cars, an important comfort factor. But that miserable dogleg seems even more obtrusive than that of the Mercury.

Head room is good, about on a par with the Dodge, and although the Olds has the smallest trunk of the three, it's still reasonably spacious.

The best part of an assignment such as this one is, of course, getting to drive the cars. We took the Dodge out first.

We were surprised to find that the Royal Lancer convertible, though a top-of-the-line car, is not equipped with power steering. That may have been a wise move on the part of the original owner, for Chrysler's power steering in the fifties was too sensitive for many drivers. In any case we found the manual steering to be light, easy and precise—

*Top left, top right and above: Olds carried rocket theme over to its hood ornament. Mercury ornament doesn't have any particular theme; Dodge used very abstract knight's helmet. **Left:** Olds headlight rim treatment gave a slightly hooded effect. **Below left:** Mercury used a very heavy hood on their lights. **Below:** Dodge treatment looks like a highly stylized eyebrow.*

though a little slow. The car, as Nick says. goes exactly where you point it.

Acceleration is handicapped by the Dodge's two-speed Powerflite transmission. Which isn't to say that the car is sluggish; it's not. But off-the-line it would do much better if the transmission had an extra gear. The shift from low to high is a smooth one; the driver is hardly aware of it.

The ride is good, very comfortable indeed. There's quite a bit of lean in the turns, but control is easy to maintain at all times.

Like its steering, the Dodge's brakes are non-powered. They take a bit of getting used to, for a lot of pedal pressure

is required. But they do their job smoothly and well.

We had forgotten that the early Merc-o-Matic transmissions start the car in second gear. We were reminded of this characteristic quickly enough, for the Mercury's acceleration from rest is less brisk than that of the Dodge. By starting off in Low, then shifting manually to Drive, performance is substantially improved.

This Merc is equipped with just about every option the company offered in 1955. The power steering preserves a fair amount of road feel, and the power brakes are—like the laxative ad says—smooth and effective. In addition, Cindy's

Right: Oldsmobile front carries typical GM combination bumper/grille styling. *Below:* Dodge uses split grille effect. *Below right:* Mercury also goes the bumper/grille route, but in a more angular manner than Olds.

car boasts power windows, power seats, a rare deluxe steering wheel, and even a factory continental kit.

If one were to stage a drag race among these three cars, the Oldsmobile would win it going away. The enormous torque of the 88 engine—largest of the three powerplants by a substantial margin—combines with the four-speed Hydra-Matic transmission to give this car a strong advantage in that department. Shifts are smooth, and so are the

The Traditional Rival: Pontiac

It had been General Motors President Alfred P. Sloan, Jr., who—back in the early twenties—had come up with the idea of arranging the corporation's various marques in the form of a "ladder." Thus, as Sloan conceived the notion, as the motorist's social, professional and financial status improved, he could progress step-by-step to ever finer and more expensive automobiles. All within the GM family, of course.

Initially there had been a couple of gaps in that ladder, and Alfred Sloan made it his business to close them. The most important of these was the considerable stretch between the price of the Chevrolet and that of the Oldsmobile. Strategically placed at the bottom of the medium-priced market, it was a segment that for years had been dominated by the Dodge Brothers four-cylinder cars.

Sloan's response to Dodge's implicit challenge was, of course, the Pontiac. (See *SIA* #44.) Introduced in 1926, it was an attractive L-head six. And it was an immediate success.

As time went along, the steps of Sloan's ladder became less well-defined. By 1939 the top-of-the-line Pontiac was actually priced substantially higher than the cheapest Olds, for instance. And by the mid-fifties, even Buick was marketing automobiles that directly competed with the upscale Pontiac models.

But still, in the public's mind—and doubtless in the thinking of the corporate planners as well—it was the Pontiac that was the traditional and natural rival of the Dodge—and of the upstart Mercury as well.

The intra-corporate rivalry among Buick,

Olds, and Pontiac is a story in itself. For years the Buick, despite the disadvantage of carrying the highest average price tag of the trio, had been General Motors' best-selling medium-priced car, followed by Pontiac and Oldsmobile, in that order. But the fifties saw some drastic shifts in the automobile market. Olds eased past Pontiac in 1954 and passed Buick in numbers of cars produced four years later. And then in 1959, with the introduction of the dramatic new "wide track" models, Pontiac leapfrogged over both of its sister divisions to take over fourth place in the industry, behind Chevrolet, Ford and Plymouth. By 1961 the Ponty was the industry's number three nameplate, a distinction it was to hold for several years to follow.

As it happened, 1955 was a banner year for Pontiac, despite the fact that the division was out-produced by both Buick and Oldsmobile. Scoring a 57 percent sales increase over the previous year, Pontiac was a country mile ahead of both Mercury and Dodge. And perhaps not surprisingly, for the car they offered was almost completely new. Fitted with GM's freshly styled A body, which it shared with Chevrolet, it featured the then-popular dogleg wraparound windshield, and was distinguished by twin "silver streaks" (a Pontiac trademark in those days) running the length of the hood. Those streaks, taken together with the comparatively massive appearance of the new model, led one critic to refer to the '55 Pontiac as "a fat man wearing suspenders." No matter; the public loved it

But significant as the new styling was, the

real change in the Pontiac was to be found under the hood. From the time of its introduction, Pontiac had used side-valve engines exclusively. There had been a short-lived and none-too-popular V-8 back in 1932, but the bulk of Pontiac's production had been of sixes and—especially—straight eights.

Pontiac's 1955 powerplant set a new direction for the marque with a modern, short-stroke, overhead-valve V-8. Not for more than a decade would Pontiac again offer a six. With a modest increase in displacement over the old L-head eight (287.2 versus 268.4 cubic inches), the new engine boasted a healthy 42 percent boost in horsepower, from 127 to 180 (as fitted to Hydra-Matic-equipped units). So, despite an extra hundred and fifty pounds of heft compared to its predecessor, the 1955 model was by far the fastest, liveliest car produced by the Pontiac Motor Division up to that time.

Three series were offered: The Chieftain 860 (Special), Chieftain 870 (Deluxe), and the Star Chief. The latter, a beautifully appointed car with two extra inches of wheelbase, measured more than seven inches longer overall than the Chieftains, the extra length taking the form of an extended rear deck. The convertible body style was offered only in the Star Chief series.

The automotive world didn't know it yet, but Pontiac was about to enter its halcyon days—the period of the marque's greatest sales success.

Left, below left, and below: All three cars will break into noticeable understeer when pushed in corners. **Below center, left to right:** Thanks to continental kit, Merc wins largest trunk contest. **Below, top to bottom:** Olds's big, round speedo is highly readable. Merc's speedo sweeps across the dial in an arc. Dodge's gauges are each carried in separate pod. All three cars boast full instrumentation as standard equipment.

brakes, and the power steering is at least the equal of the Merc's in preserving the feel of the road.

It seems to us that the Olds doesn't lean as much as either of the other cars in hard cornering. And yet it's no easier to control on winding roads. Maybe not quite as easy, in fact, as the Dodge. Hard to say; the difference between power and non-power steering could be a factor here. And in terms of ride we'd rank the Olds about equal with the Dodge—and just a bit ahead of the Mercury.

All right: so which to choose?

As usual there were characteristics in each car that had the edge over the other two, and what we would really prefer is a composite.

• We like the Oldsmobile's transmission best, though the Merc might get the edge here if only it would start off in first gear.

• It's entirely a matter of personal preference, but the sleek styling of the Dodge appeals to us. Again, the Merc is a close second—a potential winner except for that misbegotten dogleg. The curvaceous lines of the Olds are the sexiest of the lot, but they've always seemed to us to be a trifle bulbous.

• The torque output of that Oldsmobile engine is impressive, and evidently there's little penalty attached in terms of fuel mileage.

• Seating comfort up front is best in the Olds, though the margin is narrow. In the rear seat, the advantage goes to the Dodge.

• The lady at our house tends to pack everything in sight every time we go anywhere, so of course we can appreciate the Mercury's enormous trunk.

Taken all-in-all, had we been keeping a point score, perhaps the nod would have gone to the Olds—by a nose. But that's as it should be, for it was the costliest of the three, back in 1955. All three cars offer a comfortable ride, more than adequate performance, and durability that has proven itself over the years.

And when you contemplate the progress in automotive design that these cars represent, compared to their precursors of a quarter-century—or even nine years—earlier, you know it's really true: 1955 was indeed a very good year! 🐾

Acknowledgments and Bibliography

Automotive Industries, *March 15, 1955, and March 15, 1954; Thomas Bonsall,* Mercury Identification Guide, 1939-1969; *Dennis Casteele,* The Cars of Oldsmobile; *Jerry Heasley,* The Production Figure Book for US Cars; *James H. Mahoney and George H. Dammann,* American Cars, 1946-1959; *Thomas A. McPherson,* The Dodge Story.

Our thanks to Al Allande, Van Nuys,

Right, below and below right: All three engines have good accessibility to the basics, though in their day these were considered fiendishly busy engine compartments. Bottom: Dodge's tail is beginning to hint at fins; Olds looks nearly identical to '54 cars; Merc gains added inches because of wind-catching continental kit.

The Fickle Fortunes of the Lower-Medium-Priced Four

Dodge had been, from 1933 until the close of the decade of the thirties, the number-one seller in the lower-medium-price sales race—with Pontiac hard on its heels and Oldsmobile a strong third. In 1940 Pontiac took the lead, and the following year Dodge fell to third place behind Oldsmobile. Ford's new Mercury, meanwhile, was making its opening bid.

In the years just after World War II, Dodge forged ahead once again, with Pontiac, Olds, and Mercury following in that order. But fate is capricious and the public is fickle. By 1948 Pontiac had regained the lead, only to lose it to Oldsmobile six years later. Mercury, meanwhile, had slipped ahead of Dodge, leaving the one-time leader of the field in fourth place.

Calendar Year Production, 1946-1955

Year	Dodge	Mercury	Oldsmobile	Pontiac
1946	156,080	70,955	114,674	131,538
1947	232,216	124,612	191,454	222,991
1948	232,390	154,702	194,755	253,472
1949	298,399	203,339	282,885	336,466
1950	332,782	334,081	396,757	469,813
1951	325,694	238,854	285,634	345,617
1952	259,519	195,261	228,452	278,140
1953	293,714	320,369	319,414	415,335
1954	151,766	256,730	433,810	370,887
1955	313,038	434,911	643,459	581,860

Source: Jerry Heasley, *The Production Figure Book for US Cars.*

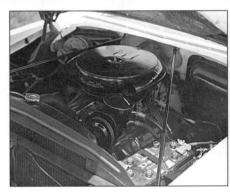

California; W.H. Braley, Santa Cruz, California; Gary Goers, Santa Fe Springs, California: Tom and Nancy Howard, Riverside, California; Franca and Vince Manocchi, Azusa, California; Jerry Olmstead, Hilltop Classics, Escondido, California; Telford and Ada Work, Pacific Palisades, California. Special thanks to Nick Dezmura, Northridge, California; Dave and Cindy Keetch, Spring Valley, California; Norb Kopchinski, Downey, California.

Color Gallery

Photograph by Vince Manocchi

Photograph by Bud Juneau

1931 F-31 Convertible Roadster

The F-31 was the only model Oldsmobile offered in 1931. It was, however, available in six variations, including the convertible roadster of which 3,500 were built. Standard power was a 65hp, 197.5-cu.in. L-head six, and a selective sliding 3-speed gearbox was standard. Options included a spotlight, spare tire cover and a backup light.

1935 L-35 Business Coupe and F-35 Town Coupe

For 1935, Oldsmobile offered one-piece, turret-top construction, longer, 115- and 121-inch wheelbases for its two models, better brakes and stronger frames. The L-35 (left) was powered by a 100hp, 240-cu.in. eight cylinder, and the F-35 (right) uses a 90hp, 213-cu.in. six.

Photograph by Bud Juneau

1938 L-38
With an increased body length of $5^1/_2$ inches, the 110hp, eight-cylinder-powered Series L shared revised nose styling that incorporated thick grille bars with the Series F six-cylinder cars. Optional equipment included a semi-automatic transmission, air-cooled battery and dual-sidemount spares.

Photograph by Don Stickles

1942 Ninety Eight B-44 Sedan
Dual front bumper grille and fade-away fenders made the Oldsmobile a very distictive car for 1942. Standard power for the upscale 98 was a 110hp, 257-cu.in. straight eight and 3-speed manual transmission. Hydra-Matic automatic transmission was a $100 option in all models.

1949 Ninety Eight Coupe

Rocket V-8 power came from Oldsmobile in 1949 and was available in Eighty Eight and Ninety Eight models. Standard equipment in the Ninety Eight Deluxe included the 135hp, 303-cu.in. V-8 engine, Hydra-Matic automatic transmission, hydraulic-powered windows, seats and tops on convertible models.

Photograph by John Lee

1953 Fiesta convertible

For 1953, Oldmobile's top offering was the Fiesta convertible. At $5,715, it was nearly $2,500 more than the second most expensive model. Fiesta featured a wrap-around windshield and modified quarter panels. Power came from a 170hp, 303-cu.in. V-8 with a Hydra-Matic transmission.

1953 Holiday coupe
With its B-pillarless design, the Holiday hardtop coupe was available in the Eighty Eight and Ninety Eight body styles. Both series used a 165hp, 303-cu.in. V-8, though a Hydra-Matic transmission, air conditioning, and hydraulic windows and seats were optional. A total of 62,500 hardtops were built in 1953.

Photograph by Terry Boyce

1954 Ninety Eight Starfire convertible
Called the Starfire, the 1954 Oldsmobile Ninety Eight convertible rode on a 126-inch wheelbase and had an overall length of 214.3 inches. Standard equipment included a 185hp, 324 cu.in. V-8, a padded dash, and chrome wheel covers, but power steering, power seats and Hydra-Matic driver were optional.

Photograph by Don Spiro

1955 Super Eighty Eight
Sharing the same 202hp, 324-cu.in. V-8 engine with the larger Ninety Eight, the Super Eighty Eight was Oldsmobile's mid-level offering for 1955. Of the 242,192 Super Eighty Eights offered this year, 62,534 were the $2,714 Holiday hardtops. They carried all of the standard Eighty Eight features plus higher quality cloth and leather interiors.

Photograph by Russ von Sauers

1957 Holiday hardtop J-2
High-performance engine option J-2 gave any 1957 Oldsmobile 300hp from a triple-carbureted 371-cu.in. V-8. Ninety Eights equipped with this $83 performance option came standard with the Jetaway Hydra-Matic transmission. Though there were more than 32,000 Ninety Eight 4-door Holiday hardtops, only a handful came with the J-2 engine.

Photograph by Robert Gross

1964 Ninety Eight convertible
The top-of-the-line Ninety Eight rode on a 126-inch wheelbase and used a 280hp, 394-cu.in. V-8 for 1964. Standard equipment included Hydra-Matic transmission, power windows, seats and steering, and special wheel covers. Of the 68,600 Ninety Eights built for 1964, only 4,004 were convertibles.

Photograph by John Lee

1957 Super Eighty Eight Fiesta station wagon
Utilitarian and spacious, the 1957 Super Eighty Eight station wagon, or Fiesta as Oldsmobile called it, rode on a 122-inch wheelbase and weighed 4,470 pounds. Standard power was a 277hp, 371-cu.in. V-8. At $3,220, the Fiesta wagon was the most expensive model in the Super Eighty Eight series.

Photograph by David Newhardt

1966 Delta Eighty Eight convertible
Introduced in 1965, the Delta Eighty
Eight was available for the first time in
convertible form in 1966. Standard
equipment included a 310hp, 425-cu.in.
V-8 and TH400 automatic, though a
375hp 425-cu.in. was optional. Cruise
control, reverb, and Guide-O-Matic
headlight dimmer were some of its convenience options.

1964 Jetstar I

Photograph by Vince Manocchi

Basically a stripped-down version of the Starfire personal luxury car, the Jetstar I
(not to be confused with the Jetstar Eighty Eight) had a 345hp, 394-cu.in. V-8, console with tachometer, and minimal brightwork. Other than the engine, all the
power amenities from the Starfire were optional.

Photograph by Robert Gross

1970 Rallye 350 Cutlass

The W-45 Rallye 350 package was ordered on just over 3,547 1970 Cutlass "S" and F-85 coupes. Powered by a 325hp, 350-cu.in. V-8, standard equipment included Sebring Yellow paint, black decals, front disc brakes, power steering and brakes, and dual exhaust.

Photograph by Robert Gross

1968 Delta Eighty Eight

Three standard and two Custom models were offered in the Delta Eighty Eight series for 1968. Dual master cylinder, energy-absorbing steering column, and four-way flashers came with the standard Delta Eighty Eight; custom models carried those plus added interior amenities. Standard power for all Eighty Eights was a 310hp, 455-cu.in. V-8.

1956 OLDSMOBILE SUPER 88 CONVERTIBLE

by John F. Katz
photos by Roy Query

IN 1951, the boom was never going to end. Harlow "Red" Curtice, formerly general manager of Buick and now executive vice president of the whole General Motors organization, was pushing a $750 million scheme to build new factories and facilities. For Oldsmobile, the Curtice plan would expand production by 25 percent. Having shipped 372,519 shiny new Oldsmobiles in 1950, the Lansing-based division held sixth place in the industry, with just under six percent of the total market. Olds had built its three-millionth car in February of that year. And despite the Korean War — which soaked up about 30 percent of the capacity Olds already had — the division would build its four-millionth automobile in May 1953.

It was a time of can-do confidence, for Oldsmobile, for General Motors, for the United States of America. At first, GM management thought the new body shells introduced in 1948-49 would sell through the end of 1954. But late in 1952, when Curtice reviewed the proposed facelifts for '54 and pronounced them a bit stale, someone suggested pushing the all-new senior and mid-

range cars slated for 1955 into production a full year early. And Curtice, who within weeks would inherit the president's chair from Charles E. "Engine Charlie" Wilson, enthusiastically agreed.

The new cars stood about three inches lower than the '53s, with flatter hoods, slab sides, and tall rear fenders that hinted at the fins to come. Windshields wrapped around for a panoramic view on flagship "C-bodies," and reached even further on mid-range "B-bodies," which featured forward-tilting windshield posts. Two-door C-bodies and all B-bodies sported a rakish dip at the beltline, echoing the very-limited-production Cadillac Eldorado, Buick Skylark, and Olds Fiesta of 1953.

Oldsmobile used only the B-body, with a wheelbase of 122 inches for the 88 and Super 88, and 126 inches for the 98. The new body required a new frame,

but Olds engineers retained the previous ladder-type configuration with its central X-brace for all body styles. While reworking the frame, the chassis department straightened the previously toed-in rear leaf springs and moved them outboard as well. They also retuned the springs and shocks for a softer ride, although chassis maven George T. Jones insisted on keeping Oldsmobile's traditional front and rear sway bars. Rotating the HydraMatic transmission 22 degrees counterclockwise gained valuable vertical clearance under the lower body. And the brakes grew in size to 11 inches.

The new Oldsmobiles weighed between 44 and 96 pounds more than their predecessors, yet Olds's new general manager, Jack Wolfram, insisted on no loss in performance. Fortunately, engine chief Gil Burrell had designed the original 303-c.i.d. "Rocket" V-8 with plenty of room for expansion, and to power the new cars he added an eighth-inch to the bore to yield a new displacement of 324 cubic inches. Compression had been climbing steadily since the engine's 1949 introduction, and now reached 8.25:1. With a longer-dwelling cam completing the changes, increased power more than compensated for the increased weight, and Olds engineers were able to specify numerically lower axle ratios for a reported 10 percent improvement in fuel economy.

It took a massive engineering effort, but the new Oldsmobiles once scheduled for 1955 debuted on January 20, 1954. And no one else, save for sister divisions Cadillac and Buick, offered an all-new look that year. *Motor Trend* joshed about "the 88 that couldn't wait," but gave the Olds high marks for performance, economy, braking, and general roominess, expressing reservations only about its indifferent handling and tight front-seat leg room. Lansing built 407,150 cars that year, clambering over both Pontiac and Plymouth to grab fourth place in the industry (behind Chevrolet, Ford, and an even faster-climbing Buick), with 7.35 percent of the total market.

Nineteen fifty-five brought refinements, both mechanical and aesthetic. A new oval air intake replaced Olds's traditional arching grille bars. Suspension engineer Jim Lewis designed new upper and lower control arms which placed direct-acting shocks inside the coil springs. Tires went tubeless, and the steering gear's Pitman arm now glided on needle bearings. New combustion chambers with higher compression and larger exhaust valves combined with a higher-lift cam to boost horsepower to 202 with a four-barrel carb. Meanwhile, the optional air conditioning moved out of the trunk and was

With its aggressive oval grille and rocket decorations there's no mistaking this car for anything but an Oldsmobile.

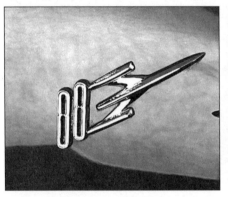

The Mid-priced Survivors
The Super 88 faces its competition

	Price	Wheelbase	C.i.d.	Bhp	Weight	Lb./bhp	Production
Oldsmobile 88	$2,226	122	324	230 @ 4,400	3,761	16.4	216,019
Studebaker President	$2,235	116	289	190 @ 4,500	3,210	16.9	10,258
Pontiac Chieftain Special	$2,294	122	317	205 @ 4,800	3,617	17.6	184,232
Mercury Medalist	$2,313	119	312	210 @ 4,400	3,500	16.7	45,812
Dodge Coronet	$2,340	120	270	189 @ 4,400	3,435	18.2	142,613
Oldsmobile Super 88	$2,363	122	324	240 @ 4,400	3,897	16.2	179,000
Pontiac Chieftain Deluxe	$2,409	122	317	205 @ 4,800	3,617	17.6	93,872
Mercury Custom	$2,410	119	312	210 @ 4,600	3,520	16.8	85,328
Buick Special	$2,416	122	322	220 @ 4,400	3,790	17.2	334,017
Hudson Wasp	$2,416	114	202*	120 @ 4,000	3,264	27.2	2,519
Nash Ambassador	$2,425	121	253*	130 @ 3,700	3,555	27.3	5,999
Dodge Royal	$2,478	120	270	189 @ 4,400	3,475	18.4	48,780
Stude President Classic	$2,489	120	289	210 @ 4,500	3,295	15.7	8,507

* Six cylinder; Hudson and Nash V-8 prices fall well outside the specified range.

Our list includes all US-built, "medium-price" nameplates priced within an admittedly arbitrary six percent of the Olds Super 88 four-door sedan. Prices and mechanical specifications are for four-door sedans with base V-8, except as noted. Horsepower listed is for automatic-transmission models where different. Wheelbase is given in inches, weight in pounds. Production is the total of all body styles in the series. Note that the Buick, Dodge, Pontiac, Mercury Custom, and Studebaker President figures include station wagons, a body style not offered by Oldsmobile (although wagons accounted for a relatively small percentage of these competitors' total production). On the other hand, the Dodge Royal, Mercury Medalist, and Pontiac Chieftain series offered no convertible; nor did Hudson or Nash.

now integrated into the dash. *Motor Trend* noted a large improvement in acceleration along with small gains in handling.

With Cadillac and Buick, Olds debuted the industry's first four-door hardtops in March '55; soon two-thirds of Olds production went pillarless — despite significantly less room relative to the four-door sedan. Oldsmobile built its five-millionth car in July, and total production for the model year peaked at 589,515 cars, for 8.22 percent of the market and a fifth-place finish behind Buick and the low-priced three.

Curtice's expansion plan continued to evolve, and was by then budgeted at $1.5 billion. Oldsmobile's share would boost the division's production capacity by half. Wolfram looked out upon the struggles of the independent automakers (Kaiser ceased production that year, Hudson became a shadow of Nash, while Studebaker and Packard made the most of their marriage of desperation) and saw only room for more Oldsmobiles.

So Olds rolled in 1956 with expanded sheet-metal, axle, and forging capacity, plus new and more automated tooling for building Rocket V-8s. The '56 models, the final facelift of the '54 theme, were shown to the press on October 26, 1955. The oval grille was now fully integrated into the bumper. Under the hood, the engine received another new camshaft, with larger journals for durability, higher lift for performance, and new contours for quiet. Still bigger exhaust

Ovals and circles, along with plenty of chrome, are the dominant styling themes up front with the Super 88. They're derived from Art Ross's oval bumper/grille theme on '53 Starfire, '54 Cutlass and F-88 show cars.

The Olds Model Lineup for '56
Production totals by series and body style

	88	Super 88	98
Two-door sedan	31,949	5,465	------
Two-door hardtop	74,739	43,054	19,433
Four-door sedan	57,092	59,728	20,105
Four-door hardtop	52,239	61,192	42,320
Convertible	------	9,561	8,581

Prices ranged from $2,166 for the 88 two-door sedan up to $3,380 for the 98 "Starfire" convertible. All hardtop models carried "Holiday" lettering in addition to their series designation.

specifications

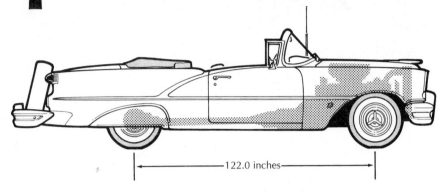

←———122.0 inches———→   ←—59.0 inches—→

1956 Oldsmobile Super 88 convertible

Base price	$2,726
Std equip includes	240 bhp "T-350" Rocket V-8, Jetaway HydraMatic transmission, automatic choke, 7.60 x 15 tires, carpeting, foam seat cushions, cloth upholstery, arm rests, sun visors, directional signals, dual horns, cigarette lighter, lined trunk, courtesy lights, unique exterior trim
Options on dR car	Power steering, $100; power brakes, $37; oil filter, $10; oil-bath air cleaner, $6; deluxe heater and defroster, $77; Super deluxe radio, $121; whitewall tires, $33; deluxe wheel discs, $28; dual exhaust, $38; exhaust extensions, $2; electric clock, $18; padded dash, $18; reverse lights, $13; deluxe steering wheel, $13; parking brake signal light, $5; windshield washers, $10; E-Z-Eye tinted glass, $30; plus glareproof tilt mirror, fender skirts, vanity mirror, outside rearview mirror, prices not available
Price as equipped	$3,400 (estimated)
Accessories	"Rocket-circle" dash plaque; external spare tire; free-flow mufflers

ENGINE

Type	V-8
Bore x stroke	3.875 inches x 3.4375 inches
Displacement	324.3 cubic inches
Compression ratio	9.25:1
Bhp @ rpm	240 @ 4,400 (gross)
Torque @ rpm	350 @ 2,800 (gross)
Taxable horsepower	48
Valve gear	Ohv
Valve lifters	Hydraulic
Main bearings	5
Carburetor	1 Rochester 4GC 4v downdraft
Fuel system	Mechanical pump w/vacuum booster
Lubrication system	Pressure
Cooling system	Pressure
Exhaust system	Dual, 2.25-inch main pipe
Electrical system	12-volt

TRANSMISSION

Type	Jetaway HydraMatic four-speed automatic with two fluid couplings
Ratios: 1st	3.97:1
2nd	2.55:1
3rd	1.55:1
4th	1.00:1
Reverse	4.31:1

DIFFERENTIAL

Type	Hypoid, semi-floating
Ratio	3.42:1

STEERING

Type	Saginaw recirculating ball with hydraulic servo
Turns lock-to-lock	4.0
Ratios	19.0:1 gear; 22.7:1 overall
Turning diameter	42 feet (curb/curb)

BRAKES

Type	Bendix 4-wheel hydraulic with vacuum servo
Front	11 x 2.5-inch drum
Rear	11 x 2-inch drum
Swept area	191.7 square inches
Parking brake	Mechanical, on rear service brakes

CHASSIS & BODY

Construction	Separate body and frame
Frame	Channel-section side rails with 5 crossmembers and I-beam X-brace
Body	Welded steel stampings
Body style	6-seat convertible coupe

SUSPENSION

Front	Independent, unequal-length control arms, coil springs, link-type anti-roll bar
Rear	Live axle, longitudinal semi-elliptic springs, link-type anti-roll bar
Shock absorbers	Delco direct-acting, front and rear
Tires	7.60 x 15 four-ply
Wheels	Stamped steel disc, 15 x 5.5

WEIGHTS AND MEASURES

Wheelbase	122 inches
Overall length	203.3 inches*
Overall width	78.6 inches
Overall height	60.5 inches
Front track	59.0 inches
Rear track	58.0 inches
Min. road clearance	6.3 inches
Shipping weight	3,947 pounds*

* without continental kit

CAPACITIES

Crankcase	5 quarts (less filter)
Cooling system	21.5 quarts (with heater)
Fuel tank	20 gallons
Transmission	22 pints
Rear axle	5 pints

CALCULATED DATA

Horsepower per c.i.d.	.74
Weight per hp	16.4 pounds
Weight per c.i.d.	12.2 pounds
PSI (brakes)	20.6
Production	9,561

PERFORMANCE**

0-30 mph	3.7 seconds
0-60 mph	10.8 seconds
Standing 1/4 mile	18.8 seconds/77 mph
Maximum speed	111.5 mph
Fuel consumption	10.2 mpg
Braking, 60-0 mph	167 feet

** Super 88 4-door hardtop with Jetaway HydraMatic, dual exhausts, 3.23:1 axle, power steering and brakes tested by *Motor Trend*, April 1956

1956 OLDSMOBILE

valves and a new T-intersection intake manifold further enhanced breathing, and re-contoured combustion chambers and slimmer head gaskets boosted compression to a mighty 9.25:1. Thus revised, the Rocket V-8 delivered 230 bhp and 340 foot pounds of torque with a two-barrel carburetor; and 240 bhp and 350 foot pounds in four-barrel form. Both carburetors were new and larger; and the four-barrel now featured vacuum-controlled secondaries and a new linkage that kicked the automatic transmission down a gear during part-throttle acceleration (instead of waiting for the driver to mash the pedal to the floor as before). Optional dual exhausts were offered for the first time, and a new "Jetaway" HydraMatic transmission promised smoother shifting.

In the chassis, thicker anti-roll bars compensated for softer, trunnion-mounted shocks, while new body mounts helped insulate passengers from any unpleasantness beneath them. A faster-ratio steering gear for power-steering cars improved handling response, and at the same time required one pound less effort before the power kicked in. A flexible coupling in the steering shaft helped absorb road shocks, and refinements to the braking system improved modulation.

Inside the cockpit, an all-new dash substituted "idiot lights" for gauges, although the optional clock now featured a sweep-second hand. A pedal-type parking brake replaced the old pull-handle, and seat belts were available at $11 a seat. There were myriad other improvements as well, including a roomier glove

Above: Even the fresh air intake below the windshield is made of the shiny stuff. Below left: Rocket taillamp design was begun in '53, reached its final iteration in '56. Below right: For Junior, who can't wait for a car of his own, a '56 Rocket 88 convertible complete with miniature drive-in tray. DriveReport Olds's owner concocted this neat pedal car by hand using various castoff trim pieces.

Getaway With Jetaway

On August 12, 1953 — just days before the start of 1954 model-year production — fire devastated the General Motors transmission factory in Livonia, Michigan. Oldsmobile management had projected that 90-93 percent of 1954 production would be equipped with HydraMatic transmission. As the smoke cleared, however, it became apparent that new HydraMatics wouldn't be available for a while. Fortunately, Buick was able to supply Dynaflow transmissions for Cadillac and Oldsmobile until GM restarted HydraMatic production at the huge Willow Run facility recently acquired from Kaiser.

Motor Trend drove a Dynaflow-equipped Olds in November 1953, and seemed more impressed by the gain in smoothness than distressed by any minor loss of performance. "You won't burn rubber," wrote the editors, "but you'll take off a lot smoother." However, the Dynaflow failed to impress Wolfram or his engineers, who preferred the fuel efficiency, engine braking, and rapid kickdown for passing afforded by the

HydraMatic. On the other hand, Oldsmobile and its sister divisions were developing more powerful engines every year — and the HydraMatic was reaching the limits of its input torque capacity.

Actually, the HydraMatic engineers had initiated a major redesign in 1952, well before the catastrophic fire. The new HydraMatic featured a second hydraulic coupling, smaller in diameter than the main coupling, and located behind the main coupling, between two sets of planetary gears. The input shaft from the engine turned the planet carrier of the forward or "front unit" gearset. In second and fourth gears, the forward gearset acted as a torque-splitting differential, dividing the incoming torque 64.4/35.6 percent between the two couplings. In first and third, the front unit acted as a reduction gear, bypassing the secondary coupling and leaving the torque splitting (60.8/39.2 in this case) to the rear gearset. This way, neither coupling ever had to withstand the full torque output of the engine, and the alter-

nate filling and draining of the secondary coupling helped cushion the HydraMatic's infamously abrupt gear changes.

At the same time, the brake bands which controlled the old HydraMatic's planetary gears gave way to sprag clutches, contributing to smoothness while eliminating the need for periodic adjustments. Other refinements included a coaxial rear oil pump and a "Park" position. As an added bonus, a smaller overall diameter allowed the new HydraMatic to fit more comfortably in lower-profile bodies.

Called "Jetaway," the new transmission debuted with the 1956 models. "We had to turn off the windshield wipers to help feel or hear (it was hard to tell which) the ultra-smooth upshifts," wrote *Motor Trend* sports editor Al Kidd. "Downshifts (pick the speed) are completely without the familiar automatic lurch of previous models.... This transmission is easily the outstanding one we've encountered in flexibility, comes very close to offering stick-shift qualities with the convenience of not using a clutch."

Above: Soft suspension and cushy ride has its price: serious, whitewall-scuffing understeer in corners. Below: Concentric-circle wheel covers were lifted from the '55 Delta show car.

1956 OLDSMOBILE

box, bigger rear-view mirror, and wipers that wiped more of the windshield. And Olds finally pitched the troublesome electric gear-position indicator of 1954-55 in favor of a more conventional, mechanically operated quadrant.

The model lineup continued as before, with all Oldsmobiles built off the mid-range B-body. The entry-level 88 came with the two-barrel carburetor "T-340" engine, three-speed manual transmission, and rubber floor mats. The four-barrel T-350 engine cost $25 extra;

HydraMatic cost $175 and Jetaway $15 more than that.

Built on the same 122-inch wheelbase, the Super 88 carried a bit more chrome and came with carpeting, the four-barrel carb, and Jetaway as standard equipment. At the top, the 98 still rode on a 126-inch wheelbase, and with its longer rear quarter panels stretched an extra nine inches overall. Standard equipment included all the features of the Super 88, plus power steering and some extra interior niceties. Somewhat cleaner and more graceful side trim further separated the 98 from the 88 models. All hardtops were badged "Holiday," as they had been since 1949.

Motor Trend sports editor Al Kidd liked the '56 Oldsmobile's large and substantial feel. Yet handling had improved significantly for '56, without the persistent tire squeal that plagued the '55. Kidd felt that the ride was smoother too, with better control on rough roads. Terming his Super 88 test car "a real road hugger," he added that "Olds has definitely jumped up a class in roadability" — although he felt that the steering ratio could be faster still, and complained that the wheel seemed lazy about centering itself. And the additional horsepower had failed to improve acceleration, a conundrum Kidd attributed to increased weight. Fuel economy suffered, though, by a whopping 20 percent.

Oldsmobile pitched its advertising at younger car buyers, featuring illustrations of thirtysomething suburbanites with captions like "More and more young folks — are getting 'Olds' ideas," and "They are enjoying their Holiday while they're young." Model-year production slipped to 485,458 units, which by itself wasn't too alarming, given that the total market had fallen from 7.2 million cars in 1955 to just under six million in 1956. At least Olds held on to fifth place. But for the first time since 1951, the basic 88 outsold the fancier, more powerful Super 88. And the division's market share dropped back to 1954's 7.35 percent.

Nineteen fifty-seven would bring another all-new, longer, and lower body; an all-new perimeter frame; another increase in engine displacement; a new anti-dive front suspension with Oldsmobile's first ball joints; and Oldsmobile's first station wagons since 1950. The conclusion of an armaments contract freed up additional production space for automobiles. The engine line now stretched 460 feet longer, and new presses packed the stamping plant.

But the market had turned against the mid-priced makes. The independents — the weakest members of the herd — had merely been the first to fall. Soon Chrysler's DeSoto would die a dramatically sudden death; and Ford's Edsel would be born without a chance. If nothing reversed the trend, then Mercury, Buick, and Olds would surely follow. In fact, Olds continued to lose market share, dropping to a low of 5.4 percent in 1960. Only a new direction in styling — and the new mid-size F-85 and Cutlass — would finally turn the division around in the early sixties.

Driving Impressions

Jim and Jerri Cartwright found our featured Super 88 convertible a few years ago in Spokane, Washington. "It was all there," Jim remembered, but rust had perforated the fenders and floor, and the car clearly needed to be stripped to its frame. Still, the Cartwrights bought the forlorn ragtop and trailered it home to Indiana in February 1991. They put in a lot of hours and had it ready to show that summer. Since then, said Jim, "it gets best of show just about every place it goes" — including some first-place national awards from the Oldsmobile Club of America.

The Cartwrights' convertible features

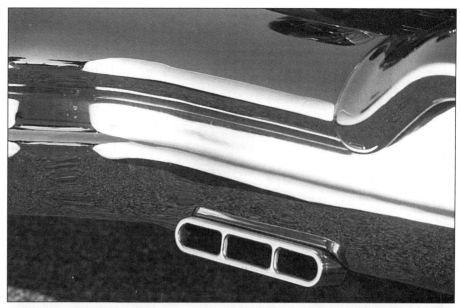

Above: Twin exhaust outlets went along with rocket theme and fed Harley Earl's love of jet plane devices on GM cars. *Below left:* Oval-shaped clock and chrome surround echo theme of grille and bumper. *Below right:* Chrome sill below side windows was the Super 88's stylistic trademark. It also provided a scratch-resistant spot for your burger and fries.

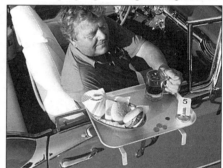

Racing the 88

Production of the Olds 88 began in February 1949, and the first major late-model stock-car race organized by the fledgling National Association for Stock Car Auto Racing (NASCAR) followed in Charlotte that June. That the 88 and NASCAR were born just four months apart was probably coincidental — but the car and the races would soon make a perfect match.

According to Jan P. Norbye and Jim Dunne in *Oldsmobile: The Postwar Years,* Olds General Manager Sherrod E. Skinner didn't design the 88 as a hot rod. Originally, Olds management considered 287- and 303-cubic-inch versions of the new V-8 for the 88 and 98 respectively. But Skinner convinced the top GM brass that it would cost less to install the big engine in both models — and to then phase out six-cylinder production, so that *all* Oldsmobiles carried essentially the same power plant. This arrangement just happened to put one of the most advanced and powerful engines made by the corporation into the relatively lightweight "A" body shell.

Even before its NASCAR debut in Charlotte, an 88 driven by three-time Indy winner Wilbur Shaw paced the 1949 Indianapolis 500. Then the 88 took NASCAR by storm, winning six out of nine late-model

events in the organization's first full season. Series champion Robert "Red" Baron drove an 88, and so did runner-up Bob Slock.

California tuner Ak Miller soon developed a solid-lifter conversion for the Olds V-8, good for at least another 500 rpm at the top. Lansing cooperated by offering synchromesh transmission on "special order" along with seven different axle ratios, ranging from 3.23 to 4.55:1. Later on, the factory developed its own "J-2" package with 8.5:1 compression; a high-lift, solid-lifter camshaft with adjustable rocker arms; and heavy-duty springs, axle, steering linkage, and engine mounts.

In 1950, 88s won ten out of 19 NASCAR national events and set a new stock-car record for the measured mile of 100.28 mph at the Daytona Speed Weeks. (The previous record of 93.88 mph, set by a Hudson Eight, had stood since 1936.) Outside of NASCAR, Herschell McGriff and Ray Elliot drove an 88 to overall victory in the first-ever Carrera Panamericana.

NASCAR expanded its schedule to 41 Grand National events in 1951 — and Oldsmobiles still won 20 of them. After that, however, the Oldsmobiles faced stiffer competition — first from the Hudson Hornets, then the Chrysler 300s, and even-

tually from high-powered models from price-leaders Ford and Chevrolet. Meanwhile, the 88 itself had grown heavier; Lansing introduced the "Super 88" on the middle-weight B-body in 1951, and then in 1952 moved the standard 88 up from the A-body to the B-body. Still, as late as 1955, Olds finished second in NASCAR's point totals and won the rival International Motor Contest Association (IMCA) championship outright. By 1957, however — the year the Automobile Manufacturers Association ostensibly withdrew from racing — Olds scored only five NASCAR Grand National victories in 53 events.

Yet Olds dealers still offered an over-the-counter camshaft and gasket kit — and 88s still set speed records. In '56, Lee Petty upped the flying-mile mark at Daytona to 144.928 mph. Major J.A. Robinson (of the US Air Force Thunderbird acrobatics team), driving his own privately entered 88, raised the mark to 146.52 in '57. And the 88 exited NASCAR with a flourish in 1959: At the inaugural 500-miler on the brand-new Daytona tri-oval, Lee Petty's Oldsmobile battled Johnny Beauchamp's Thunderbird to the closest conclusion stock-car fans had ever seen. NASCAR officials studied finish-line photos for three days before proclaiming Petty the victor.

1956 OLDSMOBILE

Above: Four-barrel carb was standard on Super 88; oil bath air cleaner cost $6 extra. *Below:* Instrument cluster also reflects the oval styling theme. For '56, idiot lights replaced gauges.

a full complement of factory options; about the only items it *doesn't* have are air conditioning and power for the seats, windows, and radio antenna. Its new owners didn't particularly like its original Rose Mist and Antique White paintwork, so they refinished it in solid Festival Red — an authentic '56 Olds color. They also added an accessory continental spare, because Jim likes continental kits, and a pair of glass-pack mufflers.

The driving position is typical of midfifties American iron, slightly short on leg room but with plenty of steering wheel looming high and close to the chest. The convertible top leaves plenty of head room, however, and the wide cabin provides lots of hip and elbow space. The soft seat back leans back a bit far for my personal taste, although the firmer bottom cushion gives good thigh support. The back seat, on the other hand, suffers from a backrest that's too vertical and a bottom cushion that's too short. And most adults would want more leg room.

Despite the dashboard's dizzying pat-

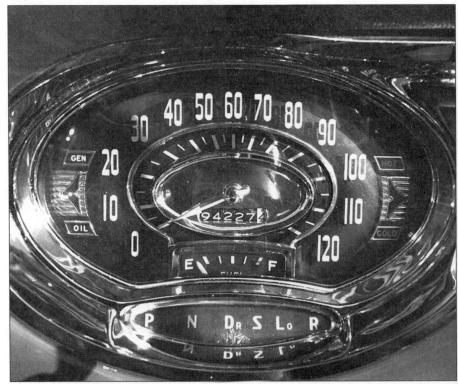

The Un-Super Alternative

Jim and Jerri Cartwright also own a very nice, mostly original '56 88 two-door hardtop, a turquoise-and-white beauty showing only some 13,000 miles. This car is powered by the base "T-340" 230-bhp engine with the two-barrel carburetor, and although it is fitted with the premium Jetaway HydraMatic transmission, its brakes and steering remain unassisted. Base two-door hardtops like this one were the best-selling 88s in '56, so naturally I asked for a drive in it as well.

The first difference I noticed, relative to the Super 88 convertible, is that the hardtop rides smoother, with somewhat less jostling from the road surface. Credit the stiffer body structure, probably. And despite its slower steering ratio (21.3:1 at the gear, 27.3:1 overall), the manual-steered car feels tighter, more connected to the road. It understeers just as heavily, but with more precise control I drove it quickly and with more confidence. Curiously, its skinnier 7.10 x 15 tires don't seem to compromise its cornering power. On the other hand, while the manual steering effort level isn't outrageous, it's high enough to make me appreciate the 18-inch wheel and the leverage afforded by its straight-across spokes.

I felt less difference in the brakes. Even without power assist, moderate effort brings an acceptable result. And of course feedback and modulation are even better.

Most surprising, though, is how little I missed those extra 10 bhp and 10 ft. lb. of torque. Stab the Super 88's throttle, and it almost skips a beat before delivering a beastly surge of power. Whereas the same move in the two-barrel 88 brings an instant flow of forward motion — less dramatic, perhaps, but probably just as effective. Of course, the base 88 hardtop weighs 232 pounds less than the Super 88 convertible — but then it's saddled with the standard 3.23:1 rear end. (Super 88 convertibles borrowed the 98's 3.42:1 gears.) I wish I could have found a contemporary comparison of acceleration times for the two cars, because I suspect they would come out dead equal.

Motor Trend did conduct a revealing 88 vs. Super 88 comparison of its own, however. In April 1956, the magazine sampled a Super 88 four-door hardtop, and obtained the test results we've listed under "Performance" on our Specifications page. Then in September, *MT* borrowed the performance figures for a base 88 tested by *Rod and Custom.* Presumably looking for maximum acceleration, *Rod and Custom* had selected a two-door sedan (only 3,705 pounds) with the rare three-speed synchromesh and the optional (on a base 88) four-barrel carburetor. This combination came with first and second gear ratios of 2.39 and 1.53, respectively — closer to second and third in the Jetaway HydraMatic. But with a shorter 3.64:1 rear end, the stick-shift Olds matched the HydraMatic hardtop's 0-30 time of 3.7 seconds, then pulled away with only 9.7 seconds to 60 mph. It scorched the quarter-mile in just 16.2 seconds. (New *Motor Trend* sports editor Paul Sorber thought that the base car's narrower tires probably helped.) Then, despite its shorter axle, the three-speed sedan turned in a top speed of 113.7 mph — a tribute to the superior efficiency of the shift-it-yourself setup.

1956 OLDSMOBILE

continued

tern of chrome and black stripes — the sort of thing that would drive a video camera bonkers — the deeply dished oval speedometer and inset fuel gauge stand out nicely for easy reading. The accessory controls *look* low and far away, but in fact they require very little reaching. The radically curved windshield keeps the A-post out of the way, and I noticed no distortion.

To imagine how the Super 88 drives, just mentally blend equal parts luxury cruiser and stock-car champion. The Olds feels enormously wide and heavy. Despite the faster steering ratio for '56, actually making a turn still requires quite a bit of cranking at the helm. Then the tires scream in protest as the Olds understeers, all heeled over and threatening to head for the trees. To thread the big car down a curvy county road, you absolutely *must* get off the brakes before you turn the wheel, or the overworked front tires have too much to do. High bumps and hump-back bridges seem to steer the rear end unsettlingly.

On the other hand, the Olds rides comfortably but considerably firmer than I expected. And the 5.3-liter V-8 bellows through its glass-packs, drowning out wind noise at an indicated 65 mph. (When *Motor Trend* sampled a new Super 88 in '56, they heard "almost no engine noise" but "considerable wind and road noise.") Even at full throttle, I could barely feel the Jetaway Hydra-Matic shift — although I *hear* the wonderful V-8 burble as the engine growls through the gears. I counted 13 seconds from 60 to 75 mph (a rather unscientific method, but in the ball park with *MT*'s figure of 11.8 seconds from 50 to 80). And at 75, the Olds felt like it was just loosening up.

And as I drove, I found I was constantly aware of the curve of the windshield, how it arched up, around, and over me; while the corner of my eye registered the twin-engine, jet-propelled hood ornament that leads the 88 down the road. This was the route to the future in 1956. Who could have known then that the future would change so much, so fast? ❑

Acknowledgments and Bibliography

Dennis Casteele, The Cars of Oldsmobile; *John A. Gunnell (editor)*, Standard Catalog of American Cars 1946-1975; *Leo Levine*, Ford: The Dust and the Glory; *Jan P. Norbye and Jim Dunne*, Oldsmobile: The Postwar Years; *Al Kidd*, "'55 Olds Super 88," Motor Trend, *May 1955;* "'56 Oldsmobile," Motor Trend, *December 1955; and* "'56 Oldsmobile Road Test," Motor Trend, *April 1956; Jim Lodge,* "'54 Oldsmobile Super 88," Motor Trend, *June 1954; Don MacDonald,* "Spotlight on Detroit," Motor Trend, *March 1954 and January 1955. Bill Neely,* "NASCAR Now!," Automobile Quarterly 26/2; *Paul Sorber,* "'56 Olds HydraMatic vs. Stick Shift," Motor Trend, *September 1956; John G. Tennyson,* "1949 Oldsmobile 98 Holiday Coupe," Special Interest Autos #121; *Walt Woron,* "Driving Around with Walt Woron," Motor Trend, *January 1955;* "An Olds with Dynaflow," Motor Trend, *November 1953.*

Thanks to Kim M. Miller of the AACA Library and Research Center; Henry Siegle, and of course Jim and Jerri Cartwright.

Previous page, top: Even with convertible top storage area intruding, trunk is gargantuan. **This page, above:** *driveReport car captures the essence of fifties American baroque styling in every line.*

SUPER 88 HOLIDAY SEDAN

Starfire Styled!

and sparkling with new ideas!

You're smart if you look ahead . . . smart if you buy a car that's styled and powered to stay new for years. *That's why it's smart to own an Olds!* For Oldsmobile has the *out-ahead* features, the *stay-ahead* styling, the *go-ahead* power of tomorrow! Just look over this "feature" line-up: Terrific Rocket T-350 Engine! Smooth, responsive Jetaway Hydra-Matic*! A brand new "Intagrille Bumper" that combines beauty and full-depth protection! And interiors are the ultimate in luxury and comfort! Come see Oldsmobile for '56 and try out the many features of the future!

Standard on Ninety-Eight models; optional at extra cost on Super 88 and 88 models.

OLDSMOBILE

TOP VALUE TODAY ... TOP RESALE TOMORROW !

75

J-2-POWERED 1957 OLDSMOBILE FIESTA WAGON

PILLARLESS PACKAGE EXPRESS

by John Lee
photos by the author

WITH nearly the entire US industry under ohv V-8 power by 1955, the horsepower race had begun. Colors were brighter. Annual styling changes were no longer limited to mere facelifts. Normal three- and four-year styling cycles dropped briefly to two years at Chrysler and Ford (and even to one, as in the case of the 1958 Chevrolets and Pontiacs). Each new model year also brought new body styles vying for public acceptance.

One gaining increasing popularity with mobile young families building houses in the suburbs was the station wagon. Previously, they were often noisy and uncomfortable, expensive, and required considerable effort to maintain their wooden bodies.

But all that began to change with the advent of the all-steel wagon from Willys in 1946, followed by Crosley in 1948, Plymouth in 1949, and other makes soon after. While still priced above all models with the possible exception of the convertible, the wagon moved out of the "lumber wagon" class in terms of both styling and upkeep.

The introduction of the Chevrolet Nomad and Pontiac Safari for 1955 demonstrated just how beautiful a station wagon could be with some effort devoted to styling rather than merely adding a cargo box onto the back of a sedan.

While all these developments were taking place, General Motors' Oldsmobile Division was absent from the station wagon market The last Olds wagon models had been built in 1950, and accounted for only 2,750 units sold.

On the other hand, corporate cousin Buick sold just 2,900 of the 1950-model wagons but had stayed in the wagon market and had seen its fortunes improve. The last to eliminate all wood trim in 1954, Buick sold nearly 22,000 Estate Wagons in its 1956 model year.

George Macfarlane, now a consulting engineer with Creative Industries in Auburn Hills, Michigan, was at the time chief engineer for Mitchell-Bentley, the firm which built station wagon bodies

Originally published in Special Interest Autos #114, Nov.-Dec. 1989

Driving Impressions

Our driveReport Olds Super 88 Fiesta wagon is owned by Jean, a teacher, and Lloyd Pettiecord, sales manager for the Pontiac-Oldsmobile-Cadillac-GMC agency in Spencer, Iowa.

The Olds was restored by a previous owner in Little Falls, Minnesota. The Pettiecords purchased it at a Minneapolis auction, and it quickly became a favorite of their collection, which includes Fords and Pontiacs from 1930 Model A's to a 1968 TransAm.

Finished in metallic green, contrasted with a white top, side-trim insert, and 14-inch tires, it's a handsome car. The upholstery is a combination of vinyl and woven acetate or nylon material in green and white.

Except for air conditioning, the Fiesta is quite fully optioned. It has the Wonderbar signal-seeking radio with controls both on the unit and a floor pedal at the driver's left, power windows, six-way power seat, and a clock set in the middle of the "upper deck" of the dashboard. Other options are the J-2 engine, kicking out 300 horsepower with progressive triple carburetion and dual exhausts, HydraMatic transmission, power steering, and power brakes.

Weighing in at over 4,500 pounds, the big Olds isn't expected to be a neck-snapper, but low gear of the HydraMatic does dig in and move it off the line in respectable fashion. There's little of the characteristic Olds lifter clatter at idle and low speeds.

Out on the open road, cruising at speed, is where the Fiesta is really in its element. Remember, some western states didn't even have a speed limit in 1957! We pushed Jean and Lloyd's Olds up to 80 briefly, and it felt smooth and solid. The power steering provides adequate road feel. While nice on a smooth road, soft springing would cause a fair amount of lean and bounce on curves and uneven surfaces.

We were disappointed that we weren't able to experience the extra carbs on the J-2 engine kicking in, but certainly understand Lloyd's decision to block off the two outboard carbs and run off the center one. They drive the car only occasionally to shows, and the end carbs have a tendency to gum up if they aren't kicked in and flushed out with fresh gas frequently.

Probably the main reason the J-2 option lasted only two years was that too many people never got their J-2s past three-quarters throttle. Consequently, the jets in the end carbs would gum up and not flow fuel at all when they were called into play. The engine would starve and falter when the throttle was floored, rather than providing the expected surge of power. As *Hot Rod*'s Ray Brock noted, "Multiple carburetion is only for those who know how to use it."

The Fiesta's dash is very glittery, which may create distracting reflections at night. However, the controls are all within easy reach and the instruments easily readable — what there are of them. The speedometer and the fuel gauge below it are the only dials, with warning lights for temperature, oil, and generator functions.

The Pettiecords' car has over 110,000 miles on it, but it is heavy, solid and well-built with none of the squeaks and rattles one expects from a 30-year-old station wagon. It's a rare, surviving example of a unique design that helped determine the shape of station wagons for years to come.

*Right: Ovals and circles everywhere. There's hardly a straight line on the Olds's front end. **Below and below right:** Fuel filler is hidden in typical late fifties GM fashion. **Bottom:** Traditional "spinner" wheel covers had been replaced by this collection of circles for 1957.*

1957 OLDSMOBILE

for Buick and other manufacturers in the Ionia, Michigan, plant that had formerly been Ionia Body Works.

Macfarlane believes the decision to get Oldsmobile back into the station wagon business came from corporate officials, cognizant of the expanding market for the model, rather than from anyone in the Oldsmobile Division itself. Oldsmobile and Buick already shared basic body structures, so it was natural that wagons be offered in both lines.

He recalls his first exposure to the proposed 1957 Buick and Olds station wagons: "I was called to a meeting at [GM] Styling. The pillarless wagon was revealed to me as what the next wagon would be. The meeting was held by Buick. I don't know if the [four-door-hardtop] design came from Buick or if styling had handed it to Buick, but someone associated with the Buick end was responsible for the styling."

Macfarlane remembers being sworn to secrecy concerning the design, which would combine station wagon utility with the sporty air of the pillarless four-doors, which had become extremely popular since their 1955 introduction by Olds and Buick.

Ironically, he said, some three weeks later he was invited to a meeting at Mercury, for which Mitchell-Bentley also built station wagon bodies. "There, they unveiled the same animal," he said, "and they also swore me to secrecy!" Macfarlane said he immediately filed away a memo describing these two events, so there would be a record in case either would later accuse him of divulging their secret pillarless station wagon concept.

DriveReport car has a look of fluid motion even when parked.

The J-2 Rocket Engine

"Another first for Oldsmobile!" proclaimed a special brochure published to announce the new J-2 Rocket engine in 1957.

With this triple-carburetor option, Oldsmobile felt it had achieved the best of both worlds — "economy when you want it, power when you need it."

Besides the three Rochester two-barrel carburetors on a dual-plane, in-line manifold, the J-2 option included a unique air cleaner and thinner head gaskets that raised the compression ratio to 10.0:1 from the standard 9.5:1. Power output was rated at 300 horsepower, compared to 277 horsepower for the standard four-barrel-equipped, 371-cubic-inch engine.

Triple carburetion and other multiple-carburetor setups had been around for years in the hot-rod industry. What the Olds engineers did was refine the concept so that the extra boost provided by increasing the flow of the air-fuel mixture would be applied only when needed.

The key is the progressive linkage connecting the three carbs to the throttle. Under normal operation, the center carb alone meters fuel to the cylinders. When the throttle is opened three-fourths of the way, vacuum opens the two outboard carburetors simultaneously. feeding additional fuel for a boost in power.

The J-2 system was most beneficial in a highway passing situation, where an extra push on the accelerator bought you a surge of power to get you safely past another vehicle. Passing range performance received much more attention in the fifties when most travel was on two-lane highways. Of course, the J-2 driver also had the extra power on tap if he felt like punching the accelerator to the floor for a quick getaway from the stop light!

Besides the economic advantage of driving most of the time on a single two-barrel, the J-2 package also required only one choke and one idle system. Therefore, it was easier to adjust, maintain, and service than some other multiple-carburetor systems.

The J-2 was the result of efforts within the Motor Group of the Oldsmobile Division to improve the efficiency of the Rocket V-8 engine. The first modern, high-compression, overhead-valve V-8 when introduced for the 1949 model run, the Rocket was the standard to which other engines were compared as they

were introduced in subsequent years.

"We had by far the greatest motor engineer in the industry — Gilbert Burrell," said Gibson "Gib" Butler, a design and development engineer, now retired from the Olds Motor Group. "He did lots of things no one else did," said Butler, and the progressive linkage tri-carb setup "may have been his idea. I don't remember."

Experimentation with multiple carburetion, as well as fuel injection, was going on throughout General Motors and the rest of the industry in the mid-1950s. Chevrolet and Cadillac both offered dual four-barrel systems, and Olds had developed one, but Butler didn't remember that any were ever put into production.

One project engineer was also following fuel-injection development, Butler recalls, but "we felt we could do as much with carburetors as with fuel injection. We didn't have the precision machining capability to produce fuel injection components for a mass-production passenger car at that time."

"What we were doing," explained the retired engineer, "was developing a progression. Once we had the four-barrel and the dual-plane manifold [developed cooperatively by Olds and the Carter and Rochester carburetor companies and introduced in the 1952 models], it was easy to develop the 3-2."

He said the decision to build the J-2 was made late in 1956, when 1957 models were

already in production. The announcement of the J-2 option, available on all models for a premium of $83, was dated January 30, 1957.

Pontiac also offered a progressive tri-carb arrangement on 1957 models, and Butler is still miffed by what he considers a technological theft by the other division.

Elliott M. "Pete" Estes, who had been an engine development engineer and was assistant chief engineer, left Olds in September 1956 to become chief engineer at Pontiac. According to Butler, he took with him the ideas of Olds's still-secret tri-carb arrangement, which was in the fine-tuning stage at that time.

"Our biggest competition was the rest of GM." said Butler. "As engineers, we were very proud of our ability to develop unique concepts."

With Pontiac certain to spring a similar option, Olds engineers hustled to get their system to market first. It became available in late January or early February as an option for the second half of 1957. Although Pontiac announced the Tri-Power in December of 1956. the option didn't hit the market until March 1957.

Oldsmobile offered the J-2 option on all models again in 1958, then dropped it in favor of improved four-barrel carburetion. It surfaced briefly again in 1966 as a 4-4-2 option before GM brass outlawed all multi-carb systems.

specifications

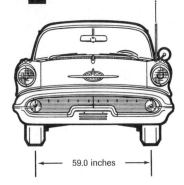

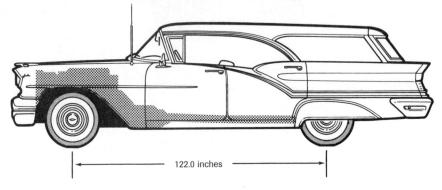

59.0 inches

122.0 inches

1957 Oldsmobile Super 88 Fiesta Station Wagon

Base price	$3,541
Options on test car	J-2 engine option, HydraMatic transmission, power steering, power brakes, tinted glass, Wonderbar radio, clock, power windows, 6-way power seat, white sidewall tires

ENGINE
Type	Overhead valve V-8
Bore and stroke	4.0 x 3.6875 inches
Displacement	371 cubic inches
Max bhp @ rpm	300 @ 4,600
Max torque @ rpm	415 @ 3,000
Compression ratio	10.0:1
Induction system	Three Rochester 2-bbl. downdraft carburetors, progressive linkage, vacuum operated secondaries
Exhaust system	Dual pipes and mufflers
Electrical system	12-volt

TRANSMISSION
Type	Four-speed automatic
Ratios: 1st	3.96:1
2nd	2.55:1
3rd	1.55:1
4th	1:1
Reverse	4.30:1

DIFFERENTIAL
Type	Spiral bevel gears
Ratio	3.42:1

STEERING
Type	Recirculating ball and nut, hydraulic power booster
Turns lock-to-lock	4.4
Turning radius	42 feet

BRAKES
Type	4-wheel drum, power assisted
Drum diameter f/r	11 inches/11 inches
Total swept area	191.7 square inches

CHASSIS & BODY
Body construction	Steel body on frame
Frame	Steel channel perimeter rails, center X-member
Body style	Four-door pillarless station wagon, six-passenger
Builder	Mitchell-Bentley, Ionia, MI

SUSPENSION
Front	Independent with ball joints, coil springs
Rear	Parallel leaf springs mounted outboard of frame
Tires	8.50 x 14
Wheels	Steel disc

WEIGHTS AND MEASURES
Wheelbase	122 inches
Overall length	208.2 inches
Overall height	60 inches
Overall width	78.5 inches
Front track	59 inches
Rear track	58 inches
Shipping weight	4,470 pounds

CAPACITIES
Fuel tank	20 gallons
Engine and filter	6.1 quarts
Cooling system	21 quarts

PERFORMANCE
0-30 mph	n/a
0-60 mph	11.2 seconds*, 10.2 seconds**
Top speed	108 mph**
Standing ¼ mile	18.2 seconds*, 18.2 seconds**

* *Consumer Reports*, June 1957, on 1957 Olds Super 88 Fiesta station wagon with 277-horsepower, 4-barrel engine.

** *Popular Mechanics* test of 1957 Olds Super 88 four-door sedan with 300-horsepower J-2 engine running premium gasoline.

This page: *Styling is actually quite conservative by standards of the time.* ***Facing page, top and above left:*** *Front end is rather mild compared to the sculpting at the rear.* ***Above right:*** *Vestigial rockets crown the front fenders.* ***Center left:*** *Dashboard is also a riot of ovals and circles bathed in chrome plate.* ***Center right:*** *Body for the wagon was farmed out rather than being built by Fisher.* ***Bottom:*** *Loading is a snap with the slop-down tailgate and high clearance on the backlight.*

1957 OLDSMOBILE

These events, Macfarlane said, would have been in late 1955, probably shortly before American Motors announced its 1956 models and scooped both GM and Ford with the four-door hardtop station wagon design.

The styling having been done at GM, the job of Macfarlane and Mitchell-Bentley was to design and build the Oldsmobile and Buick station wagons — conventional four-door pillared versions as well as the pillarless hardtop models — with as much common componentry with the rest of the line as possible.

He recalls that sedan or four-door hardtop components back to the B-pillar were used, and rear doors from the beltline down. Mitchell-Bentley then added the unique roof structures, lift gates, and glass and adapted the rear quarter panels.

The Ionia plant went ahead and built bodies for all three nameplates — Olds, Buick and Mercury — that year, turning out more than 500 station wagons a day at times, Macfarlane said.

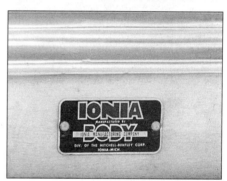

In comparison with that offered by other automakers for 1957, Oldsmobile's styling must be considered subdued. The rear pillar of the wraparound windshield slopes back at a slightly more rakish angle than the previous year's. Rather than tailfins, the rear quarters retain their familiar high crown with a redesign of the traditional Olds round taillamp. The mouth-shaped bumper and grille combination was slightly redesigned from the 1956's, and single-lens headlamp housings have less forward thrust. Although the side trim provides a natural demarcation for two-toning, that option was not promoted in factory photos and advertising.

The station wagons, both pillared and pillarless, were stylish units. The C-pillar sloped back as it did on the sedans and hardtops. The rear quarter window intersected that line, kicked up slightly, and continued straight to the rear corner.

Rather than the quarter glass curving around the corner as on the Nomad and Safari, the Olds has a wide lift gate with a one-piece curved window that wraps around the corners. This provides a larger opening at the top for loading, making it unnecessary in some instances to open the narrow lower tailgate. Arms on both sides of the lift gate lock it into a horizontal position when open and require two hands, one to lift the gate and the other to push up the catch, to close.

The rear section of the top is indented,

Right: Single air cleaner covers the three pots. Below: Clock is nearly hidden in dash cove. Below center: A sensible place to store the spare on a wagon. Who said split rear seats are new? Bottom: One of the ultimate highway haulers of the Eisenhower years.

1957 OLDSMOBILE

with stainless steel ribs running lengthwise for decoration. This panel was often painted a contrasting color. In the case of our driveReport car, it is green to match the main body color and contrast with the white top.

Inside, the back seat is split two-thirds, one-third. Each section can be folded down separately to provide a partial cargo deck with some seating or a full-length storage area. The spare tire, jack, and tools are hidden under a hatch in the rear deck floor. Oldsmobile didn't offer a third seat option in its station wagons, although many of its competitors in the upper-middle price class did.

Oldsmobile revived the name Fiesta from its 1953 limited production convertible and applied it to the 1957 station wagon models. Both pillared and hardtop-style four-door wagons were offered in the lowest-priced series, now called Golden Rocket 88. In the Super 88 series, only the pillarless version was available, and there were no wagons in the longer-wheelbase 98 series.

The public was responsive to new gimmicks in 1957, so pillarless Fiestas outsold the more conventional version by almost three to one. Total production of just under 20,000 units was not overwhelming, but still compared favorably to the 24,000 wagons sold by Buick, which had an established wagon market.

Oldsmobile was back in the station wagon market for keeps. The division would be responsible for more interesting variations on the station wagon theme In the years to come.

Acknowledgments and Bibliography *John Gunnell, Editor,* Standard Catalog of American Cars, 1946-1975; *Dennis Casteele, "The Cars of Oldsmobile,"* Hot Rod Magazine, *February 1957;* Consumer Reports, *June 1957;* Popular Mechanics, *July 1957; various Oldsmobile sales promotion publications. Our thanks to F. Gibson Butler and George Macfarlane; Helen Jones Earley and James R. Walkinshaw at the Oldsmobile History Center. Special thanks to Jean and Lloyd Pettiecord of Spencer, Iowa.*

Courtesy of O'Brien's Auto Ads

SUPER 88 FIESTA

Get in the act!

THE VERSATILE "FIESTA" PUTS THE SPOTLIGHT ON YOU!

See what happened when Oldsmobile added the happy-go-lucky look of Holiday styling to the
husky heft of a station wagon! It's the fabulous Fiesta!

This all-'round performer commands the spotlight wherever it goes. So let the Fiesta set
the stage for *your* dramatic entrance into a whole new fun-filled way of going places and doing things!

Your *first* cue is to call or visit your Authorized Oldsmobile Quality Dealer.
He'll show you how owning a Fiesta is like owning *two* Oldsmobiles in one!
OLDSMOBILE DIVISION, GENERAL MOTORS CORPORATION.

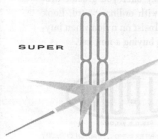

SUPER **88**

OLDSMOBILE

SEE YOUR AUTHORIZED OLDSMOBILE QUALITY DEALER

Ad originally published in *Holiday* magazine, June 1957

83

1962 OLDSMOBILE JETFIRE

TURBO BEFORE ITS TIME

by M. Park Hunter
photos by the author

OLDSMOBILE has always been a technology leader among the General Motors divisions. Hydra-Matic automatic transmissions in 1940, overhead-valve V-8s in 1949, and the front-wheel-drive Toronado in 1966 are the most obvious examples.

But there's another high-tech Oldsmobile few people remember: the 1962 Jetfire. Externally, the Jetfire looked like a gussied-up F-85. Under the hood, though, the Jetfire boasted technical specifications many modern cars could envy. A turbocharged, fluid-injected, small-displacement aluminum V-8 provided the heart and soul of this junior road rocket.

The F-85, along with Buick's Special and Pontiac's Tempest, was one of GM's second generation compacts. These cars were similar to the Corvair platform, but redesigned for conventional front-engine layouts. Befitting their status as luxury compacts, the Buick and Oldsmobile shared a new aluminum V-8 with only

215 cubic inches of displacement (see sidebar, page 88).

This engine was introduced with a two-barrel carburetor and produced 155 horsepower. Compact cars were not exempt from the horsepower race, though; so for 1962 a power-pack was available which added a four-barrel carburetor and raised compression from 8.8:1 to 10.25:1. In this guise, the little V-8 put out 185 horsepower. That was still not enough for Oldsmobile engineers.

To extract even more gusto from their little engine would have meant playing with cam timing or compression, which would have affected the smooth-running characteristics of the V-8. Increasing displacement, the other option

for more power, would add weight. And in any case, fuel economy would suffer. Oldsmobile chose a more radical route: turbocharging.

Thus, the Jetfire shares the distinction of being America's first mass-produced turbocharged car with the Chevrolet Corvair. Both cars could claim an honest one horsepower per cubic inch (145 for the Corvair, 215 for the Jetfire), but the approach they took was quite different.

The heart of a turbocharger consists of a single moving part, a shaft with turbine impellers at each end. Exhaust pressure is directed against one impeller, causing it to spin. The impeller at the other end of the shaft draws air in and flings it centrifugally into the engine's intake manifold, increasing the air pressure and providing more oxygen for combustion.

The Corvair turbo capitalized on this simplicity. However, without providing a mechanism to limit the turbo's boost,

Chevrolet engineers were forced to lower their engine's compression ratio to prevent detonation. The Corvair turbo engine packed a wallop at high rpm, but felt anemic at lower speeds and suffered from a long lag before the power kicked in.

Oldsmobile's approach was much more sophisticated. Gilbert Burrell, Oldsmobile's head engine designer, explained the philosophy in a May 1962 *Road & Track* article on the new turbochargers:

"A turbo-supercharger unit of approximately the same physical outside dimensions [as the production unit] could have been designed that would have resulted in much higher high-speed power output, but this would not have given the tremendous torque increase in the mid-speed or normal driving range. We wanted a hot-performing street job, not a high-speed race car."

Burrell researched previous turbocharger applications and found that aircraft turbochargers were fitted with wastegates, pressure valves which bled off exhaust gases to limit boost. Burrell also knew that a smaller diameter turbine would weigh less and thus react more quickly and spin faster.

Burrell worked with Garrett AiResearch, a manufacturer of industrial turbochargers, to develop these ideas. Designer Gibson Butler and tester Jim Buckley spent a lot of time polishing the details. By combining a small-diameter turbo (the compressor impeller is 2.5 inches in diameter, the exhaust impeller just 2.4 inches) with a poppet-valve wastegate, Oldsmobile's team achieved their goals.

The Jetfire turbocharger developed boost as low as 1,000 engine rpm and gained a torque advantage over the unblown V-8 at only 1,200 rpm. Maximum boost pressure of about five pounds per square inch (p.s.i.) was reached at 2,200 rpm and was then limited by the wastegate from going any higher. In contrast, the Corvair turbo didn't produce five p.s.i. until 3,100 engine rpm and hit its maximum of 11 p.s.i. at 4,500 rpm.

In operation, Oldsmobile's tiny turbo could spin as fast as 90,000 rpm (reached at 4,000 engine rpm) and accelerate to that speed almost as rapidly as the engine required. Chevrolet's somewhat larger turbo maxed out at 70,000 rpm and took a noticeable amount of time to rev up. Previous supercharger turbines, which were usually six to seven inches in diameter, had topped out at only 36,000 rpm and weren't expected to reach quickly to throttle input.

Such high speeds placed great stress on the turbine impellers, plus the exhaust side had to endure temperatures up to 1,450 degrees F. Oldsmobile had used some sophisticated materials engi-

Jetfire was the most expensive F-85 for '62 with a base of $3,049, but that included the turbocharger as well as special trim inside and out.

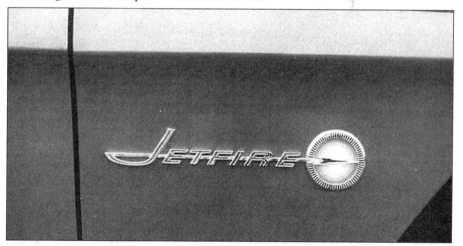

neering to handle this punishment. The exhaust impeller and shaft were made out of super-hard Haynes Stellite steel. The aluminum intake impeller was then pressed onto the shaft and the whole assembly was precision balanced.

The exhaust turbine housing was made out of ductile iron to keep it from warping at high temperatures. The center housing was cast of grey iron to reduce heat transfer to the intake side,

and the intake housing was aluminum for weight savings. The impeller shaft rode in two aluminum alloy bearings mounted in the center housing and lubricated by the engine's pressurized oil system. The bearings spun both on the shaft and in their housings, saving wear by letting them rotate at only about half the turbine's speed.

The turbocharger was mounted on the intake manifold where the carburetor

1962 OLDSMOBILE

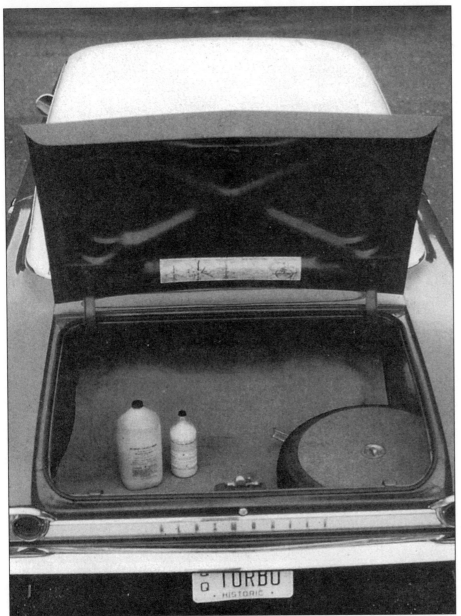

normally squatted. A single-barrel side-draft carburetor designed specifically for the Jetfire by GM's Rochester carburetor division hung off the turbocharger's side. The entire installation weighed 36 pounds.

To maintain fuel economy and low-end engine performance, Oldsmobile engineers kept the engine's compression ratio at 1.25:1, same as the four-barrel carbureted version. Even though maximum boost was limited, there were still potential problems with detonation which could quickly destroy the engine. This was solved by adding a fluid injection system. A tank of "Turbo-Rocket Fluid" (a 50-60 mix of water and alcohol with some rust inhibitor added) was mounted under the hood. When the turbocharger operated, it also pressurized this tank and caused a small amount of the fluid to be injected into the intake between the carburetor and the turbocharger. The fluid evaporated, absorbing heat from the intake air and preventing detonation.

Oldsmobile was famous for thorough engineering, and the Jetfire turbocharger installation was no exception. A warning light informed the driver when the Turbo-rocket fluid ran low. If it was allowed to run out, a butterfly valve in the throttle body closed to prevent full-power acceleration. The wastegate was operated by two diaphragms in case one failed. Even if that happened, the cap on the Turbo-Rocket fluid tank would pop off to prevent overboost. And if boost pressure was still too high, the butterfly valve would again shut down the party. One Olds engineer told *Car and Driver*, "It's 'safetied' to death."

Heavy Breathing

Most people assume that turbochargers and superchargers are two different animals. In reality, the turbocharger is just a special type of supercharger. According to HPBooks' *Auto Dictionary*, a supercharger is a "Compressor which pumps air into an engine's induction system at higher than atmospheric pressure." How it manages this trick is another story.

The first supercharger was probably fitted to a Chadwick in 1908 for use by race driver Willie Haupt. By pumping more air into the combustion chambers, Haupt hoped to overcome the six-cylinder Chadwick's poor breathing, allowing it to burn more fuel and produce more power.

Other companies picked up where Chadwick left off. Bentley in England tried it on a limited basis, as did Bugatti in France. American companies such as Auburn-Cord-Duesenberg and Franklin experimented with supercharging in the thirties. Germany's Mercedes had spectacular success with supercharged racing and sports

cars around this same time. In the fifties, both Kaiser and Ford would supercharge some engines, and Studebaker picked up the idea in the sixties.

Mechanically driven by belt, chain or gear, however, the supercharger had a serious drawback: friction. According to *Car Life*'s May 1962 technical assessment, the typical automotive supercharger sapped 10-15 bhp to pump all that air whether the extra boost was needed or not. This partially offset the power gain from supercharging and hurt fuel economy across the board.

One solution was to steal the supercharger's power source from otherwise untapped energy blowing out the exhaust pipe. A turbine could use the waste heat and pressure of exhaust gas to drive a supercharger with only a 4-5 bhp drain on the engine.

This approach, pioneered by Packard engineer Jesse Vincent way back in 1918 on Liberty aircraft engines, was common

on World War II fighter planes and postwar industrial engines. General Motors engineers were the first to seriously consider adapting an exhaust-powered supercharger to the varying demands of automotive use.

A turbine-driven supercharger has another significant advantage. Unlike mechanically driven versions, it is self-regulating. As an engine produces more power, it pumps more exhaust and the turbine spins faster. Best of all, when demand for power is low, the turbine and supercharger naturally idle along, using minimal power.

The proper name for a turbine-driven supercharger is "turbo-supercharger." In popular use the name was quickly abbreviated to turbocharger. Whatever the name, the idea is still with us. When engineers in the eighties wanted to increase power without hurting fuel economy too much, the turbocharger saw resurgent popularity.

Engines intended for turbocharging were slightly revised versions of the 185-horsepower V-8s. The pistons were redesigned, main-bearing caps were built for heavier loads, and heavy-duty aluminum alloy was used for all bearing inserts. The intake valves were aluminum coated, and the distributor and coil were revised for higher voltage. Oldsmobile also fitted all Jetfires with bigger radiators and reinforced transmissions.

All this work paid off with a 30-horse-power boost over the 185-horsepower power-pack option and a massive 70 foot-pound improvement in maximum torque (to 301 foot pounds). Better yet, torque was over 280 foot pounds from 2,000 to 3,800 engine rpm, smack in the range most drivers used. *Car Life* tests showed the Jetfire could turn 0-60 in 8.5 seconds, versus 10.9 seconds for the 185-horsepower F-85 Cutlass. They also reported the Jetfire was almost 10 seconds faster to 100 mph.

To distinguish the Jetfire from lesser F-85 siblings, Oldsmobile gave the car special aluminum side trim and two chrome spears on the hood instead of the usual one. A new Jetfire logo incorporating a rocket ship was pasted on the front fenders and trunk lid. Although a single exhaust pipe left the turbo outlet, after the muffler it split out into twin outlets.

Inside, the center console held a "Turbo Charger" gauge with a needle swinging into either economy or power ranges as manifold pressure varied. This gauge had no numbers marked on it and was roundly criticized by testers as poorly positioned and useless. The "Add Fluid" warning light for the Turbo-Rocket Fluid reservoir was incorporated into the bottom of the boost gauge.

The publicity dividend reaped by Oldsmobile from the Jetfire was amazing. Car magazines from *Hot Rod* to *Road & Track* flocked to test the Jetfire. Generally, they raved about its performance and hailed the turbo as the wave of the future. Even *Motor Trend,* which tested a Jetfire in September 1962 and was less impressed, was back in April of the next year with an article on circumventing the turbo's safeties for more performance.

Unfortunately, the Jetfire was short-lived. After selling 3,765 of them in 1962 and 5,842 in 1963 (four percent and five percent of F-85 production, respectively), Oldsmobile pulled the plug for '64. Most experts cite mechanical problems with the fluid injection, but there were other reasons as well.

As with any new technology, the turbocharger had teething problems. Bruce Sweeter is an expert on the Jetfire who owns four of the cars and sells parts to other collectors. He believes the problems were "fifty-fifty caused by people and mechanical problems."

Facing page: All GM intermediates including the F-85 had quite decent trunk space. *Above:* Rear as well as front has crisply styled sheet metal. *Below:* Model i.d. appears on trunk lid as well as front fenders.

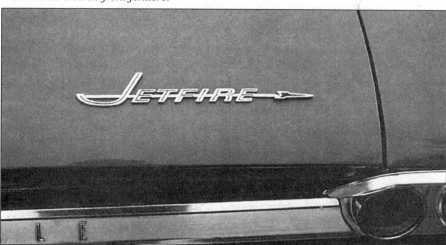

Info and Parts for Jetfire Jockeys

Clubs:

National Antique Oldsmobile Club
11730 Moffitt Lane
Manassas, VA 22111-3122
($20/year, monthly magazine, all cars 1897-1964, 2,000 members)

Oldsmobile Club of America
PO Box 16216
Lansing, MI 48901
517/321-8825 voice; 517/321-8770 fax
($25/year, monthly magazine, 6,500 members)

Information:

Oldsmobile History Center
517/885-1502
(library and resource sponsored by Oldsmobile Division; call 7-11 a.m. Michigan time)

see also: Bruce Sweeter in Parts section

Parts:

Fusick Automotive Products
22 Thompson Rd.
PO Box 655
East Windsor, CT 06088
203/623-1589 voice;
203/623-3118 fax
(reproduction parts, especially rubber parts, decals, plastics, interior trim)

Clayton T. Nelson
Box 259
Warrenville, IL 60555
708/369-6589
(NOS parts)

Bruce Sweeter
33 Hobart St.
Danvers, MA 01923
508/777-2323
(specialist in '61-63 F-85 and Jetfires, information and Jetfire parts)

1962 OLDSMOBILE

Turbocharger gave the F-85 a literal boost in power and performance, but the new technology was also faulted for being troublesome and unreliable. Factory recall converted many turbos to normal four-barrel breathing.

"People would let them run out of fluid," Sweeter says, "then complain about the performance." On the mechanical side, he says gaskets and diaphragms leaked. There were enough complaints that the factory sponsored a recall.

"In '65 they offered to convert people's turbos over to four-barrel carbs for free. They did a really good job and changed everything over," says Sweeter. New intake and exhaust manifolds, a new distributor and a new vacuum advance were all part of the package. Dealers even took out the Turbo-Rocket Fluid tank.

The Jetfires shared some other weaknesses with other F-85s. The engine suffered from cooling problems which were sometimes blamed on aluminum chips left from the casting process getting lodged in the radiator. Sweeter says the Jetfire used a larger crossflow-type radiator which helped this problem somewhat. Antifreeze occasionally reacted with the aluminum block, too.

In the driveline, the automatic transmission could get out of adjustment and shift harshly. The driveshafts were another weak link. Sweeter knows a friend who drives his car hard and always carries a spare driveshaft in the trunk.

Are these problems why Olds dropped the turbo after only two years? Sweeter disagrees.

"I don't think it was reliability," he says. "[The Jetfires] were probably ahead of their time. They were small, they were neat, but people were looking for power and cubic inches."

Ford's medium-size Fairlane was a big success in '62 and '63. For 1964, Oldsmobile radically changed the F-85 series to move into the Fairlane's market. Gone were the little unibodies and pocket rocket turbo engines. In their place was an intermediate car with body-on-frame construction. The technological *tour de force* of turbocharging was discarded in favor of brute power. As the top model, the Jetfire disappeared and was replaced by Oldsmobile's soon-to-be famous 4-4-2 package packing a hairy 330-cubic-inch, 310-horsepower V-8.

Driving Impressions

Our test car is owner Joe Lezza's second Jetfire. He bought his first one as a used car in 1967 while dating the woman who would eventually become his wife. He enjoyed the sporty little coupe, but had to sell it after a year, when he joined the military.

Fast forward to 1993: Lezza, now married and with a young son, was going to

---

The Second Life of a GM V-8

Even though GM stopped building the aluminum 215-cubic-inch V-8 in 1963, it has enjoyed a long career across the Atlantic. In the mid-sixties, the British Rover Corporation was looking to increase exports. J. Bruce McWilliams, the head of Rover's American operation, believed a more powerful engine was needed to compete in American markets. Rover gave him the okay to look at American V-8s in January of 1964.

McWilliams first looked at Chrysler powerplants, then discovered the Buick-Oldsmobile engine. The small aluminum engine would fit easily into British cars designed for lighter, smaller powerplants than most American cast-iron designs.

With help from Rover's William Martin-Hurst, McWilliams aggressively courted GM until they agreed to sell the design. In January 1965, Rover acquired rights to the V-8 and GM shipped the original drawings, some leftover tooling, and production information across the Atlantic. GM also let Joe Turley, Buick's head engine designer who was nearing retirement, move to England as a consultant.

Turley's input was important: GM production changes to the engine necessary to make it more reliable were not reflected in the drawings. Also, English manufacturers didn't have the technology to die cast the block with cast-iron cylinder lin-ings in place as GM had done. Rover finally found a supplier who could sand cast the blocks. The iron sleeves were then pressed into place.

Rover topped the engine with a new manifold supporting two SU carburetors. Lucas designed its first V-8 distributor for Rover's new engine, and a British-made oil pump was fitted. New pistons completed the makeover. Cam blanks, timing chains and gears, and hydraulic tappets were (and still are) supplied from the United States.

The Rover-ized V-8 debuted in 1965 in the old Rover P5 sedan, which was renamed the Rover 3.5 Litre after its new engine. Since then, versions of the engine have appeared in the MGB GT V-8, MG RV-8, Triumph TR8, Rover 3500, TVR Chimera, and Morgan Plus-8s. Heavily modified, the old GM design is again for sale in the United States, installed in Land Rovers and Range Rovers.

While Rover was adapting the design to its production cars, the 215 V-8 enjoyed a brief moment of glory in motorsports. Several racers used the light engine to power cars, and one of these specials became the first McLaren race car. In 1966, Jack Brabham won the world Formula I championship driving another car using an Oldsmobile block heavily modified by Britain's Repco Auto Company.

specifications

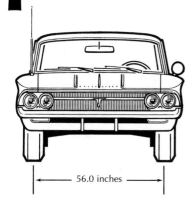

56.0 inches

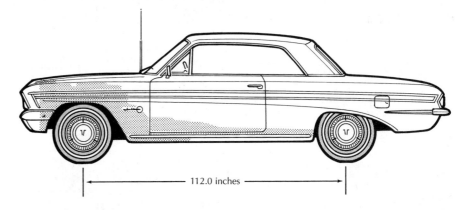

112.0 inches

1962 Oldsmobile Jetfire

Base price	$$3,049

ENGINE
Type	Turbocharged ohv aluminum V-8
Bore x stroke	3.50 inches x 2.80 inches
Displacement	215 cubic inches
Compression ratio	10.25:1
Horsepower @ rpm	215 @ 4,600
Torque @ rpm	300 @ 3,200
Valve lifters	Hydraulic
Main bearings	5
Fuel system	Vacuum pump, camshaft driven
Compression pressure	140 p.s.i.
Carburetor	Single one-barrel sidedraft Rochester
Exhaust system	Single with dual outlets
Ignition system	12-volt coil; Delco-Remy distributor; .016-inch point gap; timing: 5 degrees BTDC; spark plug type: 46FF; .035-inch spark plug gap

TURBOCHARGER
Type	Garret AiResearch
Compressor impeller/ diameter	2.5 inches
Turbine impeller dia.	2.4 inches
Idle and cruising speed	6,000 to 50,000 rpm
Full throttle	50,000 to 90,000 rpm
Maximum boost	5 p.s.i.
Boost limiter	Poppet exhaust-bypass valve
Anti-detonant system	50/50 water-alcohol fluid injection
Weight of turbocharger/ carburetor assembly	36 lb.

TRANSMISSION
Type	3-speed HydraMatic automatic
Gear ratios (trans): 1st	3.03:1
2nd	1.58:1
3rd	1.00:1
4th	1.00:1
Gear ratios (overall): 1st	10.18:1
2nd	5:31:1
3rd	3.36:1

DIFFERENTIAL
Type	Hypoid, semi-floating
Ratio	3.36:1
Drive axles	Semi-floating

STEERING
Type	Rotary valve (torsion bar) type power
Turns lock-to-lock	4.75
Ratio	26.2:1
Turning circle	37.1 feet

BRAKES
Type	Hydraulic, cast-iron drums
Drum diameter	9.5 inches
Effective area	127 square inches

CHASSIS & BODY
Body construction	Unitized, welded steel
Body style	2-door hardtop

SUSPENSION
Front	Independent coil springs, upper and lower control arms, double-acting tube shocks and anti-roll bar
Rear	Live axle, coil springs and control links, double-acting tube shocks
Tire size	6.50 x 13 4-ply rayon
Wheels	Steel disc, 4 lug

WEIGHTS AND MEASURES
Wheelbase	112 inches
Overall length	188.2 inches
Overall width	71.6 inches
Overall height	52.3 inches
Frontal area	20.8 square feet
Front track	56.0 inches
Rear track	56.0 inches
Ground clearance	5.5 inches
Curb weight	2,860 pounds
Weight distribution	54/46 percent

INTERIOR SPECS
Head room (f/r)	38.8/36.6 inches
Shoulder room (f/r)	55.2/53.2 inches
Hip room (f/r)	58.4/51.6 inches
Leg room (f/r)	43.9/36.3 inches
Knee room (r)	23.9 inches
Trunk capacity	13.5 cubic feet

CAPACITIES
Cooling system	12.5 quarts (with heater)
Engine oil	5.0 quarts
Fuel tank	16.0 gallons
Fluid injection tank	5.0 quarts (Turbo-Rocket Fluid)
Transmission	12.0 pints
Rear axle	2.5 pints

CALCULATED DATA
Horsepower per c.i.d.	1.0
Weight per bhp	14.7 pounds
Weight per c.i.d.	13.3 pounds
Stroke/bore ratio	.80
Engine revs per mile	2,860
Piston travel	1,335 ft./mile

PERFORMANCE
Top speed	107 mph
Acceleration: 0-30 mph	2.9 seconds
0-60 mph	8.5 seconds
0-100 mph	28.25 seconds
1/4 mile	16.5 seconds @ 80 mph
Fuel consumption	14.1 mpg

Sources: *Car and Driver* (6/62); *Car Life* (5/62); *Motor Trend* (9/62); *Today's Motor Sports* (6/62); *Chilton's Auto Repair Manual* 1954-1963; Joe Lezza (owner)

Above: *Bucket seats were standard, as was center console with badly positioned boost gauge.* Below: *Jetfire boasted lots of anodized trim.* Bottom: *The turbo's Achilles' heel, a need for fluid replenishment.* Facing page, top and center: *Thanks to turbo, 215 aluminum V-8 developed 215 horses.* Bottom: *Instruments were unchanged from other F-85s.*

car shows with his family. He started thinking it would be nice to have a car of his own to take to the shows. His wife, remembering the car they courted in, suggested he get another Jetfire.

Lezza took his time, looking for a nice example. Finally, at an Oldsmobile show in Somerset, New Jersey, he met a Jetfire owner who suggested he call Greg Hurley. Hurley, whose family collects Oldsmobiles, was thinking about selling a red Jetfire similar to Lezza's first car.

Hurley had purchased the car from its original owner, Raymond German, of Illinois. German had purchased the car in early 1963 and drove it until 1985, pampering it and keeping it garaged during the winters. German sent Hurley a letter in 1980 (which Lezza now has) detailing the maintenance he'd performed over the years: three sets of spark plugs, three mufflers, one new exhaust pipe, a new thermostat, and new Goodyear tires.

It was obvious German had cared for the car and taken pride in it. Hurley felt the same way. Lezza says, "He and I went back and forth for six months. I think he wanted to sell the car, but to someone who really wanted to own it."

Finally, in February 1994 the deal was made. Lezza and his young son Joey flew up to Rochester, New York. They rented a big U-Haul truck and brought the Jetfire home to New Jersey. Lezza has since put on a set of original shock absorbers and some chrome tailpipe tips. At just under 46,000 miles, the engine, transmission and turbo still do their jobs flawlessly.

Lezza has an entire spare engine which carries the Jetfire's "J" code on the block and "T" code on the heads. He also has four used turbos with the side-draft carburetors still attached and one NOS turbocharger. Lezza is particularly glad to have the extra carburetors. He says, "There's a better chance of finding a turbo than the carb."

Lezza drives the Jetfire about once a week if the weather is nice. He enjoys taking it to car shows. Nine-year-old Joey has developed an interest in the car. Father and son are fanatical about keeping the Oldsmobile polished.

For Lezza, the Jetfire's appeal is nostalgic. For Joey, the best part of the shows is "all the compliments we get on the car." He drops his chin and does a little-boy growl to imitate a typical car show spectator: "Ain't many of these around anymore!"

Out of respect to the Jetfire's age and originality, Lezza has never pushed the car to its limits. As I get behind the wheel, he encourages me to drive briskly but asks me not to "floor it."

The bucket seats are comfortable and

the cockpit is easy to settle in. This is obviously a compact car, but the hardtop styling gives the cabin an airy feel. The speedometer is right in front of me and easy to read through the steering wheel. When I start the car, suddenly it seems much newer than its 30 years would indicate. The exhaust note of the aluminum V-8 has a metallic bark rather like a modern GM performance V-6.

We cruise smoothly out to highway 36, where I dip into the throttle a bit more. Off-the-line performance doesn't sock me into my seat, but the small-displacement V-8 revs like a weed whacker and the rasping exhaust note is soon joined by the shrill whistle of the turbo. There is no flat spot in the acceleration; it feels like it will keep building until the engine spins apart. The mid-range and high end are where this car exults.

The transmission also reminds me of modern GM products. It shifts with that peculiar hesitation inherent to every GM automatic I've ever driven. Upshifts seem to take a half second or so and are accompanied by a smooth surge. It's not unpleasant, just peculiarly GM. I've been in 1960 Impalas and 1987 Trans Ams that shifted the same way.

In action, the chrome shift lever feels tall and imprecise. I have to wobble it a bit to make sure I'm in gear. The boost gauge is mounted too low to use while driving, but it isn't indexed to provide any specific information anyway. The turbo's whistle is an audible indicator of its operation.

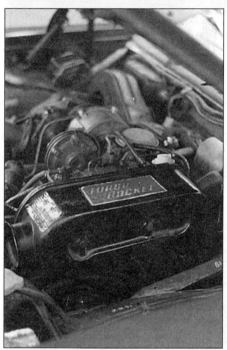

Steering is as good as any early sixties automobile. There's some lean in corners, enough to remind you that this is a compact coupe and not a true sports car. Otherwise, the handling is tight. The brakes are also more than adequate to the demands of in-town driving. I don't know how they would hold up under continuous high-speed use.

In traffic, the size of this car feels quite contemporary. It's not a land barge in the traditional American sense. Lezza tells me many people think the Jetfire is just a few years old. Driving it, I also feel like GM could have built this car yesterday. If this was my father's Oldsmobile, today's struggling division could benefit by making new cars a bit more like it.

&

Acknowledgments and Bibliography
Auto Dictionary, *John Edwards* (HPBooks, 1993); Car and Driver, *"Turbocharged Monza Spyder," June 1962;* Car and Driver, *"Turbo-Rocket Power for the Olds Jetfire," June 1962;* Car and Driver, *"Car and Driver Road Test: Oldsmobile F-85 Jetfire," May 1963;* Car Life, *"Car Life Road Test: Oldsmobile F-85 Jetfire Sports Coupe," May 1962;* Car Life, *"Car Life Road Test: Pontiac 4 Buick 6 Oldsmobile 8," December 1961;* Car Life, *"Turbo-charger," December 1961;* Cars, *"Turbo-charged F-85's Loaded With Torque," September 1961;* Chilton's Auto Repair Manual 1954-1963 *(Chilton Book Co., 1971);* Encyclopedia of American Cars From 1930, *auto editors of Consumer Guide (Publications International, 1993);* Hot Rod, *"Turbosupercharged Olds F-85," June 1962;* Lezza, Joseph *(owner of feature car);* Mechanix Illustrated, *"Car Care: The Olds F-85," July 1963;* Motor Trend, *"MT Road Test: Oldsmobile F-85 Jetfire," September 1962;* Motor Trend, *"Super Turbocharging the F-85," April 1963;* New Illustrated Encyclopedia of Automobiles, *David Wise (Wellfleet Press, 1992);* Oldsmobile History Center, *Oldsmobile Division of GM;* Popular Hot Rodding, *"Hot from Detroit: Olds Turbocharged Jetfire," November 1962;* Road & Track, *"Something for Nothing?," May 1962;* The Rover V-8 Engine, *2nd Edition, by David Hardcastle (1995, Haynes);* Sweeter, Bruce *(Jetfire collector, parts supplier);* Today's Motor Sports, *"Jetfire by Oldsmobile," June 1962.*

Special thanks to Joseph Lezza, Port Monmouth, New Jersey.

1964 OLDSMOBILE JETSTAR I

MARVELOUS MARKETING MISTAKE

Originally published in Special Interest Autos #86, Mar.-Apr. 1985

by Josiah Work
photos by Vince Manocchi

CAN it really be 21 years since The Beatles burst upon the scene? Hard to believe. But there it is: It was early 1964 when those four young men, their ages ranging from 22 to 24, arrived from Liverpool and triggered the phenomenon that came to be known as "Beatlemania." It was a form of hysteria that afflicted primarily, but by no means exclusively, the very young; and the restless, throbbing music of the Beatles both reflected and further stimulated the turbulence of the times. In near-record time (pun intended), the quartet would earn (or at any rate receive) some 56 million dollars!

Meanwhile, underdog Cassius Clay knocked out Sonny Liston, the eight-to-one favorite, to cop the heavyweight championship. Later, as Muhammad Ali, he would be stripped of the title because of his resistance — on religious grounds — to the draft. To some, the idea of a pacifist pugilist was a dichotomy not readily comprehended.

In the Panama Canal Zone 23 persons were killed in riots sparked by the raising of the US flag by a group of American students. Race riots in Harlem, Jersey City, and Philadelphia punctuated the long, hot summer. The Reverend Martin Luther King, Junior, received the Nobel Peace Prize, and President Lyndon Baines Johnson swept to a landslide victory over Senator Barry Goldwater. The Warren Commission, having duly investigated the assassination of President John F. Kennedy the previous November, announced to a somewhat dubious public that Lee Harvey Oswald had acted alone in the shooting. There was, the commission declared, no conspiracy.

A time of tranquility it was not!

Perhaps the atmosphere of violence and unrest helps to explain why, during the sixties, Americans turned as never before — nor since — to "super-cars": cars whose performance potential far outstripped the limits of the driving conditions under which motorists typically had to operate, cars whose speed and handling characteristics were well beyond the skills of the average driver in any case.

It was a prosperous time, so it comes as no surprise that this fantastic display of speed and power was accompanied, more often than not, by sumptuous luxury. A new class of automobile had come along, pioneered back in 1958 by the four-passenger, 300-horsepower Thunderbird. Ford had done exceedingly well with that one, the first in a long line of "personal luxury" cars.

Unaccountably, other manufacturers were slow to follow suit. Not until the 1963 introduction of Buick's sensational Riviera (see *SIA* #33) was there another American car that was really comparable to the 'Bird: that is, a high-styled, upscale coupe that shared its coachwork with no other automobile.

Not that some of the others had been altogether idle. Chrysler, for instance, was continuing its high-stepping letter series; and in 1961 Oldsmobile offered a smartly dressed-up convertible on the Super 88 chassis. They called it the Starfire, and it outsold the conventional Super 88 ragtop by three-to-one.

Reading the message on the sales charts, Olds added a hardtop for 1962 and established the Starfire as a series in its own right.

Although the Starfire used the same basic body as the Super 88, Olds stylists did a good job of setting it apart from its lesser brethren. Perhaps too good a job in the case of the 1962 model, for it was, as Richard Langworth has observed, "excessively flamboyant with brushed aluminum trim and garish interiors — a bit much, even in 1962." Olds advertisements even referred to the Starfire as a "sports car," which it patently was not.

But excessive or no, the public loved it; and 1962 — with a production record of 41,988 — turned out to be by far the best year ever experienced by the Starfire.

Beyond its gaudy appearance, the Starfire was a thoroughly competent performer — a driver's automobile with impeccable road manners and thundering performance. And in the years that followed Olds designers saw fit to tone

1964 Oldsmobile Price and Production Table

	Price V-6	Price V-8	Production Totals
F-85 Series (115" wheelbase, 155 hp V-6 or 230 hp V-8)			
Club Coupe	$2,332	$2,404	16,298
Sedan, 4-door	$2,386	$2,458	12,106
Sport coupe	$2,527	-------	6,594
Station wagon, 4-door	$2,678	$2,750	4,047
Vista Cruiser, 2-seat*	-------	$2,942	1,305
Vista Cruiser, 3-seat*	-------	$3,112	2,089
Deluxe Sedan, 4-door	$2,494	$2,566	49,665
Deluxe Station wagon, 4-door	$2,786	$2,858	909
Total, F-85 Series			**93,013**
Cutlass Series (115" wheelbase, 290 hp V-8)			
Coupe		$2,633	15,440
Hardtop, 2-door		$2,773	36,153
Convertible		$2,973	12,822
Vista Cruiser, 2-seat*		$3,055	3,320
Vista Cruiser, 3-seat*		$3,122	7,286
Total, Cutlass Series			**75,021**
Jetstar 88 Series (123" wheelbase, 245 hp V-8)			
Sedan, 4-door		$2,924	24,614
Hardtop, 2-door		$2,981	14,663
Hardtop, 4-door		$3,058	3,903
Total Jetstar 88 Series			62,505
Dynamic 88 Series (123" wheelbase, 280 hp V-8)			
Sedan, 4-door		$2,994	57,590
Hardtop, 2-door		$3,051	32,369
Hardtop, 4-door		$3,129	50,327
Convertible		$3,378	10,042
Station wagon, 2-seat		$3,458	10,747
Station wagon, 3-seat		$3,565	6,599
Total Dynamic 88 Series			**167,674**
Super 88 Series (123" wheelbase, 330 hp V-8)			
Sedan, 4-door		$3,245	19,736
Hardtop, 4-door		$3,472	17,778
Total, Super 88 Series			**37,514**
Jetstar 1 (123" wheelbase, 345 hp V-8)			
Hardtop, 2-door		$3,592	16,084
Total, Jetstar I			**16,084**
Ninety-Eight Series (126" wheelbase, 330 hp V-8)			
Sedan, 4-door		$3,982	11,380
Hardtop, 2-door		$4,177	6,139
Hardtop, 4-door, 4-window		$4,254	24,791
Hardtop, 4-door, 6-window		$4,331	17,346
Custom Coupe		$4,381	4,594
Convertible		$4,457	4,004
Total, Ninety-Eight Series			**68,614**
Starfire Series (123" wheelbase, 345 hp V-8)			
Hardtop, 2-door		$4,128	13,753
Convertible		$4,742	2,410
Total, Starfire Series			**16,163**
Grand Total, 1964 Oldsmobile, all series			**536,228**

*120" wheelbase

Notes: Prices include federal excise tax and preparation charges. Production figures are for model year.

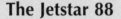

1964 OLDSMOBILE

The Jetstar 88

It's almost as though Oldsmobile deliberately set about to confuse the public. Surely it was bewildering enough that for 1964 they offered 34 distinct models in no fewer than eight series, but Olds had to compound the confusion by giving two very dissimilar automobiles the same name. There was the Jetstar 88, and there was the Jetstar I. And then as now, even comparatively knowledgeable car enthusiasts assumed that the latter was simply a gussied-up version of the former.

Nothing could be further from the truth. For, while the Jetstar I was — depending upon one's point of view — either a high-powered, upscale version of the Super 88 or a slightly less opulent rendering of the top-of-the-line Starfire, the Jetstar 88 was a totally different breed of cat.

Or rocket. Or whatever.

For, in order to provide itself with a price leader among its many full-sized cars — underselling sister-division Buick by $45 in the process — Olds had combined the body and wheelbase of the full-sized Dynamic and Super 88 with the drivetrain and brakes of the new, intermediate-sized F-85 series. Thus, instead of the 394-cubic-inch engine that, in one form or another, powered all the other full-sized Oldsmobiles, the Jet-star 88 used the 330-c.i.d. V-8 of the F-85.

A sensible move, that. The smaller engine developed 230 gross horsepower, enough — according to a road test conducted by *Motor Trend* — to propel the Jetstar from zero to 60 in 9.2 seconds; enough to give the big car a three-figure top speed. No reasonable person could ask for more than that in a family sedan!

Then there was the transmission. All Oldsmobiles in those days, save only the Ninety-Eight and the Starfire, listed three-on-the-tree as the standard gearbox. But almost nobody bought a full-scale Olds with a standard transmission. Nearly all of the big-engined Oldsmobiles left the factory equipped with the hoary-but-sturdy Hydra-Matic.

Not the Jetstar 88. In "shiftless" form it came with a new automatic gearbox known as the "Jetaway." This was a lightweight unit (thanks in part to a die-cast aluminum case), employ-

ing a variable-vane, two-speed torque converter. First gear provided a 1.76:1 ratio, while second gear was direct drive, and the variable-vane control provided increased torque between 10 and 60 miles an hour. In operation it functioned more smoothly than the heavy Hydra-Matic unit, but owners were to discover that it was not nearly as durable.

And then there were the brakes. The Jetstar 88, which outweighed the smaller F-85 by some 750 pounds, used the latter's 9½-inch drums. Lining area measured only 155.6 square inches. Thus the Jetstar had the smallest brake drums and the skimpiest lining area of any full-sized American car. The Chevrolet Impala, for instance — though 300 pounds lighter than the Jetstar 88 — had 20 percent more lining area, pressing against 11-inch drums.

It was an economy move on General Motors' part, of course. We won't dwell upon the ethics of taking chances with people's lives in the interest of effecting petty savings. We'll simply point out that the Jetstar 88's brakes faded dreadfully under heavy use. *Motor Trend* noted: "After less than 10 miles of hard mountain driving, we managed to stop from 60 mph in 187 feet. We came to a halt with the pedal against the steering column and the brakes almost completely faded away." Interesting, too, that Detroit's nemesis, Consumers' Union, found the brakes "entirely adequate."

Unfortunately, *Motor Trend*'s experience was more typical than CU's.

Evidently, to most buyers the $70 saving represented by the Jetstar over the Dynamic 88 didn't look like much of a bargain. Typically, Americans don't mind shelling out a few extra dollars if it appears that they're getting a lot more for their money. And so it was in this instance. The Dynamic 88 outsold the Jetstar by better than 2½ to 1. By 1966 that margin had grown to more than 3 to 1; and when the 1967 models were introduced, the Jetstar 88 was gone.

It had outlasted the Jetstar I, its dissimilar namesake, by only a year.

down the styling excesses of the '62 model.

In the meantime, Pontiac Division had developed a formidable competitor in the "personal luxury" field: the Grand Prix. It had started out modestly enough; the first of the series, in 1962, was distinguished from the Catalina (on which it was based) chiefly by its handsome grille. Moderately successful, it still lagged far behind Oldsmobile's Starfire in the sales race. But the 1963 Grand Prix (see *SIA* #84) was literally a sensation, and sales increased nearly 2½

times over while those of the Starfire slipped badly.

Partly, of course, the reason had to do with price, for the Grand Prix listed at several hundred dollars below its rival from Oldsmobile. But much of that difference was made up for by the Starfire's extensive list of standard equipment

The really striking thing about the 1963 Grand Prix, and the principal reason for its astounding popularity, was its styling. The public had become accustomed to seeing heavy loads of brightwork decorating the upscale models of virtually every make of car. The Grand Prix, in contrast — along with the new Buick Riviera — espoused the notion that "less is more." Chrome was applied sparingly. Suddenly, the understated look had arrived!

The message of the Grand Prix's success was not lost upon Oldsmobile, and in 1964 that division introduced a second "personal luxury" car. Nobody spoke of the Jetstar I as a "Grand Prix Fighter," but that's clearly what it was. Basically a cleaned-off version of the Starfire, it listed at only $104 more than the Grand Prix. And like its Pontiac counterpart it came with much less

standard equipment than the Starfire. The automatic transmission and the long list of power accessories with which the top-of-the-line Oldsmobile came equipped were all available on the Jetstar I, but as extra-cost options. And although it shared the unique roof styling and the concave backlight of the Starfire, the Jetstar I followed the exam-

ple of the Grand Prix in its restrained use of brightwork.

Similarly, the Jetstar I shared the Starfire's power train. The 394-c.i.d. engine, used in all the full-sized Oldsmobiles except the Jetstar 88 (see sidebar, page 94) was tuned for the two specialty models to produce 345 horsepower. Granted, that was a gross figure, arrived at with the engine stripped of all accessories. Even so, it's impressive, for the horsepower of the Starfire/Jetstar I engine was greater than that of any other General Motors car, including the Cadillac! Only those Chrysler Corporation automobiles equipped with the 413 and 426-c.i.d. engines were rated higher.

The Jetstar I was a heavy car, outweighing both the Riviera and the Grand Prix by more than a hundred pounds — and the Buick Wildcat by four times that much. In base form it was still 133 pounds lighter than the Starfire, but most of the difference was accounted for by the latter's extra equipment.

In retrospect, the Jetstar I may have been, from a marketing standpoint, a mistake. Sales of the 1964 model, which

illustrations by Russell von Sauers, The Graphic Automobile Studio
© copyright 1985, Special Interest Autos

specifications

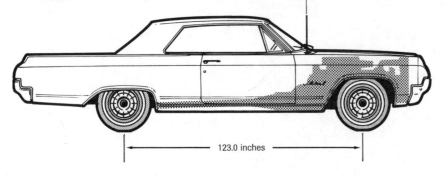

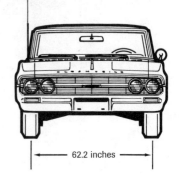

←——— 123.0 inches ———→   ←——— 62.2 inches ———→

1964 Oldsmobile Jetstar I

Price	$3,592 f.o.b. factory, with standard equipment (Federal excise tax and preparation charges included.)
Standard equipment	Console with tachometer, electric clock, rocker panel and wheel opening trim moldings, bright exterior belt moldings, bright drip moldings, chrome roof moldings, windshield washer and 2-speed wipers, wheel discs, deluxe steering wheel, foam-padded rear seat cushion, front bucket seats with bright metal moldings and foam cushions, parking brake signal lamp
Optional equipment on driveReport car	Hydra-Matic transmission, power steering, power brakes, wsw tires, remote trunk release, radio with front and rear speakers and power antenna, deluxe wheel covers, tilt steering wheel, remote control left outside mirror, right outside mirror

ENGINE

Type	Ohv V-8
Bore and stroke	4⅛ inches x 3.6875 inches
Displacement	394 cubic inches
Taxable hp	54.0
Max bhp @ rpm	345 @ 4,800
Max torque @ rpm	440 @ 3,200
Compression ratio	10.5:1
Induction system	Rochester 4GC 4-bbl carburetor, mechanical pump
Lubrication system	Full pressure
Exhaust system	Single, with crossover
Electrical system	12-volt

TRANSMISSION

Type	Hydra-Matic 3-speed automatic with stator
Ratios: 1st	3.32:1 with stator
1st	2.93:1
2nd	1.56:1
3rd	1.00:1
Reverse	3.11:1

DIFFERENTIAL

Type	Hypoid
Ratio	3.42:1
Drive axles	Semi-floating

STEERING

Type	Saginaw integral power steering
Turns lock to lock	3¼
Ratio	17.5 gear, 21.8 overall
Turn circle	45 feet 4 inches wall-to-wall, 42 feet, 10 inches curb-to-curb

BRAKES

Type	Hydraulic, drum type, power assisted
Drum diameter	11 inches
Total effective area	163.5 square inches

CHASSIS AND BODY

Frame	Perimeter type with torque boxes
Body construction	All steel
Body style	2-door hardtop coupe

SUSPENSION

Front	Independent, coil springs
Rear	One piece, coil springs
Tires	8.00 x 14
Wheels	Pressed steel

INTERIOR MEASUREMENTS

Head room	37.8 inches front; 36.5 inches rear
Leg room	41.4 inches front; 36.6 inches rear
Hip room	63.6 inches front; 55.2 inches rear
Shoulder room	58.6 inches front; 57.5 inches rear

OTHER MEASUREMENTS

Wheelbase	123 inches
Overall length	215.3 inches
Overall height	54.2 inches
Overall width	77.8 inches
Front tread	62.2 inches
Rear tread	61.1 inches
Ground clearance	4.9 inches

CAPACITIES

Crankcase	5 quarts including filter
Cooling system	20¼ quarts, including heater
Fuel tank	21 gallons

OTHER STATISTICS

Bhp per c.i.d.	.876
Weight per cu. in.	11.51 pounds
Weight per hp	13.14 pounds

PERFORMANCE

Acceleration 0-30	3.2 seconds
0-40	4.7 seconds
0-50	5.8 seconds
0-60	7.5 seconds
0-70	10.7 seconds
0-80	13.7 seconds
0-100	24.1 seconds
Standing ¼ mile	16.3 seconds @ 86 mph
Top speed (avg)	117 mph
Est. fuel consump.	11-14 mpg

(from *Car Life* road test)

There are nearly eight feet of overhang, front and rear.

1964 OLDSMOBILE

came to just 16,084 cars, appear to have been largely at the expense of the Starfire, for although the Oldsmobile Division scored a modest sales gain that year, the Starfire suffered a 37 percent decrease. And the following year, with sales of only 6,552 cars, the Jetstar I nearly dropped off the chart. By Olds standards, six thousand units is hardly more than peanuts. Not surprisingly, then, when the 1966 models arrived the Jetstar I was not among them.

The demise of this latest Olds "Super-Car," after a lifespan of only two seasons, is easy enough to explain. For, fully equipped, its price was actually higher than that of the more prestigious Starfire! (See box, this page.)

Exactly what may have been the thinking behind this apparent piece of corporate stupidity we cannot imagine. Buyers of this caliber of automobile tend to specify a full load of power equipment, so given Oldsmobile's pricing policy with the Jetstar I, the car seems in retrospect to have been doomed from the outset.

Driving Impressions

We found Dave Higby's Jetstar I to be a truly impressive automobile. Higby, who owns seven other vintage Oldsmobiles among a collection of 21 cars and trucks, found this one while he was attending the national meet of the Oldsmobile Club of America, held in Milwaukee in 1981. It was an Ohio car, all original and in beautiful condition at 56,000 miles. Its former owner, fortuitously, had stored it away during those vicious eastern winters.

Today, 10,000 miles later, the Olds still wears its original, bright red finish. The interior is likewise factory-original, and neither the engine nor the transmission has ever been opened.

Dave Higby treats all of his cars as "drivers"; there isn't a true"show" car in the lot. Least of all is the Jetstar I a pampered vehicle, for as the fastest car in his collection it is Dave's special favorite. Even so, following a Third Place Senior award at Milwaukee, the big Olds placed fourth-in-class at the World of Wheels, 1983, and took Second Place Senior honors at the Oldsmobile Club's national meet in Chicago that year. And yes, the Higbys drove the Jetstar I to Chicago from their North Hollywood, California, home. Dave reports an average of between 15 and 16 miles to the gallon on that trip, by the way, and he notes that the car delivers better fuel mileage at 70 miles an hour than at 55!

We found the Olds to be extremely comfortable. The individual front seats aren't true buckets, but they are firmly padded and angled just right for maximum support to the lower back. Leg room up front is generous, head room more than sufficient. Really, the driving position could hardly be improved upon! To the rear there's a surprising amount of knee room, though we found the seat to be a little lower than we like.

There are some nice little touches, such as courtesy lights on the transmission tunnel as well as on the rear quarter posts and under the dash. The trunk lid release is conveniently hidden in the glove compartment, and twin out-

Olds Jetstar I and Starfire Price Comparison		
	Jetstar I	Starfire
Base Price	$3,592.00	$4,128.00
Hydra-Matic transmission	242.10	Standard
Power steering	107.50	Standard
Power brakes	43.00	Standard
Power windows	108.00	Standard
Power seats	71.00	Standard
Total	**$4,163.60**	**$4,128.00**

Above: A nameplate rarely seen even when new. *Left:* Big car, but tight exit and entry in the rear compartment. *Below:* Remote trunk release is another unusual option on driveReport car. *Bottom:* Olds's powerplant has a thirst which returns mpg figures in the low teens.

Above: Jetstar I has an excellent ride/handling balance. **Right:** Doors are huge and contain safety/courtesy lamps. **Below:** Speedo needle can reach to the extreme right. **Facing page, top:** Car corners flat and fast. **Center left:** Console-mounted shifter is placed just right for easy control. **Center right:** Enough room for a month vacation's worth of luggage. **Bottom:** Handy storage bin is part of center console.

side mirrors — remote-controlled on the driver's side — contribute to the ease of guiding this huge automobile through traffic. We appreciate the tachometer, but its location, just forward of the floor-mounted transmission lever, makes it almost impossible for the driver to read when the car is under way.

Visually, the Jetstar I is a beauty. Brightwork is used sparingly, tastefully, in such areas as the wheel openings and the rocker panel. Higby's car features the impressive, extra-cost, deep-dish wheel covers. And the scarlet finish seems so appropriate for a high-performance automobile. The Starfire may have been a better value than a fully loaded Jetstar I would have been, especially if resale figures are taken into account, but we much prefer the latter's restrained good looks to the comparative gaudiness of the former.

Of course, it''s out on the road that the Jetstar I comes into its own. The big, high-compression V-8 goes like thunder, taking the car from rest to 60 miles an hour in 7½ seconds. Today's cars, by comparison, are downright anemic. The Hydra-Matic transmission shifts smoothly, though perhaps not quite as quickly as we expected. Just a little of the Oldsmobile's performance is lost here, but the enormous torque of the big engine more than makes up for it.

This is an interesting transmission, by the way. Oldsmobile advertised it as a "four-stage" unit, and even *Automottve Industries* listed it as a four-speed. That's not quite accurate, however. *Car Life* described it more precisely: "It is a three-speed Hydra-Matic with a small torque converter, which Olds labels the 'Accel-A-Rotor.' This roto-rooter gives a small amount of multiplication at low engine speed, providing more of what the engineers call 'breakaway.'" Thus,

Comparison Table: 1964 "Personal Luxury" Hardtop Coupes

	Oldsmobile Jetstar I	Oldsmobile Starfire	Pontiac Grand Prix	Buick Riviera	Chrysler 300K	Ford Thunderbird
Price, f.o.b. factory	$3,592	$4,128	$3,488	$4,374	$4,056	$4,486
Shipping weight (pounds)	4,034	4,167	3,930	3,923	3,965	4,452
Engine, c.i.d.	394.0	394.0	389.0	425.0	413.0	390.0
Horsepower @ rpm	345 @ 4,800	345 @ 4,800	306 @ 4,800	340 @ 4,400	360 @ 4,800	300 @ 4,600
Torque @ rpm	440 © 3,200	440 @ 3,200	420 @ 2,800	465 @ 2,800	470 @ 3,200	427 @ 2,800
Carburetion	1-4 bbl	1-4 bbl	1-4 bbl	1-4 bbl	1-4 bbl	1-4 bbl
Compression ratio	10.5:1	10.5:1	10.5:1	10.25:1	10.1:1	9.7:1
Automatic transmission	Optional	Standard	Optional	Standard	Standard	Standard
Power Steering	Optional	Standard	Optional	Standard	Standard	Standard
Power brakes	Optional	Standard	Optional	Standard	Standard	Standard
Braking area (square inches)	163.5	163.5	173.7	156.9	263.3	208.0
Power windows	Optional	Standard	n/a	Optional	Optional	Optional
Power seat(s)	Optional	Standard	Optional	Optional	Optional	Optional
Wheelbase	123.0 inches	123.0 inches	120.0 inches	117.0 inches	122.0 inches	113.2 inches
Overall length	215.3 inches	215.3 inches	213.0 inches	208.0 inches	215.3 inches	205.4 inches
Overall width	77.8 inches	77.8 inches	79.2 inches	76.6 inches	80.0 inches	77.1 inches
Overall height	54.2 inches	54.2 inches	54.6 inches	53.2 inches	55.1 inches	52.5 inches
Tire size	8.00/14	8.00/14	8.00/14	7.10/15	8.00/14	8.15/15
Production*	16,084	13,753	63,810	37,658	3,022	83,267

*Hardtop coupe only (model year figure)

the 2.93:1 first-gear ratio, multiplied by the torque converter's 1.13:1 boost, gives the Olds an effective first gear ratio of 3.32:1. *Car Life* continues: "As the Accel-A-Rotor is a reaction stator placed between the coupling pump and turbine, and geared to the rear wheels, its effect quickly diminishes as car speed builds up.

In short, between the 345-horsepower engine, the three-speed-plus-stator transmission and the 3.42:1 axle ratio, the Jetstar I goes like blazes!

The ride is a perfect compromise. The Oldsmobile glides along so smoothly that with Dave Higby at the wheel we were able to take fully legible notes on a clipboard held in our lap, while the car was making a tour of the town. Yet the Olds, thanks to its four-link rear struts and a 1.062-inch anti-roll bar between the front wheels, corners flat and takes the bumps with aplomb.

The power steering seems to us to be a little numb. Not bad, but a bit short of ideal. Or perhaps we're spoiled. Brakes, also power-assisted, are excellent. Powerful, but not at all touchy.

We love the deep, rich, throaty sound of the Jetstar I's exhaust. And we like the little peaks — sharp ridges, really — that ride atop all four fenders. Doubtless they're hazardous to the pedestrian in the event of a mishap, but so is getting hit by a car to begin with, and they're a great help to the driver in getting his bearings in traffic.

There are a few things about this car that we fail to understand. For instance, how could Oldsmobile have turned out a high-performance car like this one without a single instrument on the dashboard, apart from the speedometer and a fuel gauge? That, in our view, wasn't quite bright. Nor can we understand what was running through the original owner's mind when he ordered the Olds without factory air-conditioning. We've experienced Ohio weather in the sum-

mertime, and we know how much that $430 extra investment would have meant in terms of passenger comfort.

But these details aside, we found the Jetstar I to be a fine example of a mid-sixties "banker's hot rod": beautiful, comfortable, very fast and a real joy to drive. ᎧᎥ

Acknowledgments and Bibliography

Automotive Industries, *March 15, 1964;* Dennis Casteele, The Cars of Oldsmobile; Jerry Heasley, The Production Figure Book for US Cars; Journey With Olds, *April 1979 (a publication of the* Oldsmobile Club of America, Inc.); Beverly Rae Kimes and Richard Langworth, Oldsmobile, the First Seventy-Five Years; *Bob McVay, "Road Testing the Oldsmobile Jetstar 88," Motor Trend, April 1964; G. Marshall Naul,* The Specification Book for US Cars, 1930-1969; *Oldsmobile factory literature;* Popular Mechanics, *March 1964; "1964 Oldsmobile Jetstar I Sports Coupe," Car Life, May 1964.*

Our thanks to Ralph Dunwoodie, Sun Valley, Nevada; Mike Lamm, Stockton, California. Special thanks to Dave Higby, North Hollywood, California.

Behind the Scenes: The Toronado

It has seemed to some observers that neither the Starfire nor, perhaps especially, the Jetstar I have ever received from Olds the attention that these two attractive, spirited automobiles deserved. They really weren't promoted with the kind of enthusiasm that characterized, for example, Pontiac's treatment of the Grand Prix.

Perhaps this was because the attention of Oldsmobile's management was diverted elsewhere, for ever since 1959 the division's engineers had been experimenting with front wheel drive. Olds's goal, viewed by most of the industry as a risky proposition, was to provide the handling and traction characteristics of fwd in a large, heavy car — something that had never before been successfully accomplished.

(Yes, we do indeed remember the Cord [see *SIA* #35]. But the 810-812 series of 1936-37 was 800 pounds lighter than the car Oldsmobile

had in mind — and it was not without its problems. And the L-29, which actually outweighed the f.w.d. Olds, was a mechanical nightmare!)

And so, when the time came for the development of the 1966 line, Oldsmobile gave the green light to its engineering staff to take advantage of GM's forthcoming new "E" body, planned for the Buick Riviera. Olds would, of course, add its own styling touches, but the big feature distinguishing this latest Oldsmobile would be its front-wheel drive. The new car would be known as the Toronado.

Thus the attention of the entire Oldsmobile organization may have been focused upon a project that would be an engineering tour de force. The effort paid off in the long run, but perhaps Olds overlooked, in the meanwhile, the potential inherent in a couple of excellent, if thoroughly conventional, high-performance automobiles!

Toro & Cord

So different and yet so much alike!

by Michael Lamm, *Editor*

Two cars less alike would be 1936 and 1966 Chevrolets. Or 1936 and 1966 Chrysler products. Or 1936 and 1966 Lincolns. Or almost any other lineally descended American makes you can think of.

If ever two cars shared attributes, though—mechanical and spiritual—it's the coffin-nosed Cord and the 1966 Olds Toronado. Had Cord survived, the Toronado might reasonably have become its 1966 model.

We tend to think of these two front-wheel-drive cars together. It's not my intention, though, to compare them. I want to focus mainly on the Toronado, but I also do want to bring in some similarities and contrasts that involve the Cord as they come to mind.

My first glimpse of the Toronado arrived in a movie, and I clearly remember the impression. I was working at *Motor Trend* at the time—this was the summer of 1965—and a group of Olds PR people and engineers had flown in from Lansing to Los Angeles to show us a film of this new car. They didn't say so, but Olds wanted very much to have *MT*'s 1966 Car of the Year award. They later received it, of course, hands down. (The Toro also won *Car Life*'s

Engineering Excellence award and was voted *Car and Driver*'s best luxury/personal car and best all-around car of 1966.)

At any rate, as the movie began, here was this gorgeous car in motion and at various angles, and I don't mind saying that I broke out in goosebumps. The design was so pure and so striking that I sat there almost chuckling with delight.

When the conference room lights came up again, and as the other editors crowded around the Olds engineers to ask fwd questions, the one thing I wanted to know was whether the Cord had any direct bearing on the design of the Toronado. The two cars *looked* so much alike. But that question seemed pretty out of place at the time—inappropriate—and since I never have been able to put into words precisely what makes the Cord and the Toro so much alike, I let it pass.

Until now. It's nagged me down through the years, and finally, in doing this article, I did get the chance to ask some of the people involved. My first question, then, to the stylists of the 1966 Toronado, became: "Did the 1936-37 Cord directly influence the design of the first Toronado?"

David R. North is generally credited with the original Toronado styling concept He was assistant chief designer in the Olds studio in 1962, under Stanley R. Wilen. Says Dave North today:

"I think if we took any clues from the Cord, it was a hard look at the front end—and also at what made that car unique because, of course, the Cord was an extremely unique car, too. I believe you see a little bit of it in the grille. The 1966 Toronado grille wraps back into the car. It's almost hidden now, but I remember at the time having photographs on our desk of the Cord and trying to get a little of that romance into it. The Cord wasn't totally applicable, because the car we were doing had to have sheer sides instead of pontoon fenders, but we did wrap the grille as it went across the car—wrapped it back into the engine compartment. This was a direct influence from the Cord."

Stan Wilen, Dave's boss and chief designer of the Olds Studio: "Sure, we knew that the Cord was there when we were doing the Toronado. They're both identified with front-wheel drive. But this was going to be a modern car. It was going to be an American expression, an original, and we weren't out to copy anybody. But I think the same things that moved Cord to its proportions…even though in specific detail the two cars aren't alike…made them alike in architecture."

William L. Mitchell, GM's design vice president and overseer of the Toronado's original styling and subsequent facelifts, comments:

"To get a different facelift, we've made more openings in the Toronado front end over the years. But John Beltz [who at first was Olds assistant chief engineer, then chief engineer, and later general manager during and after the Toro's development]—we fought him like the devil not to make us open up that front end. That first Toronado has the Cord look. We definitely wanted a car with no air openings in front—to be different—and we happened to know they were doing wind tunnels [tests] on it. And found out we weren't so bad off. But we fought harder, and John Beltz was such a nice guy. He repeatedly said to me later, 'Bill, I'm so glad you had the guts to do it, because we've got a car like nobody else.' "

The Toronado had not one but two very distinct births. The first was mechanical and preceded the second by some seven years. Even so, I want to talk about the second birth first—the one that came in the Olds design studios in January 1962.

It began with what's called the Flame Red Car—a full-sized airbrush rendering by Dave North. The Flame Red Car turned into the 1966 Toronado by the purest chance; a piece of coincidental timing. Here's how it happened.

Stan Wilen, the Olds studio chief designer, found his people a bit bogged down in day-in, day-out routine. So as it sometimes happens, he let them,

"…blow steam at the board—just design things that meant something to them. I'd felt them tightening up, so I asked them to do something wild and exciting just to relieve the tension—but something meaningful, with real potential for Oldsmobile."

The assignment was to draw, as Bill Mitchell later wrote, "…the sort of dream car they themselves would like to own and drive."

"The designers went crazy," continues Wilen, "and designed some neat cars. I can't remember all of them, but the one I do remember was Dave North's red rendering—a red car on a black background. The thing just sang. It stood there in the room, and as people walked by it, they stopped and sat down and just studied it.

"Well, by accident, a couple of weeks later, the corporation came to Design Staff and said, 'Hey, you'll never guess what we're going to do. We're going to let you do a car like the Riviera for Oldsmobile. Let's get started.' Well, the first thing we did was to pull down the board with Dave's flame-red car, and everybody said, 'My God, that's it!' There never was a question about a second or a backup design. That design clicked immediately. Now that's unusual. Here was a case where we could do something unique, starting from scratch. We didn't have to worry about price or market. It was just an accident that we were able to do a car so soon after we had invented one."

(Talk about irony—the 1936 Cord also had its beginnings at General Motors, again in a similar but much earlier GM draw-what-you-like, blue-sky styling competition. This competition, instigated by Harley Earl, let a young designer named Gordon Buehrig put a car onto paper in 1933 that soon

evolved into the Baby Duesenberg and later became the 1936 Cord 810. That story is chronicled in Gordon's fine book, *Rolling Sculpture*, published in 1975 by Haessner Publishing Co., Newfoundland, New Jersey.)

The Flame Red Car, then, had been done without any idea of actually producing it. Dave North's original drawing had been of a Camaro-sized car or, as he puts it, "…like a 4-passenger Corvette." General Motors, though, felt the need to go to the larger E-body shell—to have Olds share the E body with the 1966 Riviera and the 1967 Eldorado. This was a cost consideration, because GM and Olds realized even then that the market for a big fwd car would be limited.

(Speaking of cost considerations, consider this. The 1936 Cord 810 was totally new from the ground up: new Lycoming V-8, new Borg-Warner 4-speed transmission, new suspension and drive system, new unitized body. The Cord shared nothing major with any other automobile. The Toronado, on the other hand, while new, was not totally new by a long shot. It shared quite a few basic components with other cars. Its V-8 engine had come from the existing Olds 88/98. Its Turbo Hydra-Matic 400 transmission was a reworked design that had been developed for other GM cars. The Toro's body—the E shell—shared tooling and stampings with the Riviera and Eldorado. Thus GM spread development, production, and tooling costs among three carmaking divisions plus half a dozen supplier divisions and could market basically similar cars under three different names. In automaking, commonality—sharing of components—means greater profit, as does using existing parts. The Cord had no commonality at all

David R. North (left) came up with basic Toronado styling in so-called Flame Red Car (right). Idea derived from a design exercise assigned by Olds studio head, Stanley R. Wilen.

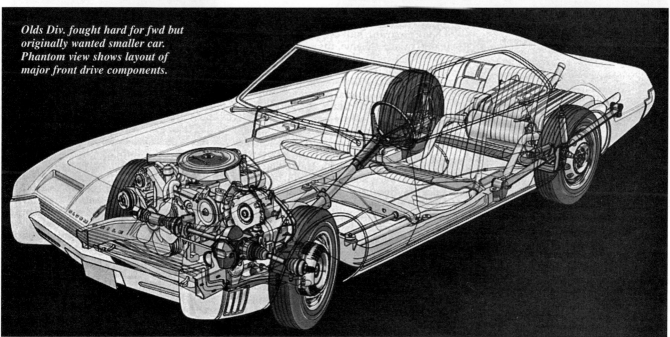

Olds Div. fought hard for fwd but originally wanted smaller car. Phantom view shows layout of major front drive components.

and no chance to use existing parts. That made the Cord so expensive to produce, especially in what were bound to be small quantities, that I'm surprised E.L. Cord attempted it at all.

On the other hand, Gordon Buehrig comments and estimates that the total cost of developing the 1936 Cord came to roughly $1 million. He notes that, "There were five of us in the styling department, and our total engineering staff numbered not over 30 people, including draftsmen." Buehrig goes on to point out several cost-saving nuances that he and his designers worked out. For example, "…normally, in a body program, half the tooling cost is for doors. In our scheme, the left rear door of the sedan was made from the same tooling as the right front door [with one extra operation]. Then too, steering wheel molds at that time cost about $10,000, so I went to Sheller Mfg. in Portland, Indiana, and looked at all their obsolete steering wheels. I then designed a horn ring with a special hub cover which, when added to an old Sheller wheel, gave a sensational new wheel with a horn ring. It started a trend. Our Cord bumpers were some we could buy from Buckeye Bumpers of Springfield, Ohio, without tooling costs. And we made new-looking inner door handles by using already existing hardware by Doehler-Jarvis, adding big, round Tenite knobs. It was little things like those that kept costs down."

Unfortunately, I'm unable to get cost figures for the Toronado, but I understand that to produce a new 5-mph bumper nowadays costs about $1 million all by itself, so you can interpolate from there.)

The Toronado decision to go with the E-body shell meant that one of the first things Stan Wilen's studio had to do was to pump up the Flame Red Car's size. The designers did this admirably, while still keeping the original proportions and aesthetic intent.

Meanwhile, as the Flame Red Car grew, Bill Mitchell and Oldsmobile lobbied in a mild way to hold the Toronado's size down. Mitchell soon prepared and proposed fwd cars in sketch and clay on the A-body shell—the GM intermediate range. Harold Metzel points out that Olds, too, wanted a smaller car. These attempts to reduce the initial Toronado's size, though, didn't pan out and were soon abandoned. The point was that the Toro had to go on the E shell.

Before his retirement in 1959, Harley Earl had proposed a fwd station wagon. Mitchell revived that idea in the Toro's early stages, and it seemed a natural, especially since the cargo area could have a very low, flat, unobstructed floor. "With the tailgate down," notes Mitchell, "you could run a motorscooter into it." Mitchell also had a 3-passenger Toronado mocked up, abbreviated in the same way that Dick Teague shortened the Javelin to become the the AMX and the Hornet to become the Gremlin.

The Toronado, as it came out, was the first American production car to take on what its designers have called the monocoque look. By that they mean a rear body section with no break between the roof and the rear fender. The 1966 Toro's upper cascades down into the haunch to form one solid piece. It's about as far from the traditional 3-box design school as you can get, and that plus the chopped tail, the bold fender lips, slotted Cord-like wheels, and the long front end give the Toronado its awesomeness.

The Toro's styling influence has, of course, been felt at least as strongly in recent years as the Cord's was back in the late 1930s. You've noticed pronounced wheel lips now on nearly every American car built since 1966. likewise, the monocoque idea has turned up on several Ford, Chrysler, AMC, and GM coupes. Ford's Maverick, for example, mirrors the Toronado in its ¾ rear aspect. But for some rea-

son, the monocoque look didn't stay with later Toronados, especially after the 1971 switch to GM's A body. Perhaps too many Toro buyers were ordering vinyl roofs, which in effect destroyed the monocoque smoothness.

Turning now to the Toronado's engineering history, the first question—with no malice aforethought—seems to be why. Why front-wheel drive in so large a car?

The Toro's SAE papers give us the accepted reasons: a totally flat floor for full 6-passenger capacity, better traction on slippery surfaces, better directional stability in crosswinds, excellent cornering, an integrated power unit.

Moot as some of those points might be, there's yet another set that enters here. Among the forces that brought about the 1966 Toronado was the fact that Oldsmobile, long considered GM's engineering division, had no "engineered" car during the early 1960s.

The '60s might go down yet as General Motors' daring decade—the years when GM was willing to climb out onto engineering limbs of various thicknesses. Every division except Olds brought out an "engineered" car of some sort back then. Chevrolet had the rear-engined, aircooled Corvair. Pontiac could point to the Tempest, with its bent driveshaft, its transaxle, its sawed-in-two V-8, and later its cogbelt ohc 6. Buick developed the aluminum V-8, the V-6, and the 1963 Riviera. Even Cadillac had recently joined GM's innovators with the gadget-filled 1957-58 Eldorado Brougham.

But Oldsmobile? Despite its reputation, Olds hadn't pulled much out of its engineering hat since Hydra-Matic before the war and the short-stroke postwar ohv V-8. The V-8 had been mostly Cadillac's effort anyway. So Oldsmobile sorely felt the need for something spectacular—a star among its cars.

This was the era when GM brought R&D out of the closet and put it on the road. Market surveys said the American public was finally ready for cars beyond the traditional front-engine/rear-drive layout. And the growing acceptance of imports with unorthodox engineering, like VW, Renault, Citroen, Saab, etc., confirmed it.

GM had been toying with fwd since the early 1930s, but the Toronado had its roots in a 1955 Motorama showcar called the LaSalle II. The LaSalle II was a joint effort by GM Engineering Staff and GM Styling. The idea was to develop a big fwd car.

Engineering Staff, through its Power Development and Transmission Development groups, had been experimenting with all sorts of far-out automotive drive systems, as it still does today. One such drive system was a compact UPP—a Unitized Power Package—that combined a V-type engine with an automatic transmission and differential/axle assembly, all of which fit into the space normally occupied by an engine alone. The LaSalle II's UPP, by the way, wasn't finished in time to install in the Motorama car, so the LaSalle II never actually ran.

However, UPP experiments continued, and around 1958, GM Engineering took a 429-cid V-8 and wrapped a fwd package very much like the Toronado's around it. It was during this period, too, that Ford started playing with big fwd cars, and Ford even assembled some fwd Thunderbird prototypes based on patents taken out by F.J. Hooven, one of Ford's engineers. Hooven's layout was remarkably like the Toronado's and was seriously considered for the 1961 T-Bird.

Olds got into fwd development in January 1958 at the behest of assistant chief engineer John Beltz. The Toronado has since been dubbed Beltz's Baby, and

although Beltz was far from alone in pushing through the car or the idea, he was one of the major forces behind it. It was through Beltz that Andrew K. (Andy) Watt, in Oldsmobile Advanced Engineering, began to look into the feasibility of making the F-85 a fwd vehicle. The F-85, of course, was a smaller car than the Toronado, and early F-85 experiments included fwd with a V-6 placed transversely and hooked to a 4-speed automatic. The V-6 was superseded by an aluminum V-8 in 1959, and several samples were tested on dynamometers. By this time, Oldsmobile Division was definitely on its way toward its own "engineered" car.

Watt wrote later: "Early in 1960, the first front-wheel-drive experimental car was built and its performance, ride, and handling were evaluated. The car had a frame-integral [unitized] body with a stub frame to carry the unitized power package [much like the Cord]. The drive shafts used constant-velocity Rzeppa joints at the wheel and non-constant velocity universal joints capable of lateral displacement at the differential. The car had a wheelbase of 112 in., an overall length of 180 in., and a weight of 3,363 lb. The performance and handling characteristics…were highly encouraging, and it exhibited good directional stability. There were areas where additional development work was needed, mainly in the driveshaft and chain."

By mid-1961, emphasis had swung from the F-85-sized fwd car to a full-sized vehicle. Oldsmobile, under general manager J. F. (Smiling Jack) Wolfram and chief engineer Harold N. Metzel, took overall charge. Comments Metzel: "The divisions had great autonomy at the time. In mid-1961, Olds started making a determined effort to get corporation approval to go ahead with fwd in a full-sized car. But it wasn't until the spring of 1964—a couple of years before we went into production—that we got full final approval for the money and the corporate go-ahead. This occurred only after we demonstrated the fully developed concept to Gordon and Donner and other GM officials out at the proving grounds."

At this point, it might be wise to unravel some of the many GM staffs and divisions that contributed to the Toronado's creation.

Olds Engineering itself was directly responsible for developing only the Toronado's engine, front suspension, and drivetrain. The Olds engine, of course, already existed—the 425-cid Olds 88/98 V-8. It did need minor revisions and picked up 10 more horses in the process. Cadillac used its own engine and handled rear suspension and subframe.

Then GM Styling (now Design Staff) and Fisher Body Division were called in to handle the Toro's body structure and passenger accommodations. Hydra-Matic Division took over the Toro's transmission and drive chain development. Buick engineers developed the Toronado's planetary differential. And Saginaw Steering Gear Division had responsibility for the fwd axles, axle joints, seals, and steering.

So you get a glimpse of how complicated, sophisticated, and coordinated a project like the Toronado comes to be. Thousands of people get involved, as do banks of computers and specialized testing equipment. And the E body program, being so thoroughly different, got the full, complete, expensive, thorough-going treatment from beginning to end, using all of GM's corporate resources. Harry Barr, who at that time was GM's engineering vice president, notes: "By 1963, under the corporate leadership of Ed Cole, Buick and Cadillac joined Olds as the divisions to share E-body development. In the beginning, GM Engineering Staff coordinated the pilot program, and we held coordination meetings weekly

Toronado was engineered around its drive chain, developed jointly by GM & Morse.

Chain allowed split Hydra-Matic, which let UPP fit into regular engine space.

Top Toro engineers were (l-r) Beltz, Dorshimer, Kehrl, Lewis, Perkins, and Watt.

Toronado has totally flat trunk, with spare behind seat and vent outlet under backlight. No tunnel divides rear floor.

Untunnelled front floors in both Cord and Toronado give extra leg room. Oldsmobile Toronado carries six in honest comfort.

Photos courtesy GM Design Staff, GM Engineering Staff, Image International, Motor Trend

In lobbying for a smaller Toro, GM Design staff cut about a foot out of 1969 model, chopped overhang, made it a 2-seater.

Olds and GM Design built several Toro wagons, all with low rear floors. Tailgate dropped down at bottom of rear bumper.

to speed major decisions and to direct the overall design. By early 1964, this program had been completed, and responsibility was returned to the three car divisions. Originally Cadillac and Buick were to share the fwd design in their 1966 models, but the Riviera kept to a conventional powertrain in the new E body, and Cadillac, wanting more development time, delayed the Eldorado until 1967, so Olds reaped the benefit of their long interest in fwd."

Oddly enough, though, the Toronado was engineered around one single, novel component—its all-important drive chain. It's a point I'd like to emphasize, because the chain became the key to the car's mechanical feasibility. Without it, fwd would never have become acceptable in so large and luxurious a car.

Gear drive had been tried earlier by both GM

Engineering and Olds, but they'd run into quite a bit of gear noise. So the silent chain, called Hy-Vo and containing 2,294 individual pieces, was developed jointly by GM's Hydra-Matic Division and Morse Chain Division of Borg-Warner Corp. It proved a master stroke and a technical breakthrough—strong, flexible, light, silent, and relatively inexpensive. The Hy-Vo chain made possible the Toronado's very compact fwd UPP, letting it fit into a space no bigger than any other engine compartment.

The chain also made possible that second master stroke of the Toronado's engineering, namely the successful separation of the Turbo Hydra-Matic's torque converter from its gearbox. Splitting those two units allowed the compactness Oldsmobile needed to stuff the entire power package into a normal-sized engine room.

To understand this separation of converter and gearbox, visualize the following. In any ordinary automatic transmission, the torque converter torus and the planetary gearbox stand in line, traditionally bolted together into one unit. But in the Toronado, the torque converter and gearbox are split apart. The converter bolts up to the engine in the usual way, but instead of the Hydra-Matic gearbox being behind the converter, there's a drive sprocket in its place. The gearbox itself now nestles below the left bank of the V-8, turned around backwards (180°), with a driven sprocket on its input shaft. The Hy-Vo chain connects the two sprockets. (Each individual Hy-Vo chain, by the way, is broken in and pre-stretched on special machines before installation in a car. Thus it never needs an idler, tensioner, or adjustment.)

What the chain meant (and means) is that the

Photos courtesy GM Design Staff, GM Engineering Staff, Image International, Motor Trend

Our article focuses on Toro, since Cord has been well chronicled elsewhere. The two, though, contain striking similarities.

Toronado could use, with minimum modification, the standard GM Turbo Hydra-Matic 400 transmission. However, to make the Hydra-Matic (H-M) work—since the gearbox was flipped end for end—the engineers had to turn all the rotating parts within the transmission around so their direction was reversed. In other words, all gears that ordinarily rotated clockwise now moved counter-clockwise, and vice-versa. Helix angles had to be reversed. Similarly, servos had to be moved to opposite sides of the transmission case, and one-way clutches now energized backwards. There were other modifications as well, but most important transmission parts still interchanged with standard H-Ms, thus keeping down costs.

Adapting the H-M, then, served three basic functions in the Toronado. First, it eliminated the need for complicated manual shift linkage—the problem Cord solved fairly well in 1936 with the Bendix remote vacuum shift. Second, the automatic trans cushioned engine firing impulses to the Hy-Vo chain and thus helped tune harshness out of the car's driving feel. Although some enthusiasts would have preferred a Toronado with a 4-speed manual gearbox as in the Cord, this would have increased roughness

Naming the Toronado

"It took us longer, as I recall, to name the car than it did to design or engineer it. We tried everything. We tried poetry, we went through books, we scanned every source you can think of. At that time we were considering Scirocco and Magnum and Raven and Cirus—things like that.

"Pretty soon, though, everybody got involved—from the guy who cleaned the studio at night to the company president. Even Ed Cole would come in and say, 'Hey, what do you think of this?'

"Finally, one day we were playing with the name. We had signs up all over the office showing different names in script, and I guess it was Bunkie Knudsen [Chevrolet general manager] who came by with Cole [GM vice president of car & truck group]. They'd just come in to look at something in the studio, and they wanted to know if we still needed a name. We said yes, and it was Knudsen who said, in a very offhand way, 'Why don't you use Toronado? We're not using it.' Toronado had been a 1963 Chevrolet showcar—a registered name that had done well in surveys. Somebody asked, 'What does it mean?' 'I don't know.' So someone chucked it out, and it was okay to use."
-Stanley P. Wilen

to a considerable degree. And third, the split H-M, as mentioned, helped make for that extremely compact UPP.

Up ahead of the transmission gear case there's the slim-line planetary differential that feeds two very carefully engineered axle shafts. The 1966 Toronado V-8 puts out nearly 4,000 foot-pounds of torque to each front axle under stall conditions. This heavy torque has to be transferred to the wheels through universal joints. Cord engineers used Rzeppa joints which, at that state of the art, gave a fair amount of trouble, needed constant attention, and sometimes caused judder under torque at severe wheel angles. Cord soon switched to Bendix-Weiss joints and solved some of those problems.

The Toronado also uses Rzeppa outer joints plus a combination of a ball-spline and Rzeppa joint inboard. Saginaw Division tested dozens of different joints and combinations before settling on the final system, and most of their experimental joints showed the same angular judder as the early Cord 810.

In a conventional rear-drive car, the driveshaft itself twists slightly to help cushion power impulses. In a fwd car, since there's no driveshaft and the axle

104

shafts are short and rigid, there's no such built-in twist cushion. So the Saginaw engineers incorporated a big, hefty rubber sleeve into the right axle shaft—a coupling that twists up to 7.5° under extreme torque. This coupling compensates for roughness and noise going into both axles from all ends.

Saginaw engineers considered the axles and joints major challenges, but the toughest components of all to develop were the axle seals. Cord, whose engineers never could work out such seals, recommended joint lubrication every 500 miles. Saginaw had to make the joints virtually ignorable, so they were lubed and sealed for life. The seals developed by Saginaw were of an oil-resistant synthetic rubber, held in place by corrosion-resistant copper snap rings. No amount of twisting, spinning, nor angulation could faze them for the normal life of the car.

The Toronado was originally aimed at the owner who appreciates automotive aesthetics—the look of cars—and also for the driver who can appreciate mechanical finesse. To that extent, the original Toronado was very much like the Cord, but the Cord contained more sports car details (4-speed gearbox, tachometer, full instrumentation, optional supercharger), while the Toro had much greater refinement and comfort. Of course, you have to recognize the difference of 30 years in development technology.

Unorthodoxy sometimes takes a while to catch on, and it's interesting to compare the Toronado's sales figures with those of the more conventionally engineered Riviera (see chart, p. 106). For the first five years, the Riv outsold the Toro by a sizable margin. Then in 1971, the tables turned and the Toronado has consistently outsold the Riviera by the same margin ever since.

Stan Wilen tells an interesting story. "I was very impressed by something that Fredric Donner [GM board chairman] once said in the studio. We were doing a facelift on the Toronado a couple of years later. There must have been 50 people in the studio. Well, my role is to stand in the back of these meetings and supply information as I'm asked. I walked to the back of the car when he did, and he nodded his head thoughtfully, indicating he considered it a good facelift. He was in a reflective mood, and I mentioned to him the fact that I was a little disappointed over then-current Toronado sales. I saw the Toronado as an *entrée* to more adventuresome and creative things, and I was apprehensive that the corporation might become conservative over the car's qualified success in the marketplace. And Donner said something I'll never forget, because it showed a scope that I never attributed to a man of his background. He said, 'You know, young man, I don't believe we should worry so much about that. It would be nice if the whole world were beating a path to our door, but the car is a unique expression, and I think it does the whole corporation good to tell its customers that we're constantly striving to do something better. We're not tired, we're not fat, and I think this car says that. It does good for the whole corporation to do a product like this every once in a while, and I feel its success is not based on volume.' I consider that a very broad view for a man with his financial background. And I feel that way myself."

The Corvair, the Tempest, the aluminum V-8, the cogbelt ohc 6, the Eldorado Brougham, and most of those other 1960s GM innovative cars are gone now, and so is that entire era. Only the Toro/Eldo and the V-6 (for the second time around) remain.

When I asked GM engineers and designers whether they felt the corporation had lost some of its spirit to innovate, the consensus was overwhelming.

Dashboard cantilevers like a shelf and wraps around passenger compartment.

Olds studio designers tried myriad variations on Flame Red Car's basic theme.

Toro was destined to share E-body shell with 1966 Riviera and 1967 Eldorado. By February 1963, this clay, called "Sidewinder," contained Toro's elements.

Everyone felt the willingness was still very much there, but government and consumer demands make innovating tougher and even riskier today than it was in the 1960s.

The groundswell for collecting early Toronados began, I'd say, a little over a year ago, when ads began to appear in the enthusiast magazines. Toronados are quickly moving from the used-car columns into the collectible category, and with good reason. I've driven new Toronados every year now since 1966, and to me, the early (1966-70) series is the best. It's more fun to drive than the later models, which tend to be too much like every other car. The early ones had tauter springing and feel more precise in their handling; also more responsive to the accelerator.

Toro wheel design, while very similar to Cord's, was arrived at by combined engineering and design efforts. Heavy-gauge 6-inch rims are deeply offset and could use no wheelcovers (discs cut off air) but were offered chromed optionally.

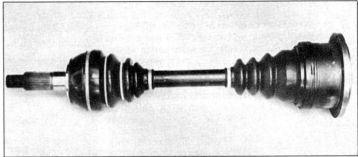

Frame ends at rear springs, carries crossmember to anchor torsion bars. Oil pan (below) is grooved for axle clearance.

Front axle uses Rzeppa and cv joints (above). Hat-section rear axle (below) has single-leaf springs plus twin shocks.

Photos courtesy Oldsmobile Div., GM Engineering Staff, GM Design Staff, Image International, Motor Trend

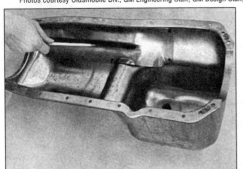

Calendar Year Sales

	Toro	Riv	Eldo
1966	32,803	45,518	3,812
1967	22,062	42,711	19,627
1968	25,536	45,152	22,292
1969	26,766	47,375	24,613
1970	16,554	24,862	16,085
1971	38,721	36,765	38,042
1972	44,118	32,217	35,613
1973	45,931	27,911	50,205
1974	23,582	18,310	36,360
1975	19,601	14,094	44,363

Source: Automotive News Almanacs, R.L. Polk & Co.

Detail shows how drive axle fits under pan, with steering damper (arrow) ahead of it and torsion bar directly to the right.

Right shaft contains rubber torsional damper that twists to take up harshness between differential and both front wheels.

specifications

Russ von Sauers. The Graphic Automobile Studio

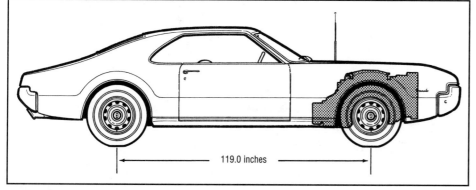

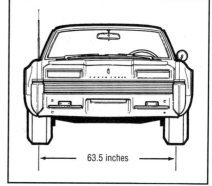

119.0 inches

63.5 inches

1966 Oldsmobile Toronado fwd 6-passenger coupe

Price when new ....$4007 f.o.b. Lansing (1966).

ENGINE
Type.........................Ohv V-8, cast-iron block, water cooled,
...............................5 mains, full pressure lubrication.
Bore & stroke ....4.126 3.975 in.
Displacement................425 cid.
Max. bhp @ rpm ....385 @4800.
Max. torque @ rpm ......475 @3200.
Compression ratio........15.5:1.
Induction system..........Single 4-bbl. carburetor, mechanical
...............................fuel pump.
Exhaust system............Cast-iron manifolds, twin exhausts,
...............................single muffler, dual resonators.
Electrical system ....12-volt battery/coil.

CLUTCH
Type.............................None.

TRANSMISSION
Type.............................Turbo Hydra-Matic 400 3-speed
...............................automatic with torque converter.
Ratios: 1st ....2.48:1.
2nd ....1.48:1.
3rd ....1.00:1.
Reverse ....2.45:1.

DIFFERENTIAL
Type.............................Spiral bevel with planetary gearset.
Ratio ....3.21:1.
Drive axles....................Independent, double jointed,
...............................front-wheel drive.

STEERING
Type.............................Semi-reversible recirculating ball nut
...............................with coaxial power assist.
Turns lock to lock..........3.4.
Ratio ....17.8:1.
Turn circle....................43.0 ft.

BRAKES
Type.............................4-wheel hydraulic drums. internal
...............................expanding.
Drum diameter ....11.5 in.
Total swept area ....328.2 sq. in.

CHASSIS & BODY
Frame ....Box-section steel, 5 cross-members,
...............................ends at rear-spring mount.
Body construction ....All steel.
Body style....................2-door, 6-passenger coupe.

SUSPENSION
Front.............................Independent, with transverse A-arms,
...............................longitudinal torsion bars, tubular
...............................hydraulic shocks, anti-roll bar.
Rear..............................Hat-section beam axle, single-leaf
...............................longitudinal springs, twin tubular shocks
...............................(vertical and horizontal).
Tires ....8.85 x 15 T-FD 4-ply.
Wheels ....Pressed steel centers, drop-center rims,
...............................offset 3 1/4 in. lug-bolted to brake
...............................drums.

WEIGHTS & MEASURES
Wheelbase....................119.0 in.
Overall length ....211.0 in.
Overall height ....52.8 in.
Overall width 78.5 in.56
Front tread....................63.5 in.
Rear tread.....................63.0 in.
Ground clearance ....5.0 in.
Curb weight...................4,860 lb. dry.

CAPACITIES
Crankcase.....................5.0 qt.
Cooling system..............18.0 qt.
Fuel tank......................24.0 gal.

FUEL CONSUMPTION
Best ....11-14 mpg.
Average..........................10-13 mpg.

PERFORMANCE (from **Car Life**, Feb. 1966):
0-30 mph ....3.2 sec.
0-40 mph ....4.9 sec.
0-50 mph ....6.8 sec.
0-60 mph ....8.9 sec.
0-70 mph ....11.5 sec.
0-80 mph ....14.5 sec.
Standing 1/4 mile ....17.8 sec. & 86.0 mph.
Top speed (av.).............135 mph.

The 1966 Toronado we borrowed for picture-taking belongs to Charles (Chuck) Holmes, a school teacher who bought his car new in August 1966. He also happens to own an 812 Cord sedan, plus several other classics and special-interest cars.

The Toro has always impressed me as a true 6-passenger grand touring car. It doesn't fudge with space—six sit in genuine comfort. I'm among those who'd prefer a 4-speed option plus more Cord-like instrumentation, but I'll gladly accept the 1966 Toronado as it is.

The car handles extremely well, but with 60% of its weight ahead of the firewall, it naturally understeers. This means that at speed, the front tires want to keep going straight even though you cock the steering wheel for a turn. I once hit loose gravel in a driveway doing about 10 mph. The wheels were cocked but the car plunged blithely straight ahead. I had the presence of mind, thank goodness, to apply power, and the front tires took me right into the driveway-no problem. Had I hit the brakes, though, I would have ended up in the ditch.

Normal driving doesn't usually induce understeer, but people have to get used to and ready for the abnormal in a Toronado. Olds originally supplied a

special tire, made by Firestone and called the T-FD (Toronado Front Drive), but modern radials are better. There's very little lean from the novel front and rear suspension systems.

This 1966 car is heavy, but the engine, with all that power, gives outstanding performance, even with the automatic. That's probably another reason why Olds never considered a manual trans. It's no trick at all to burn front tire rubber, but unlike rear-drive cars, the Toronado can't fishtail during acceleration.

It's also an extremely silent, smooth-riding automobile. I personally object to the lack of front quarter panes, and this was one of the first Detroit cars to get rid of them (they said it was for noise reasons, but give me noise and more air anytime). The flow-through ventilation system works all right, but not so well as quarter panes.

Disc brakes, both in- and outboard, were tested in early prototypes of the 1966 model, but Olds rejected discs for cost reasons until 1968, when they became optional. The finned drums do a good-enough job of stopping the car under normal circumstances, but they do fade when used on long downhill stretches. On ice and rain-slick streets, the

Toro's traction more than compensates.

To me, the Toronado's pure, timeless styling; its clever, very reliable power package; its interior roominess and great comfort; and its high degree of sophistication give it the same appeal as the coffin-nosed Cord. I believe that good examples of Toronados should be sought out and preserved for the same reasons we now covet and preserve Cords. ☙

Our thanks to William L. Mitchell, Stanley R. Wilen, David R. North, Tom Christiansen, and Jim Brady of GM Design Staff; Joseph H Karshner, GM Engineering; Harold N. Metzel,   Scottsdale, Arizona; Harry Barr, Franklin, Michigan; Gordon M Buehrig, Grosse Pointe, Michigan; R.J. Schultz and Fritz Bennetts, Oldsmobile Division, Lansing, Michigan; Strother MacMinn, Pasadena, California; John R. Bond, Escondido, California; Charles Holmes, Stockton, California; Roger von Bergen, Santa Rosa, California; the Auburn-Cord-Duesenberg Club, Fred O. Bensen, Membership Secretary, RFD 2, Hathaway Rd., Harbor Springs, MI 49740; and the Oldsmobile Club of America, Box 1498 Samp Motar Station, Fairfield, CT 06430.

1968 HURST/OLDS

CATCH-455

by John F. Katz
photos by Vince Wright

Driving Impressions

Dave Newman grew up in Hatboro, Pennsylvania, where he worked in his brother's detail shop and drag-raced early-fifties Fords and Mercurys. Of course he remembers the Hurst/Olds. "I used to admire these cars," he reminisced, "but I could never afford to buy this type of car." He remembers George Hurst, too, coming out to the races to see how "his" cars performed. When he wasn't satisfied, Hurst would service and tune a car for free. On occasion, he even gave away a Hurst shifter to an amateur with real potential. "Take this card to my shop and they'll take care of you," he'd say, "But when you start winning, I want you to tell everybody why."

Now Dave runs a successful restoration-parts business in nearby Solebury, specializing in Mustangs, GTO's and 4-2s. He acquired our driveReport car about four years ago, from restorer Troy Thornton in Telford.

The car originally belonged to Richard C. and Jeannie Bauman, who raced it at Atco in New Jersey and at Vargo Dragway in Perkasie, Pennsylvania, and had it serviced regularly at Hurst's shop in Warminster. (Thornton found ET pencils from both raceways under the rugs; Dave has kept one of each.) The Baumans last had their H/O inspected in 1979. The car was still in decent shape, with 53,000 miles, when restorer Thornton bought it from them in 1981.

Dave talked Thornton into a complete, frame-off restoration, which he now admits probably wasn't necessary. Nonetheless, they saved as many original pieces as they could, including the inner door panels, rear seats, and headliner. Dave's nephew, who runs WNJ Automobile Upholstery in Hatboro, made new front seats. Dave is very proud that his

Originally published in Special Interest Autos #164, Mar.-Apr. 1998

H/O has never been on a trailer. It won its AACA Junior at Hershey in 1996, and its senior in Maryland in 1997.

The front bucket seats are reasonably comfortable, firm for a US car, though in usual GM fashion a bit more laid-back than I like. But the relationship between the wheel and pedals is very comfortable, and over-the-shoulder visibility is better than you might think, given the fastback roofline and wide sail panels.

The dash looks clean and handsome, and the splash of wood relieves the otherwise monochrome interior. Hurst applied the wood paneling directly over the top of the existing dash, so that some controls that stood proud before are now recessed, but this doesn't seem to interfere with their operation. The gauges, however, are finely marked and deeply tunneled, which does not make them easy to read (a problem shared with the contemporary GTO).

Dave calls his Hurst/Olds "the Cadillac of muscle cars"—an amusing,

but apt, description. The 455 rumbles like a muscular V-8 should—but softly; I've driven luxury cars that didn't idle this smoothly. The wood-rimmed steering wheel looks and feels great, and the Hurst dual-gate shifter clicks solidly into Drive. Stomp the throttle, and the H/O delivers all the please-God-don't-let-me-die acceleration of a highly-tuned muscle machine—but with none of the nervous, peaky character. Power delivery is as seamless as a steamer's, and at 55 mph (2,500 rpm), at least, the Hurst/Olds is indeed as quiet as a cathedral—provided the cathedral has a big-bore V-8 throbbing somewhere in the basement. Dave reported comfortable cruising at 80-100 mph.

Roadability was considered good in its time. The power steering is utterly numb and goes light over 40 mph. Fortunately, the chassis returns some seat-of-the-pants road feel. The Hurst/Olds tends to charge into corners wanting to plow, but a gentle squeeze on the throttle brings it

back to neutral, and the H/O slithers around with the *rear* tires howling. The ride is firm but big-car comfortable; only the roughest roads jostle the occupants.

The brakes perform well for a heavy car from so long ago. Dave, who has also driven drum-braked 4-4-2s, said that the discs made a big difference.

The Hurst Dual-Gate shifter was a distant spiritual ancestor to the electronically controlled "Tiptronic" and "AutoStick" selectors that have appeared in more recent years. Keep the lever to the left, and it clunks its way through the same P-R-N-D-2-1 pattern as any other Turbo-HydraMatic. From Neutral, however, you can push the lever over to the right and pick up a second gate labeled simply 3-2-1. Now you have full manual control—once you master the technique, which I confess I was unable to do in the short time I had with the car. Manual upshifts require a crisp push forward and right, as clearly marked on the gearshift knob. From

HURST/OLDS

first, I consistently rammed the lever straight into third, anyway. But I did find the dual-gate extremely handy on curvy roads, where it slams instantly from third to second and back again with no fear of collecting first or neutral.

Dave (who has no trouble with manual upshifts) pointed out that it also allows second-gear starts in snow or on other slippery surfaces.

On the whole, Hurst and Watson achieved their goals; they built not only the biggest-displacement GM muscle car in 1968, but probably the most civi-

Top: Widely spaced headlamp design was inspired by '67 Delta 88. **Above left:** *Standard styled-steel wheels are another clue that this is not your father's Oldsmobile.* **Right:** *Medallions are only model i.d. on the car.* **Bottom:** *Hurst stripes accent the graceful window area of the Olds.*

lized and refined as well. The Cadillac of musclecars indeed!

History & Background

Oldsmobile could not have built the Hurst/Olds in 1968. Unless you understand that, nothing that follows will make any sense.

Some years earlier, GM's Engineering Policy Group had limited engine displacement for mid-size cars to 330 cubic inches or less. Pontiac slipped the 389-c.i.d. GTO around that rule in 1964, so the boys on the Fourteenth Floor raised the maximum to 400 cubes and vowed to watch the divisions more carefully. Exceptions were made for the Corvette 427, and for Buick's 401-c.i.d. V-8 (Flint had to call it a "400" in the Skylark GS), but otherwise, the rule stood firm.

Naturally, the divisions chafed at this limit, perhaps none more so than Oldsmobile. Olds engineers had stroked their big 425-c.i.d. V-8 to 455 cubes for '68, producing 320-385 bhp, depending on tune. And they had a beautiful new mid-size car just waiting for more punch.

In fact, the General redesigned all of its "A-body" intermediates for '68. Executive Vice President Ed Cole had developed an interesting strategy for these cars, stretching the wheelbase of the four-door models from 115 to 116 inches for ride and interior room, while shortening the two-doors to 112 inches for close-coupled, sporty styling. All four divisions responded with fluid, fastback forms, but Stan Wilen's Oldsmobile studio drew the fastest, smoothest, and most fluid form of all. Olds offered its new mid-size coupe in four distinct flavors: price-leading F-85, mid-range Cutlass S, luxurious Cutlass Supreme (with its own, unique, *notchback* roofline), and of course the fearsomely muscular 4-4-2. The '68 4-4-2 actually shared the new 455 block and crank, but used a reduced bore of 3.87 to maintain the officially sanctioned 400 c.i.d. In base tune, this engine developed 350 bhp and 445 foot pounds of torque; a "W-30" version, with "select-fit" internals, bigger heads, and forced-air induction from dual scoops under the bumper, produced 360 bhp at 5,400. These were impressive numbers, comparable to Pontiac's GTO or anything else the competition had to offer. But oh, to put the 455 in the 4-4-2! Oldsmobile couldn't do it. But George Hurst could.

Hurst, the undisputed master of the slick-shifting gear change, longed to put his own name on a complete automobile. In the summer of 1967, he approached Pontiac General Manager John Z. DeLorean with a bold proposal: to shoehorn Pontiac's big 428-c.i.d. V-8s into Firebird bodies at his factory in

Warminster, Pennsylvania. Pontiac couldn't build a 428 Firebird because of the same policy that prevented Oldsmobile from cataloging a Cutlass 455. But if Hurst built the cars, and sold them back to Pontiac, then GM could keep its policy (and its pretense of responsible corporate citizenship) intact—and still sell one hell of a hot rod. Elliott M. "Pete" Estes, then vice president for the Car and Truck Group, ultimately vetoed the 428 Firebird, but at the very same meeting alerted Hurst to the situation at Oldsmobile.

Hurst handed off the Oldsmobile project to Jack "Doc" Watson, his representative in Detroit. Watson envisioned the 455 Cutlass as an executive hot rod, a muscle car for more affluent buyers who wanted quiet, comfort, and road manners to go with their blistering acceleration. "Poise, personality, and performance," was how he later described it to *Motor Trend.* "I wanted a car that would give you all the acceleration you want in the straight, but wouldn't look like a floundering duck in the corners."

Now the exact sequence of events gets a little hazy, but here's what seems to have happened: In March 1968, still waiting for a decision from Oldsmobile (or perhaps from GM's upper management), Watson quit the Hurst organization. Not long after that, Olds (or GM) approved the 455 installation, agreeing to a run of 500 cars. Hurst then convinced Watson to see it through as a consultant. Somewhere along the way,

And there's a Hurst medallion on the trunk just in case you thought this was a normal Cutlass.

Watson arranged for the conversions to be done at Demmer Engineering, a Lansing tool-and-die manufacturer whose solid reputation may have helped sell the idea to Oldsmobile.

Olds engineering chief John Beltz, who had desperately wanted an Olds version of the Camaro/Firebird, saw the Hurst/Olds project as an alternative to boost his division's performance image.

Eagerly, he assigned engineers Ted Lucas, Dale Smith, and Bob Stemple to cooperate with Watson. Together, they developed a special version of the 455. Designated W-45, it borrowed the W-30's ram-air system and free breathing heads, then added a higher-lift, longer-duration cam, plus larger carburetor jets and a distributor re-calibrated for earlier advance from low speeds. A sep-

The Big-Inch Intermediates, 1968

	Hurst/Olds	4-4-2	GTO	Coronet R/T	Cyclone CJ
Price as tested	$4,298*	$3,364	$3,542	$3,353	$3,434
C.i.d.	455	400	400	440	428
Bore x stroke, inches	4.12 x 4.50	3.87 x 4.25	4.12x3.75	4.32 x 3.75	4.13 x 3.98
Compression	10.5:1	10.5:1	10.75:1	10.1:1	10.7:1
Bhp @ rpm	390 @ 5,000	350 @ 4,800	360 @ 5100	375 @ 4600	335 @ 5,600
Torque @ rpm	500 @ 3,600	440 @ 3,200	445 @ 3600	480 @ 3200	445 @ 3,400
Transmission	automatic	automatic	automatic	automatic	automatic
Axle ratio	3.91:1	3.08:1	3.55:1	3.54:1	4.11:1
Wheelbase	112 inches	112 inches	112 inches	117 inches	116 inches
Curb weight	3,603 pounds	3,603 pounds	3,707 pounds	3,800 pounds	3,880 pounds
Stroke/bore	1.09	1.10	0.91	0.87	0.96
Lb./bhp	9.2	10.3	10.3	10.1	11.6
Performance					
0-60 mph	6.6 seconds	6.7 seconds	7.3 seconds	6.0 seconds	6.1 seconds
40-60 mph	2.8 seconds	3.5 seconds	2.9 seconds	3.0 seconds	3.3 seconds
50-70 mph	3.3 seconds	3.6 seconds	3.6 seconds	3.5 seconds	3.5 seconds
1/4 mile @ mph	14.0 @ 97	15.3 @ 95	15.1 @ 90	15.1 @ 94	13.9 @ 102

*estimated

GM wouldn't put an over-400-c.i.d. engine in a mid-size car in 1968, but Ford had no trouble shoehorning 427s into Fairlanes and 428s into Cyclones, while Chrysler happily stuffed 440 Magnums (and even Hemis, if you chose) into Belvederes and Coronets. But as you can see, the Hurst/Olds still topped the biggest-engined Ford and MoPar mid-sizers for rated horsepower, rated torque, and power-to-weight ratio. Mercury's Cyclone Cobra Jet squeaked past the H/O in the quarter mile, but look at the axle ratio it needed to do it!

All of the figures above came from various issues of *Motor Trend,* so the performance numbers should be comparable. (The *MT* editors suggested that the Cyclone's published torque and horsepower were extremely conservative.) "Price as tested" is the base price plus the cost of the engine and transmission used in the test. The only 4-4-2 that *MT* tested in '68 was a standard-engine model; the W-30 would have produced 360 bhp at 5,400 rpm and 440 foot pounds at 3,600—comparable to the GTO 400 "High Output" model in the adjacent column.

specifications

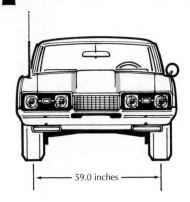
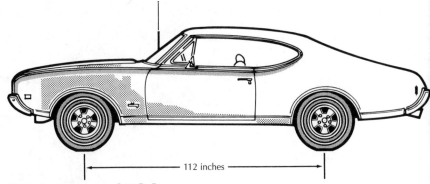

← 59.0 inches →   ← 112 inches →

1968 Hurst/Olds

Est. price as equipped	$4,432
Hurst/Olds equip. inc.	455 V-8 with forced-air induction; Turbo-HydraMatic transmission with Hurst dual-gate shifter; heavy-duty, Anti-Spin rear axle; power steering; power front disc brakes; sport steering wheel; Rally Pac gauges; unique interior and exterior trim
Options on dR car	AM/FM radio

ENGINE

Type	V-8
Bore x stroke	4.125 inches x 4.25 inches
Displacement	455 cubic inches
Compression ratio	10.5:1
Bhp @ rpm	390 @ 5,000 (gross)
Torque @ rpm	500 @ 3,600 (gross)
Taxable horsepower	54.4
Valve gear	Ohv
Valve lifters	Hydraulic
Main bearings	5
Induction	1 Rochester 4MV 4-bbl down-draft
Fuel system	Mechanical pump
Lubrication system	Pressure, gear-type pump
Cooling system	Pressure, centrifugal pump
Exhaust system	Dual
Electrical system	12-volt

TRANSMISSION

Type	TH 400 3-speed automatic with torque converter
Ratios: 1st	2.48:1
2nd	1.48:1
3rd	100:1
Reverse	2.08:1
Max. torque converter	2.36:1 @ 2,200 rpm

DIFFERENTIAL

Type	Salisbury hypoid, limited-slip differential with semi-floating axle shafts
Ratio	3.91:1

STEERING

Type	Saginaw recirculating ball witih integral hydraulic servo
Turns lock-to-lock	4.3
Ratios	17.5:1 gear; 20.7:1 overall
Turning circle	40 feet (curb/curb)

BRAKES

Type	Delco-Moraine 4-wheel hydraulic with vacuum servo
Front	11.0-inch disc
Rear	9.5-inch drum
Swept area	348.5 square inches
Parking brake	Mechanical, on rear drums

CHASSIS & BODY

Construction	Semi-unit body on separate channel-section perimeter frame with 4 crossmembers
Body	Welded steel stampings
Body style	5-seat pillarless coupe

SUSPENSION

Front	Independent, upper and lower A-arms, coil springs, anti-roll bar
Rear	Live axle, lower trailing links, upper diagonal anti-torque links, coil springs, anti-roll bar
Shock absorbers	Delco direct-acting, front and rear
Tires	Goodyear Polyglas G70 x 14
Wheels	14 x 6JK stamped steel disc

WEIGHTS AND MEASURES

Wheelbase	112 inches
Overall length	201.6 inches
Overall width	76.6 inches
Overall height	52.8 inches
Front track	59.0 inches
Rear track	59.0 inches
Min. road clearance	5.3 inches
Weight as equipped	3,750 pounds (est.)

CAPACITIES

Crankcase	5 quarts
Transmission	8 pints
Rear axle	3.7 pints
Cooling system	16.2 quarts (with heater)
Fuel tank	20 gallons

CALCULATED DATA

Bhp per c.i.d.	.85
Stroke/bore	1.03
Lb./bhp	9.6
P.S.I. (brakes)	10.8

Right: Flared exhaust trumpets were shared with 4-4-2.
Facing page: Acceleration is explosively fast yet nearly luxury-car smooth.

HURST/OLDS

arate W-46 engine was developed for air-conditioned cars, with standard 455 heads and the automatic-transmission 4-4-2 cam.

In *The Hurst Heritage*, authors Robert C. Lichty and Terry Boyce describe the W-45 and 46 engines as "some of the loosest production 455s ever built," with piston clearances of .003-.004 inch. The Hurst/Olds engines were supposed to have AISI 1049 forged steel cranks as well, but because of production problems Olds also delivered some engines with standard nodular iron cranks. Without disassembly, it was impossible to tell which were which. All H/O engines were painted red, which instantly distinguished them from the bronze-painted 400s in standard 4-4-2s.

Watson specified Oldsmobile's "G-88" heavy-duty 3.91:1 axle to make the W-45 competitive in NHRA's C/stock class. The 4-4-2 already qualified for D/Stock, and the Cutlass S "Ram Rod 350" ran E/Stock, so Olds certainly had the bases covered. Air-conditioned H/O's were set up for quiet cruising, with a 3.08:1 rear.

The Hurst engineers found little need to change the chassis. The 4-4-2 had already established a formidable reputation for roadability and, according to several sources, the 455 actually weighed 12 pounds less than the 400. Hurst added a rear anti-roll bar anyway, which in turn required box-section lower rear control links for strength. Upgrading the tires from the 4-4-2's F70 x 14 to G70 x 14 probably accounted for most of the difference in handling. Power steering and power front disc brakes, optional on 4-4-2s, were standard on the Hurst/Olds; and Hurst tweaked the brake proportioning valve for better performance. The H/O did have a unique, thicker radiator core, and Hurst recalibrated the viscous clutch for the cooling fan.

Olds Engineering approved all of these changes, so the factory warranty remained in effect; as usual, shifters carried an unconditional lifetime warranty from Hurst.

Hurst and Watson had hoped to individualize the car's exterior appearance with disappearing headlights and a movable rear spoiler, but with more than half of the model year already gone, development time was critically short and these ideas had to be abandoned. Hurst also wanted the cars painted his trademark Firefrost Gold Metallic—with black stripes—but the GM paint shop couldn't get the color right. Someone suggested reversing the

scheme to black with gold stripes, but Watson vetoed that idea, pointing out how black tended to show surface imperfections. They compromised on Peruvian Silver, a color otherwise exclusive to the Toronado, with a black rear deck and wide black stripes outlined with white pinstriping. Besides this striking color scheme, little remained to distinguish the Hurst/Olds from the garden-variety Cutlass coupe. The H/O did have a 4-4-2 hood bulge and 4-4-2-style mesh grille, but no 4-4-2 identification.

Despite its obvious ancestry, Olds never considered the H/O a 4-4-2. It was a separate model, identified by unique "Hurst/Olds" badges.

Interiors, available only in black vinyl, remained stock 4-4-2 except for a handsome panel of hand-rubbed walnut across the bottom of the dash, accented by two white-painted stripes. The 4-4-2's optional gauge package was standard on the H/O. Hurst also offered a full range of 4-4-2 options, including a reclining passenger seat, power seat

Hairy Ancestors

Ever the master promoter, George Hurst looked for ways to showcase his company's drag-race know-how without actually competing against the grassroots drag racers who bought Hurst shifters. One early solution was the Hemi Under Glass Barracuda, a mid-engine monstrosity designed to do spectacular wheelies—and not much else. A stroke of pure promotional genius, it attracted huge publicity without ever having to win an actual race.

Beginning in 1966, Hurst also built a number of exhibition specials based on the front-drive Oldsmobile Toronado. The first, and most famous, of these was the twin-engine, four-wheel-drive Hurst Hairy Oldsmobile.

Doc Watson headed the project, assisted by Dave Landrith, Paul Phelps, Bob Riggle, Dick Chrysler, and Ray Sissener. This able crew dismantled a stock '66 4-4-2 and rebuilt it as a tube-framed funny car—powered by *two* blown 425-cubic-inch Toronado V-8s, one across each axle. Milodon Engineering supplied special bearings, and modified the fuel and oil systems. Pistons, rods, and rocker arms came from Mickey Thompson, and Iskenderian ground the cams. With their Cragar blowers screaming into Sharp manifolds, the engines developed 1,050 bhp *each*. The

two Turbo-HydraMatic transmissions were suitably modified as well, and a Kelsey-Hayes disc brake installed at each corner.

Not surprisingly, Hurst painted his Hairy Olds black with Firefrost stripes. The surprise was on the inside, where most of the stock upholstery and trim had been re-installed around two custom racing seats. The driver faced dual tachometers fitted into the stock instrument nacelles, two throttle pedals, and two gear selectors built into a custom console. Veteran AA/Fuel pilot "Gentleman Joe" Shubeck, clad in a gold driving suit tailored to look like a tuxedo, debuted the car at Bakersfield on March 5, 1966, and continued to smoke all four wheels for admiring crowds until the end of the 1967 season.

Around the same time, George Hurst himself made some exhibition runs in a (comparatively) stock-appearing, metallic gold Toronado with a custom triple-carb setup poking up through its long, smooth hood. Hurst shoehorned ever-larger motors into this car, and reportedly had a 500-incher in it when it went into storage at Olds engineering. He later built the "Fouranado"—basically a '68 4-4-2 body stretched over a modified Toronado chassis.

113

Above: Hurst/Olds "W-45" power plant combined 455 block with W-30 heads. Flexible air duct leads to under-bumper scoops, **below left,** which were shared with 4-4-2 W-30 and Cutlass W-31 "Ram Rod 350." **Right:** Hurst added his own emblem inside driver's side door, just to drive restorers nuts today.

HURST/OLDS

adjusters, and cruise control.

John Demmer set up 20,000 square feet in a defunct foundry to build the cars, with large sheets of plastic screening off the painting areas. New 4-4-2s arrived sans engine and stripes but with one small surprise. Olds had pioneered polypropylene inner fender liners on its '68 intermediates; these were molded in black for all models except the 4-4-2 W-

30, on which they were red. Beltz ordered red liners for the Hurst cars, too.

By this time, however, it was already April, and Olds planned to end model-year production in June. Watson had 30 days to build 500 cars. If he pulled it off, dealers would gobble them up as end-of-season traffic builders. If he missed, and the '69s debuted in the meantime, he would be stuck with 500 unsalable lame ducks. Somehow, he pulled off a miracle. He induced a local supplier to tool and produce 2,000 emblems in a week. The custom pinstriping presented a stickier problem; it isn't a job that can be hurried. But a painter named Paul Hatton offered to stripe 20 cars every other day for $20 per car—which added up to $10,000 for 50 day's work. When Watson agreed, other plant workers grumbled about Hatton's windfall earnings. Watson silenced them by offering the same rate of pay to anyone who could paint stripes as quickly. No one could.

Even as Watson worked the kinks out of the production line, Beltz ran into resistance from his marketing staff, who didn't think Olds could sell 500 big-inch hot rods to some 3,000 dealers. Firmly, Beltz demanded an announcement to all zone managers. Two days later, the dealers had responded with 900 orders. A day after that the number rocketed to 2,600, and the sales department panicked. One Texas dealer alone had ordered 26 cars; another in Lansing had already sold eleven. Watson and Demmer ultimately assembled 515 cars,

How the Hurst/Olds Rose From a Firebird's Ashes

Hurst Performance Research had its own official story about the origin of the Hurst/Olds. According to company press releases, George Hurst asked Doc Watson to build a special car for his personal use, an Oldsmobile 4-4-2 hardtop with a 455-cubic-inch V-8 in place of the factory-approved 400. Watson then showed the car to John Demmer, who asked for two more copies for himself and his son, and to some Oldsmobile dealers—and of course they all wanted one, too.

It's a clever bit of boilerplate, neatly bypassing Hurst's false start with Pontiac while promoting his personal legend. Jim Wangers, who was there, told us that it was a load of... well, he said it *wasn't true.*

Wangers, a former NHRA Super Stock national champion, was an account executive then for Pontiac's ad agency, McManus, John, and Adams. Hurst already enjoyed a relationship with Pontiac, which had been the first make to install Hurst shifters as factory equipment. When Hurst developed his first four-speed linkage, he debuted it in a white '61 Catalina hardtop that he gave to that year's NHRA Stock-class champion. And he drove Pontiacs as his personal cars. According to Wangers, "George was driving a couple of really nice Pontiacs, a Grand Prix and a

Bonneville convertible," in late 1967, while he was supposedly cruising around in the special 455 Cutlass.

So when George Hurst wanted to put his own name on a car, he naturally approached Pontiac first, with a proposal for a Hurst 428 Firebird. "I helped him with the presentation," said Wangers. "John [DeLorean], who was then general manager of the Pontiac Division... was enthusiastic about it.

"But at that time the Engineering Policy committee had a rule that no car could be released from an assembly plant without an engine in it." Hurst planned to buy complete Firebird 400s from Pontiac, plus an equal number of crated 428s; swap the engines in his Warminster, Pennsylvania, factory; and then sell the 400-c.i.d. V-8s back to Pontiac. DeLorean responded favorably, but said he could not authorize the re-purchase of several hundred engines without approval on the corporate level.

So DeLorean, Hurst, and Wangers met with Pete Estes in the summer of 1967, hoping to launch the project with the start of the 1968 model year (see "Witness to the Creation," page 42 of *SIA* #152). Representatives from Chevrolet also attended the meeting, since Chevy controlled the F-body

(Camaro/Firebird) assembly plant in Norwood, Ohio. "At the meeting it became apparent that this was not going to be popular with Chevrolet," said Wangers. Estes turned them down flat, pointing out that Pontiac was doing quite well with the Firebird 400. Then, said Wangers, Estes "made this comment to George that Oldsmobile had been ranting and raving about not getting a version of the F-car." Estes suggested that the corporation might be more receptive ("In other words," commented Wangers, "they could shut Oldsmobile up") if Hurst instead offered to install a 455 in Oldsmobile's A-body car.

"George took that as a pretty good suggestion, and hustled up to Oldsmobile." Someone obviously changed (or bent) the rules so that Olds could deliver engineless cars to Hurst.

And the elusive 428 Firebird? It was quickly forgotten. "Frankly," Wangers continued, "Pontiac at the time didn't really care, because we were pretty satisfied with the performance we were getting out of the 400, and we had plans for a Ram Air package for both the Firebird and the GTO." The Firebird 428 "would have been a nice thing, but we didn't really need it. So there was nobody at Pontiac who was heartbroken at that time."

partly to fill those Lansing contracts.

Four hundred and fifty-nine of them were two-door hardtops, which Oldsmobile still called "Holiday Coupes." The remaining 56 were two-door sedans ("Sport Coupes" in Sales Speak), which saved serious drag racers about 20 pounds and provided needed stiffness against 500 foot pounds of torque. (A priceless period photo in *The Hurst Heritage* shows an apparently stock H/O hardtop trailering a drag-modified H/O sedan.) A single H/O, by most accounts the first, left Demmer's with a four-speed transmission, Hurst "Competition-Plus" shifter, and Hooker headers. Demmer's son bought it, and still owned it when Lichty and Boyce published their book in 1983. All remaining H/O's carried Turbo-HydraMatic trannies, with Hurst Dual-Gate shifters and modified valve bodies for crisp manual upshifts. According to *Hot Rod*, most dealers ordered automatics, anyway.

Road tests tended toward the ecstatic. *Super Stock* reported that at 75 mph, the H/O ran as quiet as "a cathedral at midnight." *Motor Trend* called the H/O the "Supercar" to buy when "you no longer make it with the Pepsi Generation—you're over 30 and nobody trusts you." According to *MT*, the 4-4-2 already provided "one of the better American-type GT suspensions" and Hurst had "tuned it to perfection." *Hot Rod* added its own accolades for handling, commenting that the H/O "feels more secure at 70 than most do at 50." The $400 premium over the price of a 4-4-2, *HR* added, would barely buy the parts if you tried to do the engine swap yourself.

In a *Car Craft* comparison test, conducted on a damp track, the single four-speed H/O turned a 12.97-second quarter mile at 108.17 mph, against 13.33 seconds and 103.56 mph for a 400-inch 4-4-2. *Hot Rod* clocked a more representative automatic H/O at 13.90 seconds and 103 mph, while *Super Stock* managed 13.77 seconds and 109 mph. *Motor Trend* measured 13.97 seconds and 97.3 mph for a W-45, and 14.28 and 94.36 for an air-conditioned W-46. The non-air car topped out at 132 mph.

The Hurst/Olds returned for '69, riding wider tires and looking rather more conspicuous in Cameo white with Firefrost accents. Two humongous hood scoops fed a slightly de-tuned 455, but aficionados still argue over how much performance really suffered. Hurst sold 906 hardtops, kept six more for company use, and built two convertibles, one of them for "Miss Golden Shifter" Linda Vaughn's promotional tour.

Then, for 1970, with emission rules already eroding performance, the Engineering Policy Group opened the cages and let the big dogs run. Pontiac and Buick released 455s of their own, Chevrolet bored and stroked its 427 to 454

Above left: '68 was first year for federally mandated side marker lamps. *Above right:* Rear seat room's adequate. Deeply recessed gauges aren't easy to read. *Below left:* Driving position feels comfortable, natural. *Right:* Plenty of room in rounded trunk. *Bottom:* Blacked-out deck was part of Hurst paint package for the H/O. Antique plates appear incongruous on such a hot car.

c.i.d., and all four divisions stuffed their biggest engines into their mid-size performance models. The new 455-c.i.d. 4-4-2 rendered the Hurst/Olds redundant. Nonetheless, special "Hurst/ Olds" Cutlasses have appeared sporadically since then, emphasizing luxury equipment and unique styling treatments rather than big-inch performance. ☞

Acknowledgments and Bibliography

Books: John A. Gunnell (editor) Standard Catalog of American Cars 1946-1975; *Robert C. Lichty and Terry V. Boyce*, The Hurst Heritage; *Jan P. Norbye and Jim Dunne*, Oldsmobile: The Postwar Years; *T. Patrick Sullivan*, Oldsmobile 4-4-2 and W-Machines Restoration Guide.

Periodicals: Steve Kelly, "Hurst-Olds," Hot Rod, *July 1968; Bill Sanders*, "Hurst/Olds," Motor Trend, *September 1968;* "Hurst-Olds," Car Craft, *July 1968;* "Hurst Olds," Super Stock, *August 1968.*

Thanks to Kim M. Miller and Kathy Armstrong of the AACA Library and Research Center; Jim Wangers of Automotive Marketing Consultants, Inc.; Henry Siegle; and of course special thanks to owner Dave Newman.

Oldsmobile Engines 1904-1980

Year	Cylinders	Displacement	Bore x Stroke	Output (Gross HP)
1901	H-1	95.4-cu.in.	4.50 x 6.00 in.	4.5
1902	H-1	95.4-cu.in.	4.50 x 6.00 in.	4.5
1903	H-1	95.4-cu.in.	4.50 x 6.00 in.	4.5
1904	H-1	117.8-cu.in.	5.00 x 6.00 in.	7
1904	H-1	142.5-cu.in.	5.50 x 6.00 in.	10
1905	H-1	117.8-cu.in.	5.00 x 6.00 in.	7
1905	H-1	142.5-cu.in.	5.50 x 6.00 in.	10
1906	H-1	117.8-cu.in.	5.00 x 6.00 in.	7
1906	H-2	196.3-cu.in.	5.00 x 5.00 in.	24
1906	I-4	269.5-cu.in.	4.25 x 4.75 in.	26, 28
1907	I-4	302-cu.in.	4.50 x 4.75 in.	35, 40
1908	I-4	302-cu.in.	4.50 x 4.75 in.	32
1908	I-4	336.7-cu.in.	4.75 x 4.75 in.	36
1908	I-6	453-cu.in.	4.50 x 4.75 in.	48
1909	I-4	165.7-cu.in.	3.75 x 3.75 in.	22
1909	I-4	302-cu.in.	4.50 x 4.75 in.	32
1909	I-4	336.7-cu.in.	4.75 x 4.75 in.	40
1909	I-6	453-cu.in.	4.50 x 4.75 in.	48
1909	I-6	505-cu.in.	4.75 x 4.75 in.	60
1910	I-4	336.7-cu.in.	4.75 x 4.75 in.	40
1910	I-6	505-cu.in.	4.75 x 4.75 in.	60
1911	I-4	336.7-cu.in.	4.75 x 4.75 in.	36
1911	I-4	471-cu.in.	5.00 x 6.00 in.	40
1911	I-6	706.8-cu.in.	5.00 x 6.00 in.	60
1912	I-4	267-cu.in.	4.00 x 5.94 in.	35
1912	I-4	471-cu.in.	5.00 x 6.00 in.	40
1912	I-6	706.8-cu.in.	5.00 x 6.00 in.	60
1913	I-4	267-cu.in.	4.00 x 5.94 in.	35
1913	I-6	380.9-cu.in.	4.125 x 4.75 in.	50
1914	I-4	192-cu.in.	3.50 x 5.00 in.	20
1914	I-6	446-cu.in.	4.25 x 5.25 in.	50
1915	I-4	192-cu.in.	3.50 x 5.00 in.	30
1915	I-6	446-cu.in.	4.25 x 5.25 in.	50
1916	I-4	192-cu.in.	3.50 x 5.00 in.	30
1916	V-8	246-cu.in.	2.875 x 4.75 in.	40
1917	I-6	177-cu.in.	2.813 x 4.75 in.	44
1917	V-8	246-cu.in.	2.875 x 4.75 in.	58
1918	I-6	177-cu.in.	2.813 x 4.75 in.	44
1918	V-8	246-cu.in.	2.875 x 4.75 in.	58
1919	I-6	177-cu.in.	2.813 x 4.75 in.	44
1919	V-8	246-cu.in.	2.875 x 4.75 in.	58
1920	I-6	177-cu.in.	2.813 x 4.75 in.	44
1920	V-8	246-cu.in.	2.875 x 4.75 in.	58
1921	I-6	177-cu.in.	2.813 x 4.75 in.	44
1921	I-4	224-cu.in.	3.688 x 5.25 in.	44
1921	V-8	233-cu.in.	2.875 x 4.50 in.	60
1921	V-8	246-cu.in.	2.875 x 4.75 in.	58
1922	I-4	224-cu.in.	3.688 x 5.25 in.	40
1922	V-8	233-cu.in.	2.875 x 4.50 in.	63
1922	V-8	246-cu.in.	2.875 x 4.75 in.	58
1923	I-6	169-cu.in.	2.75 x 4.75 in.	42
1923	I-4	224-cu.in.	3.688 x 5.25 in.	40
1923	V-8	233-cu.in.	2.875 x 4.50 in.	63
1924	I-6	169-cu.in.	2.75 x 4.75 in.	42
1925	I-6	169-cu.in.	2.75 x 4.75 in.	42
1926	I-6	169-cu.in.	2.75 x 4.75 in.	41
1927	I-6	185-cu.in.	2.875 x 4.75 in.	47
1928	I-6	197-cu.in.	2.875 x 4.125 in.	55
1929	I-6	197-cu.in.	2.875 x 4.125 in.	61
1930	I-6	197-cu.in.	2.875 x 4.125 in.	62
1931	I-6	197-cu.in.	2.875 x 4.125 in.	65
1932	I-6	213-cu.in.	3.313 x 4.125 in.	74
1932	I-8	240-cu.in.	3.00 x 4.25 in.	87
1933	I-6	221-cu.in.	3.375 x 4.125 in.	80

Year	Engine	Displacement	Bore x Stroke	Horsepower
1933	I-8	240-cu.in.	3.00 x 4.25 in.	90
1934	I-6	213-cu.in.	3.313 x 4.125 in.	84
1934	I-8	240-cu.in.	3.00 x 4.25 in.	90
1935	I-6	213-cu.in.	3.313 x 4.125 in.	90
1935	I-8	240-cu.in.	3.00 x 4.25 in.	100
1936	I-6	213-cu.in.	3.313 x 4.125 in.	90
1936	I-8	240-cu.in.	3.00 x 4.25 in.	100
1937	I-6	230-cu.in.	3.44 x 4.125 in.	95
1937	I-8	257-cu.in.	3.25 x 3.88 in.	110
1938	I-6	230-cu.in.	3.44 x 4.125 in.	95
1938	I-8	257-cu.in.	3.25 x 3.88 in.	110
1939	I-6	215-cu.in.	3.44 x 3.88 in.	90
1939	I-6	230-cu.in.	3.44 x 4.125 in.	95
1939	I-8	257-cu.in.	3.25 x 3.88 in.	110
1940	I-6	230-cu.in.	3.44 x 4.125 in.	95
1940	I-8	257-cu.in.	3.25 x 3.88 in.	110
1941	I-6	238-cu.in.	3.50 x 4.125 in.	95
1941	I-8	257-cu.in.	3.25 x 3.88 in.	110
1942	I-6	238-cu.in.	3.50 x 4.125 in.	95
1942	I-8	257-cu.in.	3.25 x 3.88 in.	110
1946	I-6	238-cu.in.	3.50 x 4.125 in.	100
1946	I-8	257-cu.in.	3.25 x 3.88 in.	110
1947	I-6	238-cu.in.	3.50 x 4.125 in.	100
1947	I-8	257-cu.in.	3.25 x 3.88 in.	110
1948	I-6	238-cu.in.	3.50 x 4.125 in.	100
1948	I-8	257-cu.in.	3.25 x 3.88 in.	110, 115
1949	I-6	257-cu.in.	3.53 x 4.38 in.	110, 115
1949	V-8	303-cu.in.	3.75 x 3.44 in.	135
1950	I-6	257-cu.in.	3.53 x 4.38 in.	110, 115
1950	V-8	303-cu.in.	3.75 x 3.44 in.	135
1951	V-8	303-cu.in.	3.75 x 3.44 in.	135
1952	V-8	303-cu.in.	3.75 x 3.44 in.	145, 160
1953	V-8	303-cu.in.	3.75 x 3.44 in.	150, 165
1954	V-8	324-cu.in.	3.88 x 3.44 in.	170, 185
1955	V-8	324-cu.in.	3.88 x 3.44 in.	185, 202
1956	V-8	324-cu.in.	3.88 x 3.44 in.	230, 240
1957	V-8	371-cu.in.	4.00 x 3.69 in.	277
1958	V-8	371-cu.in.	4.00 x 3.69 in.	265, 305, 312
1959	V-8	371-cu.in.	4.00 x 3.69 in.	270, 300
1959	V-8	394-cu.in.	4.13 x 3.69 in.	315
1960	V-8	371-cu.in.	4.00 x 3.69 in.	240, 260
1960	V-8	394-cu.in.	4.13 x 3.69 in.	315
1961	V-8	215-cu.in.	3.50 x 2.80 in.	155
1961	V-8	394-cu.in.	4.13 x 3.69 in.	250, 325
1962	V-8	215-cu.in.	3.50 x 2.80 in.	155, 185, 215
1962	V-8	394-cu.in.	4.13 x 3.69 in.	280, 330, 345
1963	V-8	215-cu.in.	3.50 x 2.80 in.	155, 185, 215
1963	V-8	394-cu.in.	4.13 x 3.69 in.	280, 330
1964	V-6	225-cu.in.	3.75 x 3.40 in.	155
1964	V-8	330-cu.in.	3.94 x 3.38 in.	230, 245, 290
1964	V-8	394-cu.in.	4.13 x 3.69 in.	280, 330, 345
1965	V-6	225-cu.in.	3.75 x 3.40 in.	155
1965	V-8	330-cu.in.	3.94 x 3.38 in.	250, 260, 315
1965	V-8	400-cu.in.	4.00 x 3.98 in.	320
1965	V-8	425-cu.in.	4.13 x 3.69 in.	360, 370
1966	I-6	250-cu.in.	3.88 x 3.53 in.	155
1966	V-8	330-cu.in.	3.94 x 3.38 in.	250, 260, 310, 320
1966	V-8	400-cu.in.	4.00 x 3.98 in.	350
1966	V-8	425-cu.in.	4.13 x 3.69 in.	300, 310, 365, 375, 385
1967	I-6	250-cu.in.	3.88 x 3.53 in.	155
1967	V-8	330-cu.in.	3.94 x 3.38 in.	250, 260, 310, 320
1967	V-8	400-cu.in.	4.00 x 3.98 in.	300, 350
1967	V-8	425-cu.in.	4.13 x 3.69 in.	300, 310, 365, 375
1968	I-6	250-cu.in.	3.88 x 3.53 in.	155
1968	V-8	350-cu.in.	4.06 x 3.38 in.	250, 310
1968	V-8	400-cu.in.	4.00 x 3.98 in.	290, 325, 350, 360
1968	V-8	455-cu.in.	4.13 x 4.25 in.	310, 320, 365, 375, 400
1969	I-6	250-cu.in.	3.88 x 3.53 in.	155
1969	V-8	350-cu.in.	4.06 x 3.38 in.	250, 310, 325

Oldsmobile Engines 1904-1980
continued

Year	Type	Displacement	Bore x Stroke	Horsepower
1969	V-8	400-cu.in.	4.00 x 3.98 in.	325, 350, 360
1969	V-8	455-cu.in.	4.13 x 4.25 in.	310, 365, 375, 390, 400
1970	I-6	250-cu.in.	3.88 x 3.53 in.	155
1970	V-8	350-cu.in.	4.06 x 3.38 in.	250, 310, 325
1970	V-8	455-cu.in.	4.13 x 4.25 in.	310, 320, 365, 370, 375, 390, 400
1971	I-6	250-cu.in.	3.88 x 3.53 in.	145
1971	V-8	350-cu.in.	4.06 x 3.38 in.	240, 260
1971	V-8	455-cu.in.	4.13 x 4.25 in.	280, 320, 340, 350

Starting in 1972 horsepower is listed as a Net rating

Year	Type	Displacement	Bore x Stroke	Horsepower
1972	V-8	350-cu.in.	4.06 x 3.38 in.	160, 180
1972	V-8	455-cu.in.	4.13 x 4.25 in.	225, 250
1973	I-6	250-cu.in.	3.88 x 3.53 in.	100
1973	V-8	350-cu.in.	4.06 x 3.38 in.	160, 180
1973	V-8	455-cu.in.	4.13 x 4.25 in.	250, 275
1974	I-6	250-cu.in.	3.88 x 3.53 in.	100
1974	V-8	350-cu.in.	4.06 x 3.38 in.	180
1974	V-8	455-cu.in.	4.13 x 4.25 in.	180, 210
1975	V-6	231-cu.in.	3.80 x 3.40 in.	125
1975	I-6	250-cu.in.	3.88 x 3.53 in.	100
1975	V-8	260-cu.in.	3.50 x 3.39 in.	150
1975	V-8	350-cu.in.	4.06 x 3.38 in.	180
1975	V-8	455-cu.in.	4.13 x 4.25 in.	210
1976	V-6	231-cu.in.	3.80 x 3.40 in.	105
1976	I-6	250-cu.in.	3.88 x 3.53 in.	105
1976	V-8	260-cu.in.	3.50 x 3.39 in.	110
1976	V-8	350-cu.in.	3.80 x 3.85 in.	140, 155
1976	V-8	350-cu.in.	4.06 x 3.38 in.	170
1976	V-8	455-cu.in.	4.13 x 4.25 in.	190, 215
1977	I-4	140-cu.in.	3.50 x 3.63 in.	84
1977	V-6	231-cu.in.	3.80 x 3.40 in.	105
1977	V-8	260-cu.in.	3.50 x 3.39 in.	110
1977	V-8	305-cu.in.	3.74 x 3.48 in.	145
1977	V-8	350-cu.in.	4.00 x 3.48 in.	170
1977	V-8	350-cu.in.	4.06 x 3.38 in.	170
1977	V-8	403-cu.in.	4.35 x 3.39 in.	185
1978	I-4	151-cu.in.	4.00 x 3.00 in.	85
1978	V-6	231-cu.in.	3.80 x 3.40 in.	105
1978	V-8	260-cu.in.	3.50 x 3.39 in.	110
1978	V-8	305-cu.in.	3.74 x 3.48 in.	145, 160
1978	V-8	350-cu.in.	4.00 x 3.48 in.	160
1978	V-8	350-cu.in.	4.06 x 3.38 in.	120, 170
1978	V-8	403-cu.in.	4.35 x 3.39 in.	185
1979	I-4	151-cu.in.	4.00 x 3.00 in.	85
1979	V-6	231-cu.in.	3.80 x 3.40 in.	115
1979	V-8	260-cu.in.	3.50 x 3.39 in.	90, 105
1979	V-8	301-cu.in.	4.00 x 3.00 in.	135
1979	V-8	305-cu.in.	3.74 x 3.48 in.	130, 160
1979	V-8	350-cu.in.	4.00 x 3.48 in.	160
1979	V-8	350-cu.in.	4.06 x 3.38 in.	125, 160, 165
1979	V-8	403-cu.in.	4.35 x 3.39 in.	175
1980	I-4	151-cu.in.	4.00 x 3.00 in.	85
1980	V-6	173-cu.in.	3.50 x 3.00 in.	115
1980	V-6	231-cu.in.	3.80 x 3.40 in.	110
1980	V-8	260-cu.in.	3.50 x 3.39 in.	105
1980	V-8	265-cu.in.	3.75 x 3.00 in.	120
1980	V-8	301-cu.in.	4.00 x 3.00 in.	135
1980	V-8	305-cu.in.	3.74 x 3.48 in.	155
1980	V-8	307-cu.in.	3.80 x 3.39 in.	150
1980	V-8	350-cu.in.	4.06 x 3.38 in.	105, 160
1980	V-8	403-cu.in.	4.35 x 3.39 in.	175

Oldsmobile Model Year Production, 1901-2000

Year	Production
1901	425
1902	2,500
1903	4,000
1904	5,508
1905	6,500
1906	1,600
1907	1,200
1908	1,055
1909	6,575
1910	1,850
1911	1,250
1912	1,075
1913	1,175
1914	1,400
1915	7,696
1916	10,507
1917	22,613
1918	19,169
1919	39,042
1920	34,504
1921	19,157
1922	21,499
1923	34,811
1924	44,854
1925	19,506
1926	53,015
1927	82,955
1928	84,635
1929	104,007
1930	51,384
1931	47,316
1932	19,239
1933	36,673
1934	79,814
1935	126,768
1936	200,546
1937	200,886
1938	99,951
1939	137,249
1940	192,692
1941	270,040
1942	67,999
1943	0
1944	0
1945	0
1946	119,328
1947	194,388
1948	173,661
1949	288,586
1950	408,060
1951	285,616
1952	213,420
1953	334,464
1954	354,002
1955	583,181
1956	485,459
1957	384,392
1958	296,375
1959	382,865
1960	347,141
1961	318,550
1962	447,594
1963	476,753
1964	546,112
1965	592,804
1966	586,756
1967	546,242
1968	648,293
1969	679,393
1970	633,473
1971	558,889
1972	758,711
1973	938,970
1974	619,168
1975	628,720
1976	874,618
1977	1,135,909
1978	1,015,805
1979	1,068,155
1980	910,306
1981	940,655
1982	789,454
1983	939,157
1984	1,179,656
1985	**1,192,549***
1986	1,157,990
1987	806,915
1988	562,920
1989	520,981
1990	447,177
1991	474,837
1992	482,998
1993	367,999
1994	435,172
1995	480,998
1996	394,016
1997	329,742
1998	346,462
1999	352,000
2000	280,000

*Oldsmobile's biggest year ever

Oldsmobile Clubs & Specialists

For a complete list of all regional Oldsmobile clubs and national clubs' chapters, visit **Car Club Central** at **www.hemmings.com**. With nearly 10,000 car clubs listed, it's the largest car club site in the world! Not wired? For the most up-to-date information, consult the latest issue of *Hemmings Motor News* and or *Hemmings' Collector Car Almanac*. Call toll free, 1-800-CAR-HERE, Ext. 550.

OLDSMOBILE CLUBS

Curved Dash Oldsmobile Club
3455 Florida Ave. N
Minneapolis, MN 55427
612-533-4280

National Antique Oldsmobile Club
13903 Roanoke St.
Woodbridge, VA 22191-2416
703-491-7060

Oldsmobile Club of America
P.O. Box 80318
Lansing, MI 48908-0318
517-663-1811
(45 regional chapters)

Other Important Clubs

Antique Automobile Club of America
501 W. Governor Road
Hershey, PA 17033
717-534-1910
(311 regional chapters, 7 international chapters)

Horseless Carriage Club of America
3311 Fairhaven Dr.
Orange, CA 92866-1357
661-326-1023
(91 regional chapters, 7 international chapters)

Veteran Motor Car Club of America
4441 W. Altadena Ave.
Glendale, AZ 85304-3526
800-428-7327
(82 regional chapters)

OLDSMOBILE SPECIALISTS

Brothers Automotive Products
7275 W. 162nd St. Ste. 103
Stilwell, KS 66085
800-442-7278
1964-1972 Cutlass and 4-4-2 parts

Fusick Automotive Products
P.O. Box 655HM
East Windsor, CT 06088-0655
860-623-1589
Full supply of parts for all 1935-1975 models

Kanter Auto Products
76 Monroe St
Boonton, NJ 07005
800-526-1096
Engine, electrical and suspension components

Mondello Performance Products
1103 Paso Robles St.
Paso Robles, CA 93446
805-237-8808
V-8 performance parts

Original Parts Group
17892 Gothard St.
Huntingdon Beach, CA 92647
800-243-8355
Cutlass and 4-4-2 parts supplier

Pro Antique Auto parts
50 King Spring Rd.
Windsor Locks, CT 06096
860-623-8275
New and reproduction parts for 1929-1964 models

Parts Place
217 Paul St.
Elburn, IL 60119
800-442-0411
4-4-2 and Cutlass new and reproduction body and trim parts

SMS Auto Fabrics
2325 SE 10th Ave.
Portland, OR 97214
503-234-1175
1940-1980 upholstery and interior supplies

Steele Rubber Products
6180 Hwy 150 East
Denver, NC 28037-9735
800-544-8665
Weatherstripping and bushings

Tanson Enterprises
2508 J St.
Sacramento, CA 95816-4815
916-448-2950
1930-1970 body, interior and mechanical parts

U.S. Parts Supply
8505 Euclid Ave.
Manassas, VA 20111
703-335-1935
1941-1945 body and mechanical parts

Year One
P.O. Box 129
Tucker, GA 30085-0129
800-932-7663
1964-1972 new and reproduction mechanical and body parts for Cutlass and 4-4-2